MANHATTAN PREP

Sentence Correction

GMAT Strategy Guide

This essential guide takes the guesswork out of grammar by presenting all of the major grammatical principles and minor grammatical points known to be tested on the GMAT. Do not be caught relying only on your ear; master the rules for correcting every GMAT sentence.

guide **8**

Sentence Correction GMAT Strategy Guide, Sixth Edition

10-digit International Standard Book Number: 1-941234-07-0
13-digit International Standard Book Number: 978-1-941234-07-5
eISBN: 978-1-941234-28-0

Copyright © 2014 MG Prep, Inc.

10 9 8 7 6 5 4

Note: *GMAT, Graduate Management Admission Test, Graduate Management Admission Council,* and *GMAC* are all registered trademarks of the Graduate Management Admission Council, which neither sponsors nor is affiliated in any way with this product.

Layout Design: Dan McNaney and Cathy Huang
Cover Design: Dan McNaney and Frank Callaghan
Cover Photography: Alli Ugosoli

SUSTAINABLE FORESTRY INITIATIVE Certified Sourcing
www.sfiprogram.org
SFI-00756

GMAT® STRATEGY GUIDES

0 GMAT Roadmap

1 Fractions, Decimals, & Percents

2 Algebra

3 Word Problems

4 Geometry

5 Number Properties

6 Critical Reasoning

7 Reading Comprehension

8 Sentence Correction

9 Integrated Reasoning & Essay

STRATEGY GUIDE SUPPLEMENTS

Math

GMAT Foundations of Math

GMAT Advanced Quant

Verbal

GMAT Foundations of Verbal

MANHATTAN
PREP

December 2, 2014

Dear Student,

Thank you for picking up a copy of *Sentence Correction*. I hope this book gives you just the guidance you need to get the most out of your GMAT studies.

A great number of people were involved in the creation of the book you are holding. First and foremost is Zeke Vanderhoek, the founder of Manhattan Prep. Zeke was a lone tutor in New York City when he started the company in 2000. Now, well over a decade later, the company contributes to the successes of thousands of students around the globe every year.

Our Manhattan Prep Strategy Guides are based on the continuing experiences of our instructors and students. The overall vision of the sixth edition of the GMAT guides was developed by Stacey Koprince, Whitney Garner, and Dave Mahler over the course of many months; Stacey and Dave then led the execution of that vision as the primary author and editor, respectively, of this book. Numerous other instructors made contributions large and small, but I'd like to send particular thanks to Josh Braslow, Kim Cabot, Dmitry Farber, Ron Purewal, Emily Meredith Sledge, and Ryan Starr. Dan McNaney and Cathy Huang provided design and layout expertise as Dan managed book production, while Liz Krisher made sure that all the moving pieces, both inside and outside of our company, came together at just the right time. Finally, we are indebted to all of the Manhattan Prep students who have given us feedback over the years. This book wouldn't be half of what it is without your voice.

At Manhattan Prep, we aspire to provide the best instructors and resources possible, and we hope that you will find our commitment manifest in this book. We strive to keep our books free of errors, but if you think we've goofed, please post to manhattanprep.com/GMAT/errata. If you have any questions or comments in general, please email our Student Services team at gmat@manhattanprep.com. Or give us a shout at 212-721-7400 (or 800-576-4628 in the United States or Canada). I look forward to hearing from you.

Thanks again, and best of luck preparing for the GMAT!

Sincerely,

Chris Ryan
Vice President of Academics
Manhattan Prep

HOW TO ACCESS YOUR ONLINE RESOURCES

IF YOU ARE A REGISTERED MANHATTAN PREP STUDENT

and have received this book as part of your course materials, you have AUTOMATIC access to ALL of our online resources. This includes all practice exams, question banks, and online updates to this book. To access these resources, follow the instructions in the Welcome Guide provided to you at the start of your program. Do NOT follow the instructions below.

IF YOU PURCHASED THIS BOOK FROM MANHATTANPREP.COM OR AT ONE OF OUR CENTERS

1. Go to: **www.manhattanprep.com/gmat/studentcenter**
2. Log in with the username and password you chose when setting up your account.

IF YOU PURCHASED THIS BOOK AT A RETAIL LOCATION

1. Go to: **www.manhattanprep.com/gmat/access**
2. Create an account or, if you already have one, log in on this page with your username and password.
3. Follow the instructions on the screen.

Your one year of online access begins on the day that you register your book at the above URL.

You only need to register your product ONCE at the above URL. To use your online resources any time AFTER you have completed the registration process, log in to the following URL:

www.manhattanprep.com/gmat/studentcenter

Please note that online access is nontransferable. This means that only NEW and UNREGISTERED copies of the book will grant you online access. Previously used books will NOT provide any online resources.

IF YOU PURCHASED AN EBOOK VERSION OF THIS BOOK

1. Create an account with Manhattan Prep at this website:

www.manhattanprep.com/gmat/register

2. Email a copy of your purchase receipt to **gmat@manhattanprep.com** to activate your resources. Please be sure to use the same email address to create an account that you used to purchase the eBook.

For any questions, email **gmat@manhattanprep.com** or call **800-576-4628**.

Please refer to the following page for a description of the online resources that come with this book.

YOUR ONLINE RESOURCES

YOUR PURCHASE INCLUDES ONLINE ACCESS TO THE FOLLOWING:

1 FULL-LENGTH GMAT PRACTICE EXAM

The full-length GMAT practice exam included with this book is delivered online using Manhattan Prep's proprietary computer-adaptive test engine. The exam adapts to your ability level by drawing from a bank of more than 500 unique questions of varying difficulty levels written by Manhattan Prep's expert instructors, all of whom have scored in the 99th percentile on the Official GMAT. At the end of the exam you will receive a score, an analysis of your results, and the opportunity to review detailed explanations for each question.

Important Note: The GMAT exam included with the purchase of this book is the same exam that you receive upon purchasing any book in the Manhattan Prep GMAT Complete Strategy Guide Set.

5 FREE INTERACT™ LESSONS

Interact™ is a comprehensive self-study program that is fun, intuitive, and directed by you. Each interactive video lesson is taught by an expert Manhattan Prep instructor and includes dozens of individual branching points. The choices you make determine the content you see. This book comes with access to the first five lessons of GMAT Interact. Lessons are available on your computer or iPad so you can prep where you are, when you want. For more information on the full version of this program, visit **manhattanprep.com/gmat/interact**.

SENTENCE CORRECTION ONLINE QUESTION BANK

The Online Question Bank for Sentence Correction consists of 25 extra practice questions (with detailed explanations) that test the variety of concepts and skills covered in this book. These questions provide you with extra practice beyond the problem sets contained in this book. You may use our online timer to practice your pacing by setting time limits for each question in the bank.

ONLINE UPDATES TO THE CONTENT IN THIS BOOK

The content presented in this book is updated periodically to ensure that it reflects the GMAT's most current trends. You may view all updates, including any known errors or changes, upon registering for online access.

The above resources can be found in your Student Center at manhattanprep.com/gmat/studentcenter.

TABLE *of* CONTENTS

guide **8**

Official Guide Problem Sets

As you work through this Strategy Guide, it is a very good idea to test your skills using official problems that appeared on the real GMAT in the past. To help you with this step of your studies, we have classified all of the problems from the three main *Official Guide* books and devised some problem sets to accompany this book.

These problem sets live in your Manhattan Prep Student Center so that they can be updated whenever the test makers update their books. When you log in to your Student Center, click on the link for the *Official Guide Problem Sets*, found on your home page. Download them today!

The problem sets consist of four broad groups of questions:

1. A mid-term quiz: Take this quiz after completing **Chapter 4** of this guide.

2. A final quiz: Take this quiz after completing this entire guide.

3. A full practice set of questions: If you are taking one of our classes, this is the homework given on your syllabus, so just follow the syllabus assignments. If you are not taking one of our classes, you can do this practice set whenever you feel that you have a very solid understanding of the material taught in this guide.

4. A full reference list of all *Official Guide* problems that test the topics covered in this Strategy Guide: Use these problems to test yourself on specific topics or to create larger sets of mixed questions.

As you begin studying, try one problem at a time and review it thoroughly before moving on. In the middle of your studies, attempt some mixed sets of problems from a small pool of topics (the two quizzes we've devised for you are good examples of how to do this). Later in your studies, mix topics from multiple guides and include some questions that you've chosen randomly out of the *Official Guide*. This way, you'll learn to be prepared for anything!

Study Tips:

1. DO time yourself when answering questions.

2. DO cut yourself off and make a guess if a question is taking too long. You can try it again later without a time limit, but first practice the behavior you want to exhibit on the real test: let go and move on.

3. DON'T answer all of the *Official Guide* questions by topic or chapter at once. The real test will toss topics at you in random order, and half of the battle is figuring out what each new question is testing. Set yourself up to learn this when doing practice sets.

Chapter 1
of

Sentence Correction

The SC Process

In This Chapter...

Chapter 1

The SC Process

Sentence Correction (SC) is one of three question types found in the Verbal section of the GMAT. Sentence Correction tests your mastery of both grammar and meaning as it applies to conventional written English.

SC questions typically comprise a bit more than one-third of the questions in the Verbal section, so a strong performance on SC is an important part of a great score.

Question Format

Take a look at this SC problem:

> Although William Pereira first gained national recognition for his movie set designs, <u>including those for *Reap the Wild Wind* and *Jane Eyre*, future generations remember</u> him as the architect of the Transamerica Tower, the Malibu campus of Pepperdine University, and the city of Irvine.
>
> (A) including those for *Reap the Wild Wind* and *Jane Eyre*, future generations remember
>
> (B) like that for *Reap the Wild Wind* and *Jane Eyre*, future generations will remember
>
> (C) like those for *Reap the Wild Wind* and *Jane Eyre*, future generations remembered
>
> (D) including that for *Reap the Wild Wind* and *Jane Eyre*, future generations remembered
>
> (E) including those for *Reap the Wild Wind* and *Jane Eyre*, future generations will remember

1

The question consists of a given sentence, part of which is underlined. The underlined segment may be short, or it may include most or even all of the original sentence. The five answer choices are possible replacements for the underlined segment.

In all SC questions, choice (A) is exactly the same as the underlined portion of the sentence above it; in other words, you would choose choice (A) if you think nothing is wrong with the original sentence. The other four choices will always offer different options. Your task is to choose the answer that, when placed in the given sentence, is the best option of those given, in terms of grammar and meaning.

By the way, the original sentence, choice (A), is the correct answer just as often as the other answer choices—about 20% of the time.

The SC Process

Because the other two Verbal question types, Critical Reasoning (CR) and Reading Comprehension (RC), require so much reading, you're going to have to move quickly on SC. In fact, you'll need to average just 1 minute and 20 seconds per SC question.

As a result, you'll need a standard process to help you work through any SC question efficiently and effectively.

Here's the basic process:

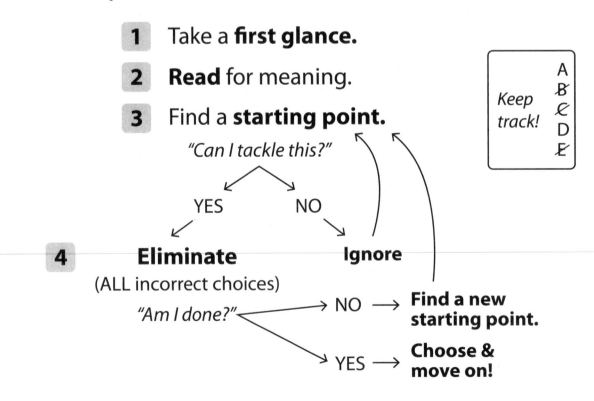

Try the process out with the William Pereira example:

> Although William Pereira first gained national recognition for his movie set designs, <u>including those for *Reap the Wild Wind* and *Jane Eyre*, future generations remember</u> him as the architect of the Transamerica Tower, the Malibu campus of Pepperdine University, and the city of Irvine.

(A) including those for *Reap the Wild Wind* and *Jane Eyre*, future generations remember

(B) like that for *Reap the Wild Wind* and *Jane Eyre*, future generations will remember

(C) like those for *Reap the Wild Wind* and *Jane Eyre*, future generations remembered

(D) including that for *Reap the Wild Wind* and *Jane Eyre*, future generations remembered

(E) including those for *Reap the Wild Wind* and *Jane Eyre*, future generations will remember

Step 1: Take a first glance.

Take a first glance to spot clues that may help you answer the question. (You may not notice much at first; you'll get better with practice!)

Don't read—just glance briefly at the entire problem. How long is the underline? What's happening where the underline starts?

In the Pereira problem, the underline is relatively short. It begins right after a comma and the first word is *including*.

The first word of the five answers will *always* contain at least one difference, so glance down the first word of each choice. The "split," or difference among the answers, here is *including* vs. *like*.

The word *including* is used to introduce examples. The word *like* is used to indicate a similarity between two or more things. Keep these in mind as you move to your next step.

Step 2: Read the sentence for meaning.

While you read the sentence, keep an eye out for both grammar and meaning issues. The object of this step emphasizes *meaning* because many people forget to think about what the sentence is trying to say.

A sentence can be grammatically correct and yet illogical or ambiguous:

> Anne and Millie went to the movies in her car.

Wait a minute…whose car did they take? Anne's? Millie's? Someone else's? The sentence is unclear.

What does the William Pereira sentence say?

The sentence begins with a contrast word (*although*), so make sure the rest of the sentence does convey a contrast. Although he gained recognition for one thing, he was remembered for other, quite different things. That basic meaning does make sense.

Step 3: Find a starting point.

Most SC problems test multiple issues and those issues can appear anywhere in the sentence. Where do you start?

Initially, you're likely to have one of two starting points:

1. You spot an error (or suspected error) in the original sentence.
2. You notice splits, or differences, in the answers.

If you think you've found an issue in the original sentence, immediately look through the answers to make sure you're offered at least one split for that issue. If all five are identical, then you haven't actually found an error. If you are offered splits, go ahead and tackle that issue.

You might get to the end of the original sentence without spotting an error. In this case, start comparing the answers to find splits. If you don't know how to decide about a particular split, ignore it and find another.

The first two steps—first glance and read for meaning—will usually help you to find your first starting point. For instance, in the Pereira problem, the first glance showed a split between *including* and *like*, so as you read, ask yourself: why does the sentence mention these two films? They represent examples of Pereira's movie set designs, and examples should be introduced using the word *including*, not the word *like*.

Step 4: Eliminate all incorrect choices.

Scan down the options. Answers (B) and (C) both use *like*; eliminate them.

A
B̶
C̶
D
E

Repeat!

There are still three choices left, so find another starting point and repeat steps 3 and 4. After a repetition or two, you'll either get down to one answer or get stuck. Either way, pick an answer and move on to the next problem.

If you spot a difference but don't know how to deal with it, ignore that difference and look for some other difference instead.

Now, where are you going to find these new starting points? You have two main options:

1. Tackle errors that you spotted in the original sentence.

2. Compare the remaining answer choices vertically, looking for differences, or splits. If you know how to tackle a particular split, do so!

In the Pereira example, you might note that the answers split on *that* vs. *those*. What is at the heart of that difference?

The two words are pronouns, but one is singular and one is plural. The pronoun is intended to refer back to the plural word *designs*, so the singular *that* is incorrect. Eliminate answer (D).

Now, compare the last two answers, (A) and (E). The only difference is at the end: *remember* vs. *will remember*. Pereira first gained recognition for one thing, but the author postulates that *future generations* are going to remember him for something else. The future tense, *will remember*, fits that meaning.

Eliminate (A) and pick (E).

"Best" Does Not Mean Ideal

Sentence Correction questions ask for the best option *among those given*, not the best option in the universe. Sometimes you may feel—and rightly so—that all the answers, including the correct one, aren't very good. Correct GMAT Sentence Correction answers never break strict grammatical rules, but these answers can sound formal or even awkward. Expect that, at times, a correct answer won't sound or feel very good to you.

SC Timing

In order to have adequate time for RC and CR questions, you'll need to average about 1 minute and 20 seconds per SC problem.

How can you possibly move that quickly and still get the right answer? Here's how:

• Most wrong answers contain more than one error; you only need one valid reason to cross off any wrong answer.

• The same error is often repeated in two or more choices.

• The SC process described earlier capitalizes on the first two points above to get you through the problem as efficiently as possible.

1

In general, try to spend at least 40 seconds on any SC question; if you work more quickly than that, you are more likely to make careless mistakes. Speed is never an advantage if it causes you to miss problems that you know how to answer.

If you're approaching the two-minute mark, wrap the problem up. If you need that long to answer, chances are good that you're missing something or have already made a mistake. Don't cross the two-minute mark on SC; instead, guess from among the remaining answers and move on.

Using This Book

Complete the chapters in the order in which they are presented, because later material sometimes builds on material presented earlier in the book.

At the end of this chapter, you'll find a section called *How to Get Better at the SC Process*. Every chapter or two, return to the *How to Get Better* section and do some drills to hone your skills on the various steps of the process.

When answering practice questions, if you are completely confident that an answer is wrong even though you can't articulate exactly why, go ahead and cross that answer off. When you are reviewing your work afterwards, check to make sure that you were correct. If so, you may be able to trust your "ear" for that type of error in future.

If not, however, then you will need to dive into the grammar or meaning issues, possibly including learning some technical grammar terminology and rules, so that you can retrain your ear for future problems.

The first two chapters of this guide cover strategy and overall lessons for SC, while the subsequent chapters teach specific grammar and meaning concepts that you need to know for the GMAT.

Beginning with Chapter 2, you will have problem sets on which to test your skills. Try about half of the problems included in the end-of-chapter set; save the rest for future study. After you complete each problem, check the answer. Whenever necessary, return to the lessons in the chapter to solidify your understanding before trying the next problem.

You also have online access to problem set lists that refer to questions found in the three *Official Guide* books published by the test makers. If you have access to these other books, then you can use our problem set lists in your practice.

How to Get Better at the SC Process

First Glance

Your first glance at a problem is, by definition, quick and superficial, but—if you get good at this step—you can pick up some very useful clues that will help you read the original sentence with an idea already in mind of what the sentence may be testing.

For SC, pay attention to three issues during your first glance:

Clue	Possible Implication
1. Is the underline very long? Very short?	Very long underlines often signal issues with sentence structure, meaning, modifiers, and parallelism. Very short underlines (less than five words) may lead you to compare the answers in full before reading the original sentence.
2. What is the first underlined word? What is the word right before?	The nature of the first underlined word (or the word just before) can give you a clue about one of the issues tested in the sentence. For example, if the word *has* is the first underlined word, the sentence is likely testing either subject-verb agreement or verb tense, since *has* is a verb.
3. What are the differences among the first word or two of each answer?	There will always be at least one difference at the beginning of the answers (as well as one at the end). It's easy to glance down the first word or two of each answer, so do so. If the first word switches between *has* and *have*, for example, then you know the sentence is testing singular vs. plural. Now, you can actively look for the relevant subject when you read the original sentence.

After you've studied SC for a few weeks and tried some problems from any of the three *Official Guide* books published by the test makers, you can add a first glance drill to your study regimen. Find some lower-numbered (easier) problems that you've already tried in the past. Give yourself a few seconds (no more than five!) to glance at a problem, then look away and say out loud what you noticed in those few seconds.

Afterwards, look at the full problem and remind yourself what it tests. Did your first glance unearth any of those issues? Examine the first underlined word, the one just before, and the first words of each choice more carefully, and ask yourself whether there are any clues, or markers, you missed. If so, write them down on a flash card. Here's an example:

1

(front)	(back)
When I see:	**I'll think:**
and	Parallelism: X and Y X, Y, and Z Could be: a list, a modifier, compound subject or verb, two independent clauses

Sometimes, there are no good clues at the first glance level, so don't expect that this strategy will always help you. Still, don't skip this step; good clues exist for more than 50% of problems, so this quick step is quite valuable.

Read the Sentence for Meaning

Your default strategy is to read the entire original sentence, all the way to the period, noting possible grammar or meaning issues along the way. The non-underlined portion contains very valuable information that can help you decide how to proceed. Once you're done, decide which issue to tackle first. If you think you've spotted an error in the original, verify, then cross off answer (A) as well as any other answers that repeat that same error.

You might, though, choose to break this strategy for one very good reason: you spot an early error in a longer underline and you are 100% sure that you've found a definite error. In that case, go ahead and eliminate choice (A) immediately and glance through the remaining answers to eliminate any with that same error. At that point, though, return to the original sentence and finish reading it, keeping an eye out for any additional errors that you could use to eliminate other answers.

Either way, read the entire original sentence so that you can spot overall issues with meaning or sentence structure. If you don't, you'll be much more likely to fall into a trap.

To drill yourself on meaning, pull out your *Official Guide* again and look at some problems you've done in the past. Read only the original sentence (not the answers), then look away and try to articulate aloud, in your own words, what the sentence is trying to say. (You don't need to limit your rephrase to a single sentence.)

Do actually talk out loud. You'll be able to hear the conviction in your own voice when you know what the sentence is trying to say and you'll also know if you don't really know what the sentence means.

In the latter case, examine the problem again. Either you just didn't understand it or there was actually a meaning issue in that sentence. Which is it? Check the solution: does it say that there is a meaning problem? If so, then great—no wonder you had trouble rephrasing it. If not, then the explanation itself

1

may help you to understand what the sentence is trying to say. (If you don't like the official solution, you can find many *Official Guide* solutions in our *GMAT Navigator*™ program.)

Find a Starting Point

Most of the time, you'll have to find multiple starting points on SC problems—one of the annoying things about this problem type. There are two primary ways to find a starting point: read the original sentence and compare answers.

To drill the latter skill, open up your *Official Guide* again and look at some problems you have done before. This time, do NOT read the original sentence. Instead, cover it up.

Compare the answers and, based on the splits that you spot, try to articulate all of the things that the problem is testing.

You usually won't be able to pick an answer, but you can often tell *what* is being tested even when you can't tell *how* to answer. For example, you might see a verb switching back and forth between singular and plural. If the subject isn't underlined, then you can't know which verb form is required (because you haven't read the sentence!), but you do know that subject-verb agreement is an issue.

When you're done, read the underlined portion of the sentence or check the solution. How good were you at figuring out what the problem was testing? What clues did you miss? Consider making flash cards for those clues.

Eliminate All Incorrect Choices

One of the most annoying moments in SC occurs when you've narrowed the answers down to two… and then you don't know how to decide. When this happens to you, don't waste time going back and forth repeatedly, agonizing over the answers. Pick one of the two and move on.

Afterward, review the problem and learn how to make that choice. Add the following analysis to your overall review of SC problems:

1. Why is the right answer right? Why are each of the four wrong answers wrong?
2. How would someone (mistakenly) justify *eliminating* the right answer? What is the trap that would lead someone to cross out the correct answer?
3. How would someone (mistakenly) justify *picking* any of the wrong answers? What is the trap that would lead someone to pick a wrong answer?

When you learn how you (or someone) would fall into the trap of thinking that some wrong answer looks or sounds or feels better than the right one, you'll be a lot less likely to fall into that same trap yourself in future.

1

Throughout this guide, you will encounter both wrong and right examples to teach you the precise differences:

Wrong: The value of the stock ROSE by a 10% INCREASE.

Right: The value of the stock INCREASED by 10%.

Don't just glance over those examples. Cement the wrongness of the wrong options in your brain by crossing or X-ing them out as you read and even adding a note as to why they're wrong:

Wrong: ~~The value of the stock ROSE by a 10% INCREASE.~~

Redundant! Rose or increase, not both.

Right: The value of the stock INCREASED by 10%.

MANHATTAN
PREP

Chapter 2

of

Sentence Correction

Grammar & Meaning

In This Chapter...

Chapter 2
Grammar & Meaning

Sentence Correction (SC) appears on the GMAT because business schools want to be sure that their admitted applicants grasp the two principles of good business writing:

1. **Grammar:** Does the sentence adhere to the rules of standard written English?
2. **Meaning:** Does the sentence clearly indicate the author's intended meaning?

These principles are equally important and actually overlap quite a bit. Certain grammar rules exist in order to convey a logical and unambiguous meaning. You'll learn some of these principles in this chapter and others as you work your way through this guide.

Grammar: Much of the language that you hear in everyday speech actually violates one rule or another. The GMAT tests your ability to distinguish between good and bad grammar, even when the bad grammar seems natural.

Consider this example: *Does everyone have their book?* You likely hear similar sentences all the time, but the question actually violates the rules of standard written English. It should read: *Does everyone have his or her book?*

Meaning: Confusing writing is bad writing. If you have to read a sentence more than once to figure out what the author is saying—or if the sentence lends itself to multiple interpretations—it is not a good sentence.

What about the often-cited "principle" of concision? It is true that the GMAT does not like to waste words. If an idea expressed in 10 words can be expressed clearly and grammatically in 6, the GMAT prefers 6. However, this is a *preference*, not a rule.

Test-takers focus far too quickly and broadly on concision. As a result, the GMAT often makes the right answer *less* concise than an attractive wrong answer. Furthermore, *Official Guide* (OG) explanations often label a sentence wordy or awkward without additional explanation; typically, these sentences have a meaning problem or an idiom error. In general, focus your efforts on grammar and meaning; concision is unlikely to help much.

2

Grammar: A Closer Look

This guide will steer you through the major points of standard written English on the GMAT. Each chapter will present a major grammatical topic in depth: sentence structure, modifiers, parallelism, comparisons, pronouns, verbs, and idioms. You will learn both the overarching principles of each grammatical topic and the nitty-gritty details that will help you differentiate correct grammar from poor grammar. You will also complete practice exercises designed to hone your skills in that topic.

For your reference, a glossary of common grammatical terms appears in Appendix B of this book. Do *not* be overly concerned with the names of the grammatical terms, as the GMAT will never require you to know what the rules are called. The terms are simply necessary to explain various grammatical rules. Focus on understanding and applying these rules, not on memorizing terms.

The Five Grammar Terms You Need to Know

We try to keep fancy terms to a minimum in this book, but there's no way to discuss grammar without using at least a few actual grammar terms. Here are the five terms you absolutely need to know:

1. Clause

A **clause** is a set of words that contains a subject and a working verb. This is a clause:

> She applied for the job.

She	*applied*
Who applied for the job? She did.	What did she do? She applied.

She is the **subject** because she is the one performing the action. *Applied* is the **working verb** because it describes what the subject did. For any sentence, you could ask, "Who (or what) did what?" and the (correct) answer will point to the subject and working verb.

Together, the subject and working verb create a complete, stand-alone sentence, or an **independent clause**. Independent clauses have, at the very least, a subject and a verb. Every correct sentence must have at least one independent clause.

A **dependent clause** also contains a verb but cannot stand alone as a sentence.

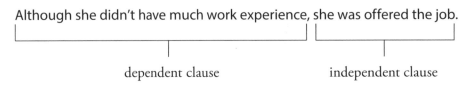

A complete sentence requires one independent clause, but more complex sentences will also include something else: another independent clause, a dependent clause, or other modifiers.

Without an independent clause, you have a **sentence fragment**. This is a fragment:

> Although she didn't have much work experience.

You'll learn more about clauses in Chapter 3, "Sentence Structure," of this guide.

2. Modifier

A **modifier** provides additional information in a sentence, beyond the core subject and verb. The simplest example is an adjective. For example, in the phrase *the happy child*, the word *happy*, an adjective, is a modifier.

Modifiers can also be more complex:

> The large dog, which has black fur, is a Labrador.

The modifier *which has black fur* is called a **nonessential modifier**. If you remove it from the sentence, the core of the sentence still makes sense: *The large dog is a Labrador.*

Compare that to this sentence:

> The job that she started last week is much harder than her previous job.

In this sentence, *that she started last week* is called an **essential modifier**. Why is this one essential? Look what happens when you remove it from the sentence:

> The job is much harder than her previous job.

The *job*? What *job*? If you haven't already specified a particular job, then the meaning of the sentence is murky. This is the hallmark of an essential modifier: the modifier is necessary in order to understand the meaning of the sentence.

You can find a full discussion in Chapter 4, "Modifiers," of this guide.

3. Sentence Core

The **core** of a sentence consists of any independent clauses along with some essential modifiers. This is the bare minimum needed in order to have a coherent sentence.

Any nonessential modifiers are stripped out of the sentence core. See more on sentence core in Chapter 4 of this guide.

4. Conjunction

Conjunctions are words that help to stick parts of sentences together. Here's an example:

> He worked hard, **and** a raise was his reward.

2

Coordinating conjunctions, such as *and*, can glue two independent clauses together. Both *he worked hard* and *a raise was his reward* are independent clauses. The most common coordinating conjunctions are the FANBOYS: *for, and, nor, but, or, yet, so*.

Modifiers can be connected to independent clauses by **subordinating conjunctions**. You saw an example of this before:

> Although she didn't have much work experience, she was offered the job.

The word *although* is a subordinating conjunction. Other examples include *because, while, though, unless, before, after,* and *if*.

You'll learn more about conjunctions in Chapters 3 and 4 of this guide.

5. Marker

This one is not an official grammar term, but it's important. A **marker** is a flag or clue that a certain kind of issue is being tested. On occasion, this book will talk about certain kinds of markers. For example, the word *unlike* is a comparison marker; when you see *unlike*, you should think about comparisons.

Let's say you read an explanation and think, "Hmm, I didn't know that that word was a marker for that kind of grammar issue." If this happens, immediately write that marker down! Keep a list, make flash cards, record it however you prefer—but do record (and study) the fact that this particular marker should have made you think about a certain grammar issue.

That's all to start. (Yes, technically, we did sneak more than five terms into that list. The terms are all related, though.)

If you run across other unfamiliar terms, you can look them up in the glossary at the end of this guide.

Meaning: A Closer Look

A clear sentence is transparent—the author's intended meaning shines through. On the GMAT, however, either the original sentence or its variations may muddy the waters. One of your tasks is to choose the answer choice that conveys a logical and clear meaning. Consider this sentence:

> Tomorrow, she bought some milk.

No grammar rule is violated in that sentence, but the sentence doesn't make any sense! Either she bought the milk in the past or she will buy the milk in the future. You know the sentence is wrong because the *meaning is illogical*.

If the meaning of the original sentence is clear, start looking for grammar issues.

If, however, the original sentence is confusing, you will need to discern the author's intent. Fortunately, this intent will not be buried too deeply. After all, the correct sentence has to be one of the five choices. Thus, the GMAT tends to make use of "small" errors in meaning that can be easy to overlook.

Most instances of *meaning errors* fall into one of three major categories:

1. Choose your words
2. Place your words
3. Match your words

Choose Your Words

Did the author pick the right words out of the dictionary? If a word has more than one meaning, is the author using that word correctly, to indicate the right meaning? The GMAT rarely tests you on pure vocabulary, but very occasionally, it tries to pull a trick on you by switching a particular word and its cousin. For example:

> My decision to drive a hybrid car was motivated by ECONOMIC considerations.
> ECONOMICAL considerations motivated my decision to drive a hybrid car.

The second sentence, which is shorter and punchier, may look preferable. Unfortunately, it is wrong! *Economical* means "thrifty, efficient." Notice that this meaning is not too distant from what the author intends to say: he or she wants an efficient automobile. But the appropriate phrase is *economic considerations*—that is, *monetary* considerations.

Consider the following pairs of "cousin" words and expressions, together with their distinct meanings:

> *aggravate* (worsen) vs. *aggravating* (irritating)
> *known as* (named) vs. *known to be* (acknowledged as)
> *loss of* (no longer in possession of) vs. *loss in* (decline in value)
> *mandate* (command) vs. *have a mandate* (have authority from voters)
> *native of* (person from) vs. *native to* (species that originated in)
> *range of* (variety of) vs. *ranging* (varying)
> *rate of* (speed or frequency of) vs. *rates for* (prices for)
> *rise* (general increase) vs. *raise* (a bet or a salary increase in American English)
> *try to do* (seek to accomplish) vs. *try doing* (experiment with)

Big changes in meaning can be accomplished with switches of little words. Certain **helping verbs**, such as *may*, *will*, *must*, and *should*, provide another way for the GMAT to test meaning.

These helping verbs express various levels of certainty, obligation, and reality. Simply by swapping these verbs, the GMAT can completely change the meaning of the sentence.

2

Example 1

Absolutely Necessary: The court ruled that the plaintiff MUST pay full damages.

Morally Obliged: The court ruled that the plaintiff SHOULD pay full damages.

Notice that the second sentence <u>cannot</u> be correct. Why? The word *should* means "moral obligation"—something that a court cannot impose. On the other hand, the use of *must* in the first sentence indicates a legally binding obligation imposed upon the plaintiff. Thus, you should go with *must*, whether the original sentence used *must* or not. On the GMAT, *should* almost always indicates "moral obligation," <u>not</u> "likelihood." In everyday speech, you can say *The train should arrive now* to mean that the train is <u>likely</u> to arrive now, but the GMAT doesn't agree with this usage.

Example 2

Actual: If Chris and Jad met, they DISCUSSED mathematics.

Hypothetical: If Chris and Jad met, they WOULD DISCUSS mathematics.

The first sentence could be said by someone who is unsure whether Chris and Jad have actually met: "If this did indeed happen, then that is the consequence." The second sentence, however, predicts the consequences of a hypothetical meeting of the two people: "If this were to happen, then that would be the consequence."

Pay attention to the original sentence's helping verbs—and only change them if the original sentence is obviously nonsensical.

For more on helping verbs see Chapter 8, "Verbs" of the guide.

Place Your Words

Beware of words that move from one position to another. The placement of a single word can alter the meaning of a sentence. For example:

> ALL the children are covered in mud.
> The children are ALL covered in mud.

In these sentences, changing the placement of *all* shifts the intent from *how many* children (all of them) to *how* the children are covered in mud (all over). Consider another example:

> ONLY the council votes on Thursdays.
> The council votes ONLY on Thursdays.

In the first sentence, *only* indicates that the council alone votes on Thursdays (as opposed to the board, perhaps, which can vote any other day, but not Thursdays). In the second sentence, *only* indicates that the council does not vote on any day but Thursday.

If a word changes its position in the answer choices, consider whether the change has an impact on the meaning of the sentence. Look out especially for short words (such as *only* and *all*) that quantify nouns or otherwise restrict meaning.

At a broader level, pay attention to **overall word order**. All the words in a sentence could be well-chosen, but the sentence could still be awkward or ambiguous. For example:

> The council granted the right to make legal petitions TO CITY OFFICIALS.

What does the phrase *to city officials* mean? Did the city officials receive the right to make legal petitions? Or did someone else receive the right to make petitions *to the officials*? Either way, the correct sentence should resolve the ambiguity:

> The council granted CITY OFFICIALS the right to make legal petitions.
> OR
> The right to make legal petitions TO CITY OFFICIALS was granted by the council.

Match Your Words

Sentences generally contain pairs of words or phrases that must match. As you saw in an example earlier in this chapter, a verb must match the time frame of the overall sentence.

These matches also have grammatical implications. What's wrong with the following comparison?

> Unlike Alaska, where the winter is quite cold, the temperature in Florida rarely
> goes below freezing.

Though you know that the author is trying to say that Alaska and Florida are dissimilar, technically, the sentence says that *Alaska* and the *temperature* in Florida are dissimilar. It's illogical to compare a state to the temperature in another state.

A similar matching principle holds for other grammatical connections (e.g., pronouns and the nouns to which they refer). Future chapters will explore each type of connection in turn; for now, remember to test the *meaning* of any potential connection. Connected words must always make sense together.

Avoid Redundancy

Another aspect of meaning is redundancy. Each word in the correct choice must be necessary to the meaning of the sentence. If a word can be removed without subtracting from the meaning of the sentence, it should be eliminated. Redundancy goes beyond mere concision—redundancy confuses the meaning, causing the reader to ask: "Did I read that right?" No right answer on the GMAT will contain redundant words.

A common redundancy trap on the GMAT is the use of words with the same meaning:

> Wrong: The value of the stock ROSE by a 10% INCREASE.
> Right: The value of the stock INCREASED by 10%.
> Right: The value of the stock ROSE by 10%.

Since *rose* and *increase* both imply growth, only one is needed.

> Wrong: The three prices SUM to a TOTAL of $11.56.
> Right: The three prices SUM to $11.56.
> Right: The three prices TOTAL $11.56.

Since *sum* and *total* convey the same meaning, only one is needed. Consider this example:

Pay attention to expressions of time. It is easy to sneak two redundant time expressions into an answer choice (especially if one expression is in the non-underlined part, or if the two expressions do not look like each other):

PAST:	Previously	Formerly	In the past	Before now
PRESENT:	Now	Currently	Presently	At present
YEARLY:	Annual	Each year	A year (e.g., *three launches a year*)	

A sentence should include only one such expression. This does not mean that you can never repeat time expressions in a sentence; just be sure that you are doing so for a meaningful reason.

Also pay attention to transition words, such as contrast words. What is wrong with the sentence below?

> Although she studied night and day for three months, yet she did not do well on her exam.

The word *although* already conveys the coming contrast; it is unnecessary to use the second contrast word, *yet*.

Problem Set

The underlined portion of each sentence below may contain one or more errors (including illogical or ambiguous meaning). Each sentence is followed by a **boldface** sample answer choice. Select **(A)** if the original version is correct, **(B)** if the boldface version is correct, **(C)** if neither is correct, and **(D)** if both are correct.

If you select **(A)**, explain what is wrong with the boldface version. If you select **(B)**, explain how the boldface version corrects the original version. If you select **(C)**, explain why both versions are incorrect. Some questions refer to rules and distinctions that will be discussed in upcoming chapters.

1. <u>No matter how much work it may require</u>, getting an MBA is an investment that pays off for most people.
    Though it doesn't require much work

2. The driver picked up <u>the people at the airport who had been waiting</u>.
    the people who had been waiting at the airport

3. Rising costs of raw materials <u>may result in fewer employees on the assembly line or product volume</u>.
    could resolve itself in fewer employees on the assembly line or in lower product volume.

4. She is the most dedicated gardener on the block, watering <u>the more than 50 plants in her yard every day</u>.
    more every day than the 50 plants in her yard

5. Hector remembers San Francisco <u>as it was when he left 10 years ago</u>.
    as though time has stood still in the 10 years since he left

6. Students at Carver High School are encouraged to pursue only those extracurricular activities from which <u>stems success in college applications</u>.
    success in college applications stems

Fix the following four sentences. Look for issues outlined in this chapter.

7. After the test format was changed, scores subsequently dropped by more than a 25% decrease.

8. It is possible that the earthquake may have caused the building's collapse.

9. Though canals have experienced a severe decline in barge traffic over the past several decades, yet with the rise in fuel costs, "shipping" by actual ships may once again become an important means of transporting goods within the country.

10. Orinoco.com, a major internet retailer, announced mixed results for the second quarter: the number of people shopping at Orinoco.com grew by a 34% rise, but profit per customer fell sharply as consumers shifted to lower-margin items in response to uncertain economic conditions.

MANHATTAN
PREP

Solutions

1. (A): The original sentence indicates that getting an MBA might be a lot of work, but it still turns out to be a good investment for most people. The boldface version loses this contrasting idea: getting an MBA is not a lot of work, *though* (or *but*) it still turns out to be a good investment? It would be more logical to connect two positives with *and*, not the contrast word *though*: it's not a lot of work *and* it's a good investment!

2. (C): In the original sentence, the modifier *who had been waiting* does not clearly modify *the people*. It appears, illogically, to modify the closer noun (*the airport ride*). The boldface version moves *who had been waiting* next to *the people*, thus making clear that it is *the people* who *had been waiting*. However, this change introduces a new problem: an ambiguous meaning. Did the taxi driver *take for a ride* the people who had been waiting for something unspecified (maybe they were waiting for the sun to set)? Or did the taxi driver take the people who had been *waiting for someone to give them a ride*?

3. (C): Neither is correct! The original sentence offers two possible results of the rising costs of raw materials: the company in question may put *fewer employees on the assembly line* or it may have...*fewer product volume*. Product volume is uncountable, so it should say *lesser* or *lower* product volume. You can learn more about countable and uncountable nouns in the Modifiers chapter.

The boldface version corrects this error but introduces a new one: *resolve itself* means fix itself, but the rising costs are not going to fix themselves. Nor is the abstract situation going to fix itself. Some human will have to take steps to fix the situation.

4. (A): The original version contains the phrase *the more than 50 plants*. Here the words *more than* modify the number 50. The sentence therefore means that she waters her own (more than 50) plants daily. In the boldface version, the phrase changes to *more every day than the 50 plants in her yard*. Is she watering more and more as each day passes? Is she watering additional plants every day beyond her own 50, or is she watering more than 50 plants a day somewhere else (not in her own garden)? The meaning is ambiguous.

5. (D): Both versions use different words to convey the same idea. Hector left San Francisco 10 years ago and he remembers it as he left it. As far as his memories are concerned, nothing has changed in San Francisco in the last 10 years!

6. (D): Both versions are correct. The original sentence inverts the normal order of subject (*success*) and verb (*stems* = "originates"). This inversion is perfectly acceptable in this sentence construction, even if it sounds a bit funny.

7. After the test format was changed, scores dropped by more than 25%. Eliminate redundancy. You do not need both *dropped* and *decrease*, since both words convey the same idea. For the same reason, you do not need both *after* and *subsequently*.

2

8. **The earthquake may have caused the building's collapse.** Eliminate redundancy. *It is possible that* and *may* both express the same level of uncertainty, so you can remove one of them without changing the intended meaning.

9. **Canals have experienced a severe decline in barge traffic over the past several decades, yet with the rise in fuel costs, "shipping" by actual ships may once again become an important means of transporting goods within the country.** (No *Though* at the beginning of the sentence.)

Using both *Though* and *yet* is redundant. It is preferable to keep *yet* in order to delineate the contrast clearly; otherwise, you might mistakenly consider the phrase *with the rise of fuel costs* as part of the first clause.

10. **Orinoco.com, a major internet retailer, announced mixed results for the second quarter: the number of people shopping at Orinoco.com grew by 34%, but profit per customer fell sharply as consumers shifted to lower-margin items in response to uncertain economic conditions.**

Eliminate redundancy. *By a 34% rise* should be *by 34%*. The verb *grew* already conveys the idea of an increase, so there is no need to use the noun *rise*.

Chapter 3 of Sentence Correction

Sentence Structure

In This Chapter...

Chapter 3
Sentence Structure

Every sentence must have a **subject** and a **verb**. The subject is the noun that performs the action expressed by the verb:

The DOG with the gray ears RUNS out of the house.
    Subject   Verb

The subject, the *dog*, is performing the action of *running*. Moreover, the subject and the verb must agree in number: in this case, both *dog* and *runs* are singular.

How does the GMAT make things more complicated?

Subject and Verb Must Both Exist

If a sentence is missing the subject or the verb, the sentence is a **fragment**; in other words, it is not a complete sentence! On the GMAT, the correct answer must be a complete sentence, or **independent clause.**

The GMAT might disguise the error by dropping the verb:

Wrong: The cat sitting by the stairs.

Wait a minute, what about *sitting*? *Sitting* certainly looks like a verb. It is not, however, a **working verb**, a verb that can run a sentence by itself. Here's an example of a working verb:

Right: The cat sitting by the stairs WATCHED the mouse.

In this sentence, the word *watched* is a working verb. Here's another example of a working verb:

Right: The cat WAS SITTING by the stairs.

In this sentence, the words *was sitting* make up the full verb form. The word *sitting* is called a **present participle** and you'll see more of these "-*ing*" words throughout this book. For now, just remember that an -*ing* word by itself is never a working verb: *The cat sitting by the stairs* is not a sentence.

These are also not complete sentences:

Wrong:	BECAUSE the dog was never mine.
Wrong:	WHICH will be approved tomorrow.

Because and *which* are connecting words. They add extra information to a sentence, but they are not sentences by themselves. They're examples of **modifiers**, which you will learn about in the next chapter.

The correct answer must contain at least one independent clause; if an answer choice does not, eliminate it!

Subject and Verb Must Agree in Number

A singular subject requires a singular verb form:

The <u>dog runs</u> out of the house.

A plural subject requires a plural verb form:

The <u>dogs run</u> out of the house.

You already know this; you would never write *the dog run out* or *the dogs runs out*. The GMAT, therefore, has to try to obscure these errors so that some people will fall into a trap.

How? The GMAT might hide the subject, so that you are unsure whether the subject is singular or plural. If you do not know the number of the subject, then you will not be able to select the verb form that agrees with it. Consider this example:

The discovery of new medicines (was/were) vital to the company's growth.

What is the subject, *discovery* or *new medicines*? If you ask yourself, "What is/are vital to the company's growth?" you may be able to talk yourself into either choice. It makes as much sense to say the *discovery was vital* as it does to say the *new medicines were vital*.

In this case, *The discovery … was* is the correct subject–verb pair because the noun *medicines* is part of the **prepositional phrase** *of new medicines*. A noun in a prepositional phrase cannot be the subject of the sentence.

Are these sentences both correct?

> Lin and Guy drive to work.
> Lin, as well as Guy, drive to work every day.

The first sentence is a correct example of a **compound subject**: Lin and Guy together function as the subject of the sentence. Compound subjects are always plural because at least two nouns function as the subject.

A compound subject <u>must</u> be connected by the word *and*, but the second sentence uses the modifier *as well as Guy*. Only Lin qualifies as the subject, so the sentence is incorrect. It should read:

> Right: LIN,   as well as Guy,   <u>drives</u> to work every day.
>   Subject   Modifier   Verb

A sentence can also contain a **compound verb** (two or more verbs that all point to the same subject). For example:

> Right: Lin   *drove* to work   *and*   *said* hello to his co-worker.
>   Subject Verb   Conjunction   Verb

> Right: *Lin*   *and*   *Guy*   *drive* to work together every morning *and*
>   Subject Conjunction Subject Verb   Conjunction
>
>   *greet* their co-workers cheerfully.
>   Verb

That last sentence contains both a compound subject and a compound verb. If the writer inserts enough distance between the two portions of a compound subject or verb, it could be easy to make a mistake. Read on to learn how the GMAT does this.

Eliminate the Middlemen and Skip the Warmup

The most common way to hide a subject is to insert words between the subject and the verb; we call these words the **middlemen**. If you learn to ignore these words when looking for a subject, you'll be much less likely to pick the wrong noun as the subject.

Further, the GMAT often puts a significant number of words in front of the subject you want. In these cases, you have to ignore the **warmup** that comes before the subject of the sentence.

There are a few common types of middlemen and warmups.

1. Prepositional Phrases

A prepositional phrase is a group of words headed by a **preposition**. For example:

of mice	for milk	by 1800
in Zambia	with her	at that level
to the store	on their orders	from the office

The prepositions underlined above are among the most common in the English language. A list of common prepositions is included in Appendix B.

Prepositions are followed by nouns or pronouns, which complete the phrase. Prepositional phrases modify or describe other parts of the sentence. A noun in a prepositional phrase will not be the main subject of the sentence.

> Near Galway, the houses on the road to Spiddle is/are gorgeous.
> ~~Near Galway~~, the HOUSES ~~on the road to Spiddle~~ ARE gorgeous.

In the example above, the subject is *houses* (plural) and the correct verb is *are* (also plural).

2. Dependent Clauses

Dependent clauses, which begin with connecting words such as *who* or *because*, cannot stand alone as sentences. Nor are they part of the main subject or main verb; rather, they are always attached to independent clauses. Look at the first sentence in this paragraph: can you find the dependent clause? (Hint: examine the commas.)

> Dependent: *which begin with connecting words such as* who *or* because
> Independent: *Dependent clauses cannot stand alone as sentences.*

If a dependent clause is stripped out of a sentence, what remains is still a complete sentence.

Try another example:

> Because she studied hard, she earned a good score on the test.

What is the dependent clause? What is the independent clause (complete sentence)?

> Dependent: *because she studied hard*
> Independent: *She earned a good score on the test.*

3. Other Modifiers

Other words can also function as modifiers, which add extra information to the sentence. Modifiers will be covered in depth in Chapter 4.

Use Structure to Decide

Consider the following sentence:

> In the waning days of the emperor's life, the conquest of new lands on the
> borders of the empire was/were considered vital.

To find the subject of the verb *was* or *were considered*, you might be tempted to ask yourself, "What *was* or *were considered* vital?" This method will get rid of obviously inappropriate subjects, such as *the emperor's life* or *the waning days*, but you could fall into the trap of thinking that *new lands* is the subject. However, *new lands* is in a prepositional phrase modifying the noun *conquest*. Since a noun in a prepositional phrase cannot be the subject of the sentence (with limited idiomatic exceptions that you'll learn about later), the subject must be *conquest*:

Wrong: ~~In the waning days of the emperor's life,~~ the CONQUEST ~~of new lands on the borders of the empire~~ WERE CONSIDERED vital.

Right: ~~In the waning days of the emperor's life,~~ the CONQUEST ~~of new lands on the borders of the empire~~ WAS CONSIDERED vital.

Do not fall for tempting nouns, such as *new lands*, inserted to distract you! Instead, use the structure of the sentence to eliminate the middlemen and find the subject.

Now consider this example:

> The tidal forces to which an object falling into a black hole is/are subjected is/are
> sufficient to tear the object apart.

You have to match up two subject–verb pairs on this one. First, find the main subject and match it with the appropriate verb:

Better: The tidal FORCES ~~to which an object falling into a black hole is/are subjected~~ ARE sufficient to tear the object apart.

Next, match up the subject and the verb in the dependent clause:

Right: The tidal forces to which an OBJECT ~~falling into a black hole~~ IS SUBJECTED are sufficient to tear the object apart.

Mid-Chapter Quiz: Test Your Skills

Fix the following sentences. Look for issues outlined in this chapter.

1. The recent string of burglaries, in addition to poor building maintenance, have inspired the outspoken resident to call a tenants meeting.

2. A new textbook focused on recent advances in artificial intelligence assigned by our instructor.

3. The proliferation of computer games designed to involve many players at once were first developed before the widespread availability of high-speed internet connections.

Answer Key: Test Your Skills

Changes made to the original sentence are underlined.

1. The recent string of burglaries, in addition to poor building maintenance, <u>has inspired</u> the outspoken resident to call a tenants meeting. [*String* is used here as a singular noun. Omit the middlemen *of burglaries* and *in addition to poor building maintenance.*]

2. A new textbook focused on recent advances in artificial intelligence <u>was assigned</u> by our instructor. [The original is a fragment. A simple fix is to add a form of the verb *to be*, such as *was*.]

3. Computer games designed to involve many players at once were first developed before the widespread availability of high-speed internet connections. [This is a tricky one! The subject and verb have to make sense together, but the original sentence says that *the proliferation … were first developed*; this is illogical. Rather, the *computer games were developed*. The corrected sentence is just one possible rewrite.]

You may want to pause to let the first half of this chapter sink in before you continue with the rest. Consider picking up this lesson again later today or tomorrow.

Building Complex Sentences

How else can the test writers add complexity to sentences? Take a look at this example:

> Despite some initial concerns, the teacher is confident that her students mastered the lesson.

The core structure of the sentence is this:

> *The teacher is confident that her students mastered the lesson.*
>   Subject   Verb   THAT   Subject   Verb   Object

When the word *that* appears just after a working verb, it acts as a "re-set" button in the sentence: a new subject–verb–object structure will follow.

Note: the word *that* can also serve other roles, which you'll learn about throughout this guide.

In the real world, people will often drop the word *that* from the sentence structure:

> Wrong on the GMAT: **The teacher is confident her students mastered the lesson.**

This is acceptable in the real world, but it doesn't follow the strictest grammar conventions. Technically, the missing *that* can make the sentence ambiguous; consider this example:

> Wrong: **I know Meryl Streep is an actor.**

Do you actually know Meryl Streep herself? Or do you know something about Meryl Streep?

> Right: **I know that Meryl Streep is an actor.**

When a sentence is trying to convey something more complex, the word *that* signals to the reader that more information is coming. The teacher isn't just confident in her students in general. She is confident *that they mastered the lesson.*

Two Independent Clauses

Two complete sentences can be connected into one long sentence. For example:

> Right: **Lin drove to work,   but   Guy rode his bike.**
>   Independent Clause Conjunction Independent Clause

Lin drove to work is a complete sentence. So is *Guy rode his bike.* Two complete sentences can be connected using a comma plus a conjunction (such as *but*) to create a **compound sentence**.

But is part of a group of seven conjunctions called the FANBOYS:

> <u>F</u>or
> <u>A</u>nd
> <u>N</u>or
> <u>B</u>ut
> <u>O</u>r
> <u>Y</u>et
> <u>S</u>o

The English language contains many conjunctions; these seven are special because they are very common in the English language and because they can also be used to connect two independent clauses into one complex sentence.

It is not acceptable, however, to connect two sentences using only a comma:

Wrong: Lin drove to work   ,   Guy rode his bike.
             Independent Clause   Comma without Conjunction!   Independent Clause

The above is called a **run-on sentence** or a comma splice. Any GMAT answer choice that connects two independent clauses via only a comma is incorrect.

Pop quiz! Can you spot the error in the sentence below?

Wrong: The latest statistics released by the Labor Department indicate that producer prices rose rapidly last month, despite a generally weakening economy, some analysts contend that the economic slowdown in the euro zone and in Asia will stem the rise in commodity prices, reducing inflationary pressures in the United States.

The sentence above is a run-on. The example below strips the sentence to its core subject and verb components and adds the necessary conjunction:

Right: The latest statistics ... indicate that producer prices rose ... ,   BUT
                        Independent Clause   Conjunction

            some analysts contend that the economic slowdown ... will stem the rise in
                  Independent Clause

            commodity prices.

Here's another type of error the GMAT might throw at you:

Wrong: The term "Eureka," meaning "I have found it" in ancient Greek and famously uttered by Archimedes, and ever since then, scientists have exclaimed the same word upon making important discoveries.

What's the problem with that sentence? It may look fine because it correctly contains a comma along with the conjunction *and*.

Unfortunately, the first half is not a complete sentence. Try to make it stand alone:

Wrong: The term "Eureka," meaning "I have found it" in ancient Greek and famously uttered by Archimedes.

The term "Eureka" could be a subject, but the rest is only a modifier; it does not contain a working verb.

You could fix the sentence by turning the first part into an independent clause:

Right: The term "Eureka," meaning "I have found it" in ancient Greek, WAS famously uttered by Archimedes, and ever since then, scientists have exclaimed the same word upon making important discoveries.

In sum, use a comma plus a FANBOYS conjunction to connect independent clauses. Cross off any answers that connect two independent clauses using only a comma.

Semicolon

You can also connect two independent clauses using a semicolon. The semicolon (;) connects two closely related statements. Each statement must be able to stand alone as an independent sentence. For instance:

Right: Earl walked to school; he later ate his lunch.

Consider another example:

Wrong: Andrew and Lisa are inseparable; doing everything together.

The second part of this sentence cannot stand on its own. Therefore, the two parts may not be connected by a semicolon.

Right: Andrew and Lisa are inseparable; they do everything together.

In the corrected example above, the two sentence parts can each stand alone. Therefore, they may be connected by a semicolon.

The semicolon is often followed by a transition expression, such as *however, therefore,* or *in addition.* In this way, the writer can modify the equal relationship that a bare semicolon implies. Note that these transitional elements are not true conjunctions like *and.* As a result, you must use semicolons, not commas, to join the sentences:

Wrong: Andrew and Lisa are inseparable, THEREFORE, we never see them apart.
Right: Andrew and Lisa are inseparable; THEREFORE, we never see them apart.

A rare but correct use of the semicolon is to separate items that themselves contain commas:

Wrong: I listen to *Earth, Wind & Fire, Wow, Owls,* and *Blood, Sweat & Tears.*
Right: I listen to *Earth, Wind & Fire; Wow, Owls;* and *Blood, Sweat & Tears.*

You'll learn about colons and dashes, which are less common, in Chapter 10.

Adding Modifiers

Quick quiz: what do you remember about dependent clauses? (You first learned about them earlier in this chapter, in the *Eliminate the Middlemen* section.) Glance back through that section if your brain is swimming in all of these new grammar terms.

Dependent clauses are modifiers; they add extra information to the sentence. In addition to independent clauses, GMAT SC sentences will also contain dependent clauses in order to make these sentences as complex (and annoying!) as possible.

You'll learn all about these modifiers in the next chapter. For now, concentrate on learning the core sentence structures discussed in this chapter so that you are fully prepared to add even more complexity when you move to Chapter 4.

Problem Set

In each of the following sentences, (a) (circle) the verb and (b) <u>underline</u> the subject. Then (c) determine whether the subject and the verb make sense together and (d) determine whether the subject agrees in number with the verb. If the subject is singular, the verb form must be singular. If the subject is plural, the verb form must be plural.

If the sentence is a fragment, or if the subject and verb do not make sense together, or if the subject and verb do not agree, (e) rewrite the sentence correcting the mistake. If the sentence is correct as it is, mark it with the word CORRECT.

3

1. A venomous snake designated the emblem of the rebellion by the insurgency.

2. A number of players on the team have improved since last season.

3. Jack, along with some of his closest friends, is sharing a limo to the prom.

4. There is, according to my doctor, many courses of treatment available to me.

5. After all the gardening we did, the sun shining on the flowerbeds make a beautiful sight.

6. The decision to place the beautiful artifacts in out-of-the-way nooks around the mansion's various rooms was inspiring.

7. Just around the corner is a fantastic bakery and a small supermarket.

Fix the following sentences if necessary. Look for issues outlined in this chapter.

8. The music company was afraid of the accelerating decline of sales of compact discs would not be compensated by increased internet revenue.

9. The petroleum distillates were so viscous, the engineers had to heat the pipe by nearly 30 degrees.

10. The municipality's back-to-work program has had notable success, nevertheless, it is not suitable for a state-wide rollout for several reasons.

11. Historically, the Isle of Man had an economy based primarily on agriculture and fishing; now, one based on banking, tourism, and film production.

12. The Bentley trench, situated more than a mile and a half below sea level and completely covered by Antarctic glaciers, and it is the lowest point on the planet not under the oceans.

Solutions

Answers labeled CORRECT were already correct as written.

1. A venomous <u>snake</u> (was designated) the emblem of the rebellion by the insurgency. [The original is a fragment, with *designated* as a past participle. A simple fix is to add a form of the verb *to be*, such as *was*.]

2. A <u>number</u> of players on the team (have improved) since last season. CORRECT [A *number of* is plural.]

3. <u>Jack</u>, along with some of his closest friends, (is sharing) a limo to the prom. CORRECT [Omit middlemen beginning with words such as *along with*.]

4. There (are), according to my doctor, many <u>courses</u> of treatment available to me. [The subject *many courses* comes after the verb with *there is* or *there are*.]

5. After all the gardening we did, the <u>sun</u> shining on the flowerbeds (makes) a beautiful sight. [Omit the middleman *shining on the flowerbeds*.]

6. The <u>decision</u> to place the beautiful artifacts in out-of-the-way nooks around the mansion's various rooms (was) inspiring. CORRECT. [Omit middleman phrases beginning with *to*, *in*, and *around*.]

7. Just around the corner (are) a fantastic <u>bakery</u> AND a small <u>supermarket</u>. [If you rearranged the sentence, it would read: *A fantastic bakery AND a small supermarket ARE just around the corner.* The word *and* makes a compound subject, which is plural.]

8. **The music company was afraid THAT the accelerating decline of sales of compact discs would not be compensated by increased internet revenue.**

The original sentence has an independent clause (*The music company was afraid of the accelerating decline of sales of compact discs*) with another verb phrase—*would not be compensated by increased internet revenue*—inappropriately tacked on. One way to fix the sentence is to replace the preposition *of* with *that*.

9. **The petroleum distillates were so viscous THAT the engineers had to heat the pipe by nearly 30 degrees.**

The original sentence is a run-on sentence. To fix the sentence, you need to insert *that*.

10. **The municipality's back-to-work program has had notable success; nevertheless, it is not suitable for a state-wide rollout for several reasons.** [semicolon before *nevertheless*]

The word *nevertheless* is not a FANBOYS conjunction (such as *and*). As a result, you need to use a semicolon, not a comma, before *nevertheless*.

11. **Historically, the Isle of Man had an economy based primarily on agriculture and fishing; now, IT HAS one based on banking, tourism, and film production.**

Just like the words that come before a semicolon, the words that come after a semicolon must constitute a complete sentence. In the original sentence, the second part of the sentence does not form a valid independent clause.

12. **The Bentley trench, situated more than a mile and a half below sea level and completely covered by Antarctic glaciers, IS the lowest point on the planet not under the oceans.**

The original sentence has an independent clause linked to a sentence fragment by the use of *and*. In the corrected version, one main clause combines all of the information given.

Chapter 4 *of*
Sentence Correction

Modifiers

In This Chapter...

Chapter 4
Modifiers

A **modifier** describes or provides extra information about something else in the sentence. Although modifiers can be as simple as a single word (an adjective or an adverb), GMAT sentences often contain several complex modifiers. For example:

> Tired out from playing basketball, CHARLES decided to take a nap.

The modifier *Tired out from playing basketball* describes the noun *Charles*. It provides additional context as to *why* Charles decided to take a nap. Many modifiers answer the questions *who, what, when, where,* or *why*. Incorrectly used modifiers can lead to ambiguity or illogical meaning.

Adjectives and Adverbs

Adjectives and adverbs are one-word modifiers. An **adjective** modifies only a noun or a pronoun, whereas an **adverb** modifies almost anything but a noun or a pronoun. These two types of modifiers illustrate the two broad categories of modifiers. **Noun modifiers**, such as adjectives, modify only a noun or a pronoun. **Adverbial modifiers**, such as adverbs, can modify verbs, adjectives, prepositional phrases, even entire clauses, but they do not modify plain nouns. For example:

> The smart STUDENT WORKS quickly.

Here the adjective *smart* modifies the noun *student*, while the adverb *quickly* modifies the verb *works*. Many adverbs are formed by adding *-ly* to the adjective.

The GMAT will sometimes offer answers that use an adjective where an adverb is grammatically required and vice versa. All of the following examples are correct, although they differ in meaning:

> Amy is a good PERSON. (*Good* is an adjective that modifies the noun *person*.)
> AMY is well. (*Well* is an adjective that modifies the noun *Amy*.)
> Amy WRITES well. (*Well* is an adverb that modifies the verb *writes*.)

On harder questions, the GMAT could provide two grammatically correct phrasings. For instance, which of these sentences is more logical?

> Max's grandmother is his supposed Irish ancestor.
> Max's grandmother is his supposedly Irish ancestor.

In the first option, the adjective *supposed* points to the noun *ancestor*, implying that Max's grandmother is not actually his ancestor. In the second option, the adverb *supposedly* points to the adjective *Irish*, implying that Max's grandmother is not actually Irish.

Logically, Max's grandmother has to be his ancestor; if she weren't, the sentence would call her his *supposed grandmother*. Only the second option, then, has a sensible meaning: Max's grandmother is *supposedly Irish* but she may not be after all.

Adjectives that have been observed alternating with their corresponding adverbs in released GMAT problems include *corresponding, frequent, independent, rare, recent, seeming, separate, significant, supposed,* and *usual*. If you spot an answer switching back and forth between the adjective and adverb forms of the same word, ask yourself what the word is modifying. If it's modifying a noun by itself, use the adjective form. If it's modifying anything other than a noun (or pronoun), use the adverbial form.

Noun Modifiers

Adjectives are the most simple noun modifiers. Other types of noun modifiers act like long adjectives. Consider these examples (you don't need to memorize the grammar terms):

Type	Example	Meaning
Preposition	The CAT <u>on the couch</u> loves dogs.	Which cat? (the one on the couch)
Past Participle	The CAT <u>owned by Sue</u> is playful.	Whose cat? (the one owned by Sue)
Present Participle without Commas	The CAT <u>sleeping on the rug</u> belongs to Sue.	Which cat? (the one sleeping on the rug)

Many modifiers answer a specific question, as shown in the *Meaning* column above. When you can ask a *who, what, which,* or *where* question about a noun, and the answer points to the modifier, you have a noun modifier.

Think about the circumstances in which you would use each of the two sentences below:

> The cat, which lives next door, is very noisy.
> The cat that lives next door is very noisy.

In the first example, you would already have to know which cat the speaker is talking about. The modifier provides extra information, as though the speaker is saying, "Oh, by the way, that cat that we're talking about lives next door. Just thought I'd mention it." The second example, by contrast, would be

used to distinguish between multiple cats when you don't already know which cat the speaker wants to discuss. If three cats are playing in front of you, the speaker would specify *the cat that lives next door*, not the other two cats.

The "comma which" structure is an example of a **nonessential modifier**. If you take a nonessential modifier out of the sentence, you still retain the full meaning of the main part of the sentence: the cat is very noisy (and you already know which cat is under discussion). Nonessential modifiers are usually separated out from the rest of the sentence by commas.

The second sentence includes an example of an **essential modifier**. If you remove it from the sentence, then the meaning may be compromised. For instance, if there are three cats and you say only, "The cat is very noisy," nobody will know which cat you mean. Essential modifiers are *not* usually separated out by commas.

Position of Noun Modifiers

The placement of modifiers is really a function of meaning. Place the modifier incorrectly and the sentence may have an illogical or ambiguous meaning.

There are typically many nouns in a long sentence, so a noun modifier has to be placed in such a way that the reader knows exactly which noun is being modified. The practical result is that nouns and noun modifiers must be placed either right next to each other or very close together. Remember this rule:

Place a NOUN and its MODIFIER as close together as possible—the closer, the better!

Here's what can happen when a noun and its modifier break this rule:

Wrong: A hard worker and loyal team player, the new project was managed by Sue.

The sentence begins with an **opening modifier** set off from the rest of the sentence by a comma. Who is *a hard worker and loyal team player*? Not the *project*! That's illogical.

Instead, move the appropriate noun closer to the modifier:

Right: A hard worker and loyal team player, Sue managed the new project.

The majority of the time, a noun and its modifier will be placed right next to each other, with no other words intervening. In certain circumstances, though, a noun and its modifier may be separated by another modifier. For example:

The box of nails, which is nearly full, belongs to Jean.

The noun *box* has two modifiers: *of nails* and *which is nearly full*. They can't both be placed right after the noun; one has to come first.

An essential modifier trumps a nonessential modifier. *Of nails* is an essential modifier (which box? the box of nails), so it is placed immediately after *box*. The "comma which" modifier is a nonessential modifier, so it can come second. In this case, the *which* modifier refers to the closest preceding *main* noun, *box*.

Which of the options below is better?

> Jim biked along an old dirt road to get to his house, which cut through the woods.
> To get to his house, Jim biked along an old dirt road, which cut through the woods.

4

What *cut through the woods*? The *road*. Modifiers should be as close as possible to the nouns they modify, so the second option is preferable.

In the first sentence, *to get to his house* is not a noun modifier referring to *road*, so it should not be placed in between the "comma which" modifier and the noun that it modifies. (*To get to his house* refers to the verb *biked*: how did he get to his house? *He biked*. You'll learn more about adverbial modifiers later in this chapter.)

Possessive Nouns Are Not Nouns!

Can you spot the error in the sentence below?

> Wrong: Happy about his raise, Bill's celebration included taking his friends out to dinner.

Logically, the modifier *happy about his raise* should describe *Bill*. However, possessive nouns are actually adjectives, not nouns, and a noun modifier has to point to a noun. As it stands, the sentence technically (and illogically) says that Bill's *celebration* is *happy about his raise*. Here is a corrected sentence:

> Right: Happy about his raise, Bill celebrated by taking his friends to dinner.

Noun Modifier Markers: Relative Pronouns

Noun modifiers are often introduced by **relative pronouns** such as the following:

Which   That   Who   Whose   Whom   Where   When

The words above always signal noun modifiers with the exception of the word *that*, which sometimes signal other structures. A noun followed immediately by the word *that* signals a noun modifier. A verb followed immediately by the word *that* signals the more complex sentence structure subject–verb–THAT–subject–verb–object (see Chapter 3 for more).

The pronouns *who* and *whom* must modify people. On the other hand, the pronoun *which* cannot modify people.

Perhaps surprisingly, the pronoun *whose* <u>can</u> modify either people or things: *the town <u>whose water supply was contaminated</u>*.

Which or *whom* sometimes follow prepositions: *the canal <u>through which water flows</u>; the senator <u>for whom we worked</u>*.

The pronoun *where* can be used to modify a noun place, such as *area*, *site*, *country*, or *Nevada*. *Where* cannot modify a "metaphorical" place, such as *condition*, *situation*, *case*, *circumstances*, or *arrangement*. In these cases, use *in which* rather than *where*.

> Wrong: We had an <u>arrangement</u> WHERE he cooked and I cleaned.
> Right: We had an <u>arrangement</u> IN WHICH he cooked and I cleaned.

The pronoun *when* can be used to modify a noun event or time, such as *period*, *age*, *1987*, or *decade*. In these circumstances, you can also use *in which* instead of when.

Noun Modifier Markers: Prepositions and Participles

Both prepositional phrases and participle modifiers can be noun modifiers or adverbial modifiers, but they do follow some specific rules.

In general, if a preposition immediately follows a noun, then the prepositional phrase modifies that noun. For example:

> The executive DIRECTOR <u>of the company</u> resigned three days ago.

Can you spot the noun modifiers in the following sentence?

> Researchers discovered that the most common risk factor resulting in cholera epidemics is the lack of a clean water supply.

The adjective *common* describes the *risk factor*. (The adverb *most* refers to *common*.) What about the more complex noun modifiers?

The word *resulting* is a participle. Note that it is not separated out from the rest of the sentence by a comma. Therefore, *resulting in cholera epidemics* signals a noun modifier; it refers to the *risk factor*.

The prepositional phrase *of a clean water supply* modifies the noun *lack*.

Researchers discovered that the <u>most common</u> RISK FACTOR <u>resulting in cholera epidemics</u> is the LACK <u>of a clean water supply</u>.

Participles can be present or past:

Verb	Present Participle (-ing)	Past Participle
to play	playing	played
to manage	managing	managed
to begin	beginning	begun

Present participles always end in *–ing*. Past participles most commonly end in *–ed*, but there are a number of irregular verb forms. These participles can function as verbs, nouns, or various types of modifiers. For example:

She is playing soccer.	*is playing* = verb form
Playing soccer is fun.	*playing* = subject (noun)
The girl playing soccer is my sister.	*playing soccer* = noun modifier
She stayed all day, playing soccer until she was the only one left on the field.	*playing soccer … field* = adverbial modifier

Any *–ing* word functioning as part of the verb form will have another verb immediately before it, as in the *is playing* example. If no prior verb exists, then the *–ing* word is not acting as a verb.

Any *-ing* words that are not verbs and not separated from the rest of the sentence by a comma will either be a noun, as in *Playing soccer is fun*, or modify another noun, as in *The girl playing soccer is my sister*.

Finally, any *"comma –ing"* structures are adverbial modifiers; you'll learn more about these later in the chapter.

Past participles, or *–ed* words, are not tested as frequently as *–ing* words, but follow the same general rules, except that a past participle can be a verb all by itself but it cannot function as a noun.

She played the lottery yesterday.	*played* = verb
She accidentally bought an expired lottery ticket.	*expired* = noun modifier
Exhausted from her job, she bought a lottery ticket with hopes of winning big.	*exhausted … job* = adverbial modifier

You could also think of *exhausted from her job* as a noun modifier of *she*. Who was *exhausted*? *She* was. However, the context of the rest of the sentence matters. A sentence such as *exhausted from her job, she has red hair* would not be acceptable on the GMAT. As a result, it is better to think of this modifier as applicable to the whole main clause. Because she was *exhausted, she bought a lottery ticket*?

MANHATTAN
PREP

Adverbial Modifiers

As their name indicates, **adverbial modifiers** modify verbs and adverbs. They can also modify adjectives, prepositional phrases, clauses...anything that isn't just a plain noun. These modifiers also answer questions, such as how, when, where, or why an action occurred, but this time, the answer will point to something other than a plain noun. Here are a few examples:

Type	Example	Meaning
Adverb	The engineer <u>rapidly</u> IDENTIFIED the problem.	How did the engineer *identify* the problem? (rapidly)
Prepositional Phrase	The TEAM ATTENDS staff meetings <u>on Mondays</u>.	When does *the team attend* staff meetings? (on Mondays)
Present Participle with Commas	The ENGINEER FIXED THE PROBLEM, <u>earning himself a promotion</u>.	What happened when the *engineer fixed the problem*? (he earned himself a promotion)
Past Participle with Commas	<u>Exhilarated by the successful product launch</u>, the TEAM CELEBRATED after work.	Why did the *team celebrate*? (the team was exhilarated by the successful launch)

Adverbial modifiers do not have the same placement constraints as noun modifiers. A sentence typically contains only one or two main clauses, so adverbial modifiers can be placed more freely without creating meaning issues in the sentence. As long as the adverbial modifier clearly points to one particular verb or clause, the placement is acceptable. In fact, only the first example in the list above places the modifier right next to the verb, and even that was not required. *The engineer IDENTIFIED the problem rapidly* is also correct.

It is possible to place adverbial modifiers poorly, though. What's wrong with this sentence?

> He walked and caught up with his sister more rapidly.

The placement of the modifier *rapidly* indicates that he *caught up with his sister more rapidly*...than what? Logically, he walked more rapidly than he had been walking before in order to catch up with his sister. Try a harder one:

> The CEO declared that everyone had to work every day through the holidays to make the production deadline, but in calling for such an extreme measure, the company's employees were upset to the point of mutiny.

The phrase *in calling for such an extreme measure* is a *"comma –ing"* modifier. Such modifiers refer to the entire clause to which they are attached.

Which clause is that? The sentence has two:

Independent Clause	*Conjunction*	*Independent Clause*
The CEO declared that everyone had to work every day through the holidays to make the production deadline,	but	the company's employees were upset to the point of mutiny.

in calling for such
an extreme measure,
Modifier

Logically, the CEO called for this extreme measure, not the employees. However, because the *–ing* modifier falls after the conjunction connecting the two clauses, the modifier refers to the *employees*, not to the *CEO*. The sentence could be fixed in multiple ways:

> Right: In an extreme measure, the CEO declared that everyone had to work every day through the holidays to make the production deadline; her employees were upset to the point of mutiny.
>
> Right: The CEO declared that everyone had to work every day through the holidays to make the production deadline, but in calling for such an extreme measure, she upset her employees to the point of mutiny.

Both of the correct sentences properly attribute the extreme move to the CEO, not to the employees.

In short, an adverbial modifier points to the right verb or clause as long as it is not structurally closer to some other verb or clause. An adverbial modifier does not necessarily have to be placed as close as possible to what it modifies.

Check the Sequence in Participle Modifiers

The final two examples in the earlier list illustrate an additional requirement that applies specifically to adverbial modifiers that use participles: the information presented earlier in the sentence leads to or results in the information presented later in the sentence.

For example:

The engineer fixed the problem, earning himself a promotion.

Main Clause   *comma -ing* Modifier

Because the engineer fixed the problem, he earned a promotion. Fixing the problem resulted in earning the promotion. Consider this example:

Exhilarated by the successful product launch, the team celebrated after work.

comma -ed Modifier   Main Clause

Because the team was exhilarated, it celebrated. The exhilaration led to the celebration.

Whichever statement comes first in the sentence, whether modifier or main clause, is the instigating action, and whichever comes second, is the effect or result.

Picture a woman ice skating. She loses her balance, crashes to the ice, and then clutches her ankle in pain. Which of these three sentences correctly describes this scenario?

> Slipping on the ice, she broke her ankle.
> Breaking her ankle, she slipped on the ice.
> She slipped on the ice, breaking her ankle.

Although they have different structures, the first and third sentences both correctly describe what happened: the woman slipped on the ice, and this action caused her to break her ankle.

The middle sentence is illogical because it implies that she broke her ankle first, then slipped on the ice.

Subordinators

Take a look at this sentence:

> *Although the economy is strong,* the RETAIL INDUSTRY IS STRUGGLING.

The first part of the sentence is called a **subordinate clause**. It is almost exactly like a complete sentence, but it has a subordinator (*although*) at the beginning.

Subordinate clauses are *not* complete sentences:

> Wrong: Although the economy is strong.

Subordinate clauses modify the main clause to which they are attached. In the correct example presented first in this section, the subordinate clause provides additional information about the main clause: despite the fact that the overall economy is doing well, one particular industry is not.

Common subordinator markers include:

after	although	because	before	if	since
so that	that	unless	until	when	while

Pay attention to the meaning of the chosen word. If the word indicates a contrast, for example, then make sure the sentence actually conveys a contrast:

> Wrong: Although the economy is strong, the retail industry is doing well.

Subordinators are similar to the FANBOYS conjunctions: in both cases, you need to make sure that the chosen word logically connects the two pieces of information. (The two types of conjunctions are not interchangeable, though; see Chapter 3 to learn how to use FANBOYS.) The GMAT will test you to make sure that you are paying attention to this kind of meaning!

Use only one connecting word per "connection":

Wrong:	ALTHOUGH I need to relax, YET I have so many things to do!
Right:	ALTHOUGH I need to relax, I have so many things to do!
Right:	I need to relax, YET I have so many things to do!

Make sure that clauses are connected by a sensible connecting word:

Wrong:	She is not interested in playing sports, AND she likes watching them on TV.

In the example above, the connecting word *and* is not sensible, because the two sentence parts are in opposition to each other. This meaning error can be corrected by choosing a different connecting word:

Right:	She is not interested in playing sports, BUT she likes watching them on TV.
Right:	ALTHOUGH she is not interested in playing sports, she likes watching them on TV.

Finally, be on the lookout for sentences that join a main clause to something that should be a clause but is not actually a clause:

Wrong:	Citizens of many countries are expressing concern about the environmental damage caused by the widespread release of greenhouse gases may be impossible to reverse.

The main clause in this sentence is *Citizens of many countries are expressing concern about the environmental damage caused by the widespread release of greenhouse gases.* There is nothing wrong with this main clause. What about the rest of the sentence, which consists of the verb phrase *may be impossible to reverse*? This verb phrase has no subject. The GMAT wants you to think that *environmental damage* is the subject of *may be impossible to reverse*, but *environmental damage* is part of a prepositional phrase (*about the environmental damage*). Nouns in prepositional phrases cannot also be subjects.

One way to fix the sentence is to change the preposition *about* to the subordinator *that*:

Right:	Citizens of many countries are expressing concern THAT the environmental damage caused by the widespread release of greenhouse gases may be impossible to reverse.

In this correct version, the main clause is *Citizens ... are expressing concern*. The subordinate clause begins with the word *that* and extends to the end of the sentence. Within that subordinate clause, *environmental damage* is the subject of *may be*.

Another way to fix the sentence is to put *may be impossible to reverse* inside a modifier:

> Right: Citizens of many countries are expressing concern about the environ-
>   mental damage caused by the widespread release of greenhouse gases,
>   <u>DAMAGE THAT may be impossible to reverse.</u>

In this correct version, the main clause ends right before the comma. The words *damage that may be impossible to reverse* provide additional information about the damage mentioned earlier in the sentence.

Which vs. the Present Participle *-ing*

Sentences such as the following are common in speech, but they are wrong in writing:

> Wrong: Crime has recently decreased in <u>our neighborhood, WHICH has led to a
>   rise in property values</u>.

The recent decrease in crime has led to a rise in property values, but *decreased* is a verb in the sentence. Whenever you use *which*, you must be referring to a noun. Here, the *neighborhood* has not led to anything, nor has *crime* by itself. Remember the rule:

> Use WHICH *only* to refer to nouns—never to refer to an entire clause.

One way to correct the sentence is to turn the first thought into a noun phrase and make this phrase the subject of the verb in the *which* clause, eliminating *which* altogether:

> Right: The recent <u>decrease</u> in crime in our neighborhood <u>has led</u> to a rise in
>   property values.

Another way to correct the sentence is to use an adverbial modifier to refer to the whole clause:

> Right: <u>Crime has recently decreased</u> in our neighborhood, <u>leading</u> to a rise in
>   property values.

Again, in speech, people often break these rules, incorrectly using *which* to refer to a previous thought that is <u>not</u> a noun. In fact, the GMAT has made the same mistake in Sentence Correction explanations and even in a Reading Comprehension passage! Do not use your ear for this one. Always test *which* clauses to make sure that the *which* refers to the closest preceding main noun and not the whole clause.

Modifier vs. Core

Two long nonessential modifiers in a row can lead to awkward or incorrect phrasings:

> Wrong: George Carlin, <u>both shocking and entertaining audiences across the nation</u>, <u>who also struggled publicly with drug abuse</u>, influenced and inspired a generation of comedians.

Here's a better way to convey the same information:

> Better: <u>Both shocking and entertaining audiences across the nation</u>, George Carlin, <u>who also struggled publicly with drug abuse</u>, influenced and inspired a generation of comedians.

In this better sentence, one nonessential modifier is placed before the noun and the other is placed after.

On harder questions, GMAT answers are more likely to rephrase the sentence so that one of the modifiers becomes part of the core of the sentence; that is, it is no longer a modifier. Here's an example:

> Best: <u>Both shocking and entertaining audiences across the nation</u>, George Carlin influenced and inspired a generation of comedians yet struggled publicly with drug abuse.

Here's the core sentence:

> Carlin influenced and inspired yet struggled.

Two FANBOYS conjunctions connect the three verbs (*influenced*, *inspired*, *struggled*), so that final portion is now part of the core sentence, not a modifier. If you've forgotten the FANBOYS or the concept of compound verbs, review these lessons in Chapter 3.

If your first glance reveals a long underline, expect portions of the sentence to move around or even change roles completely in the answers. Here are some examples of correct sentences in which the core and modifier portions change:

> Right: Employing the new lab equipment, the engineer identified the problem quickly.

> Right: The engineer employed the new lab equipment, identifying the problem within minutes.

Both of these sentences convey the same information, but the first sentence has a modifier–core structure while the second has a core–modifier structure. Neither one is better than the other; both would be acceptable on the GMAT.

Right: <u>Pushed to justify his decision,</u> <u>the manager froze and was unable to say anything,</u>
                        Modifier   Core

            <u>eventually breaking down in tears.</u>
                        Modifier

Right: <u>The manager froze and was unable to say anything</u> <u>when he was pushed to justify</u>
                        Core   Modifier

            <u>his decision;</u> <u>he eventually broke down in tears.</u>
                                        Core

Both of these sentences are acceptable as long as the meaning is logical and unambiguous.

Quantity

In the English language, words and expressions of quantity are subject to strict grammatical rules.

Rule #1: Words Used for *Countable* Things vs. Words Used for *Uncountable* Things

Some nouns in the English language are countable, such as *hat(s)*, *feeling(s)*, and *person/people*. Other nouns are uncountable, such as *patience*, *water*, and *furniture*. If you are unsure as to whether a particular word is countable, try to count it out:

For *hat*:   **One hat, two hats, three hats**. This works. *Hat* is countable.
For *patience*:   **One patience (?), two patiences (?), stop**. This does not work. *Patience* is not countable.

Here are some examples of words and expressions that modify countable things and those that modify uncountable things:

Countable Modifiers	Uncountable Modifiers
MANY hats	MUCH patience
FEW stores	LITTLE merchandise
FEWER children	LESS money
FEWEST shoes	LEAST greed
NUMBER of chairs	AMOUNT of furniture
NUMEROUS books	GREAT courage

More, most, enough, and *all* work with both countable (plural) and uncountable (singular) nouns: *more hats*; *more patience*; *most people*; *most furniture*; *enough hats*; *enough patience*; *all people*; *all furniture*.

Do not use the word *less* with countable items. This error has become common in speech, and in the signs above express lines in grocery stores: *10 items or less*. Since the noun *item* is countable, the sign should read *10 items or <u>fewer</u>*. For example:

Wrong: There were <u>less</u> Numidian KINGS than Roman emperors.
Right: There were <u>fewer</u> Numidian KINGS than Roman emperors.

Be careful with unit nouns, such as *dollars* or *gallons*. By their nature, unit nouns are countable: *one dollar, two dollars, three dollars*. Thus, they work with most of the countable modifiers. However, unit nouns represent uncountable quantities: *money, volume*. (You can count money, of course, but you cannot count the <u>noun</u> *money*: *one money (?), two moneys (?)*, stop.) As a result, use *less* with unit nouns, when you really want to indicate something about the underlying quantity:

Right: We have less than 20 DOLLARS.

The amount of money, in whatever form, totals less than $20. If you write *We have FEWER THAN twenty dollars*, you would mean the actual pieces of paper. (You would probably say *fewer than twenty dollar <u>bills</u>* to make the point even clearer.)

Rule #2: Words Used to Relate *Two* Things vs. Words Used to Relate *Three* or More Things

To relate two things, use comparative forms of adjectives and adverbs (*better, worse, more, less*). For example, the rabbit is *faster* than the toad. Use superlative forms (*best, worst, most, least*) to compare three or more things or people. For example, the rabbit is the *fastest* of all of the animals at the farm.

In addition, use *between* only with two things or people. When you are talking about three or more things or people, use *among*:

Right: I mediated a dispute BETWEEN Maya and Kalen.
Right: I mediated a dispute AMONG Maya, Logan, and Kalen.

Rule #3: The Word *Numbers*

If you wish to make a comparison using the word *numbers*, use *greater than*, not *more than* (which might imply that the quantity of numbers is larger, not the numbers themselves):

Right: The rare Montauk beaked griffin is not extinct; its NUMBERS are now sus-
            pected to be much GREATER than before.

Rule #4: *Increase* and *Decrease* vs. *Greater* and *Less*

The words *increase* and *decrease* are not the same as the words *greater* and *less*. *Increase* and *decrease* express the change of one thing over time. *Greater* and *less* signal a comparison between two things. For example:

Right: The price of silver INCREASED by 10 dollars.

Right: The price of silver is five dollars GREATER than the price of copper.

Watch out for redundancy in sentences with the words *increase* and *decrease*:

Wrong: The price of silver FELL by a more than 35% DECREASE.

Right: The price of silver DECREASED by more than 35%.

Right: The price of silver FELL by more than 35%.

Decrease already includes the notion of falling or lowering, so *fell* is redundant. Similarly, *increase* includes the notion of rising or growing, so *rise* or *growth* would be redundant as well.

Problem Set

Each of the following sentences contains one or more underlined modifiers. For each of these modifiers, ·
(a) identify the word or words, if any, that it modifies, and (b) indicate whether the modifier is correct.
If the modifier is incorrect, suggest a way to correct the error.

1. <u>Upon setting foot in the Gothic cathedral</u>, the <u>spectacularly</u> stained-glass windows amazed the <u>camera-wielding</u> tourists.

2. A <u>recent</u> formed militia, consisting of <u>lightly</u> armed peasants and a few <u>retired</u> army officers, is fighting a <u>bitterly</u> civil war against government forces.

3. Angola, <u>which was ravaged by civil war for many years after it gained independence from Portugal</u>, <u>which is now one of Africa's success stories</u>, has an economy that grew by 21% last year, <u>where parliamentary elections are to be held later this week</u>.

4. Mary buys cookies made with SugarFree, <u>an artificial sweetener</u>, <u>which tastes as sweet as the corn syrup that her brother loves</u> but <u>having fewer calories than in an equivalent amount of corn syrup</u>.

5. People <u>that are well-informed</u> know that Bordeaux is a French region <u>whose most famous export is the wine</u> <u>which bears its name</u>.

6. People, <u>who talk loudly on their cell phones in crowded trains</u>, show little respect for other passengers.

7. Of all the earthquakes in European history, the earthquake, <u>which destroyed Lisbon in 1755</u>, is perhaps the most famous.

8. The tallest mountain on Earth is Mount Everest <u>that is on the border between Nepal and Tibet</u>.

9. <u>Unaccustomed to the rigors of college life</u>, James's grades dropped.

10. Regina returned the dress to the store, <u>which was torn at one of the seams</u>.

11. Last night our air conditioner broke, <u>which caused great consternation</u>.

The following four sentences contain circled sections. Use the rules in this chapter to correct any errors
that you can find in the circled sections. Do not change anything that is not circled.

12. The negotiations (between) the company, the union, and the city government were initially contentious but (ultimately) amicable.

13. Jim is trying to reduce the (number) of soda that he drinks(,) at last night's party, however, his resolve to drink (fewer) soda was sorely tested(,) he found himself quaffing (many) of sodas.

14. (Between) 1998 and 2003, there was heavy fighting in Parthia (between) numerous armed factions (yet) this conflict, so much more complicated than a conventional war (between) two states, involved no (less) than eight countries and twenty-five militias.

15. Most legislators—including (much) in the governor's own party—realize that the governor's budget would imperil the state's finances(, nonetheless,) the budget is likely to be approved(, because) few legislators want to anger voters by cutting spending or raising taxes.

4

Solutions

1. <u>Upon setting foot in the Gothic cathedral</u>, the <u>spectacularly</u> stained-glass windows amazed the <u>camera-wielding</u> tourists.

Upon setting foot in the Gothic cathedral: INCORRECT. *Upon* is a preposition. The phrase *Upon setting foot in the Gothic cathedral* contains the gerund *setting*. Who or what set foot in the cathedral? Logically, it must be the *tourists*, not the *windows*. However, the noun *windows* is the subject of the sentence, and so *windows* seems to be the subject of *setting*.

spectacularly: INCORRECT. An adverb such as *spectacularly* can modify many parts of speech, but not a noun. The phrase *spectacularly stained-glass windows* seems to imply that the windows were *spectacularly stained*—that is, *spectacularly* seems to modify *stained*. However, *stained-glass* is a material. The author intended to say that either the *stained glass* itself or the windows were *spectacular*. The adverb should be replaced with the adjective *spectacular*.

camera-wielding: CORRECT. This participle modifies *tourists*.

Correction: **Upon <u>entering the Gothic cathedral</u>, the <u>camera-wielding</u> tourists were amazed by the <u>spectacular</u> stained-glass windows.**

2. A <u>recent</u> formed militia, consisting of <u>lightly</u> armed peasants and a few <u>retired</u> army officers, is fighting a <u>bitterly</u> civil war against government forces.

Recent: INCORRECT. The adjective *recent* modifies *militia*, whereas logic calls for an adverb, *recently*, to modify *formed*.

Lightly: CORRECT. The adverb *lightly* modifies the past participle *armed*, which is being used as an adjective (*armed* modifies the noun *peasants*).

Retired: CORRECT. *Retired* is an adjective that modifies *army officers*. (You can also argue that *retired* is a past participle being used as an adjective.)

Bitterly: INCORRECT. The adverb *bitterly* modifies *civil*, but the writer surely meant to use an adjective (*bitter*) to modify the noun phrase *civil war*.

Correction: **A <u>recently</u> formed militia, consisting of <u>lightly</u> armed peasants and a few <u>retired</u> army officers, is fighting a <u>bitter</u> civil war against government forces.**

3. Angola, <u>which was ravaged by civil war for many years after it gained independence from Portugal</u>, <u>which is now one of Africa's success stories</u>, has an economy that grew by 21% last year, <u>where parliamentary elections are to be held later this week</u>.

Which was ravaged ... from Portugal: CORRECT. This relative clause modifies the noun *Angola*.

which is now one of Africa's success stories: INCORRECT. This relative clause illogically modifies *Portugal* (which is in Europe).

where parliamentary … this week: INCORRECT. A relative clause that begins with *where* must modify a noun that names a physical place, so this clause cannot modify *year*. The clause is too far away from *Angola*, however, to perform its intended role of modifying *Angola*.

Repairing this deeply flawed sentence involves rearranging its components and incorporating some of the modifiers into main clauses:

Correction: **Ravaged by civil war for many years after it gained independence from Portugal, Angola is now one of Africa's success stories: its economy grew by 21% last year, and parliamentary elections are to be held later this week.**

4. Mary buys cookies made with SugarFree, <u>an artificial sweetener</u>, <u>which tastes as sweet as the corn syrup that her brother loves</u> but <u>having fewer calories than in an equivalent amount of corn syrup</u>.

an artificial sweetener: CORRECT, but can be better. This appositive noun phrase modifies *SugarFree*, though it should be moved so that the *which* modifier is closer.

which tastes … brother loves: CORRECT. Now that *artificial sweetener* has been moved, this modifier clearly modifies *the artificial sweetener SugarFree*.

having … corn syrup: INCORRECT. The *-ing* modifier *having … corn syrup* is meant to be parallel to the relative clause *which tastes … brother loves*. When relative clauses are parallel, they should start with the same relative pronoun.

Correction: **Mary buys cookies made with <u>the artificial sweetener</u> SugarFree, <u>which tastes as sweet as the corn syrup that her brother loves</u> but <u>which has fewer calories than does an equivalent amount of corn syrup</u>.**

5. People <u>that are well-informed</u> know that Bordeaux is a French region <u>whose most famous export is the wine</u> <u>which bears its name</u>.

that are well-informed: INCORRECT. This clause uses the relative pronoun *that* to refer to people. *Who* must refer to human beings. Another problem with *that are well-informed* is that it is wordy. Avoid relative clauses whose only verb is a form of *to be*, because they can generally be expressed more succinctly.

whose most famous … bears its name: CORRECT. This clause modifies *region*. Notice that *whose*, unlike *who* and *whom*, can correctly modify non-human entities.

which bears its name: INCORRECT. The context of this sentence calls for an essential clause to modify the wine, since the point of the clause is to identify *the wine*. If the sentence ended with the wine, it would be incomplete. The clause should therefore begin with *that* rather than *which*.

Correction: **Well-informed people know that Bordeaux is a French region whose most famous export is the wine that bears its name.**

6. People, who talk loudly on their cell phones in crowded trains, show little respect for other passengers.

who talk … crowded trains: INCORRECT. This clause is wrong because the commas that enclose it make it a nonessential clause. The logic of the sentence calls for an essential clause, because the rest of the sentence would change its meaning without the information in the relative clause. (The sentence *People show little respect for other passengers* makes a sweeping claim about every human being.) To correct this error, remove the commas.

Correction: **People who talk loudly on their cell phones in crowded trains show little respect for other passengers.**

7. Of all the earthquakes in European history, the earthquake, which destroyed Lisbon in 1755, is perhaps the most famous.

which destroyed Lisbon in 1755: INCORRECT. This clause is wrong because the commas that enclose it make it a nonessential clause. The logic of the sentence calls for an essential clause to make clear which earthquake is the most famous. (If you remove the relative clause, you get the very mysterious sentence *Of all the earthquakes in European history, the earthquake is perhaps the most famous.*) To correct the sentence, remove the commas and replace *which* with *that*.

Correction: **Of all the earthquakes in European history, the earthquake that destroyed Lisbon in 1755 is perhaps the most famous.**

8. The tallest mountain on Earth is Mount Everest that is on the border between Nepal and Tibet.

that is on … Tibet: INCORRECT. This clause is wrong because it is essential. The logic of the sentence calls for a nonessential clause for two reasons: (1) the information about Mount Everest being *on the border between Nepal and Tibet* is hardly necessary to identify which mountain this sentence is talking about, since the sentence gives both the mountain's name (*Mount Everest*) and a unique description of the mountain (*the tallest mountain on Earth*); and (2) the meaning of the rest of the sentence would not change in any significant way if the information in the relative clause were removed. To correct this sentence, put a comma after *Everest* and change *that* to *which*.

Correction: **The tallest mountain on Earth is Mount Everest, which is on the border between Nepal and Tibet.**

9. <u>Unaccustomed to the rigors of college life</u>, James's grades dropped.

Unaccustomed to … college life: INCORRECT. As a noun modifier, the past participle *unaccustomed* modifies the noun phrase *James's grades*. However, the author of the sentence intends *unaccustomed* to modify *James* himself. If you wish to begin the sentence with the noun modifier, you must rephrase the sentence to make *James* the subject.

Correction: **<u>Unaccustomed to the rigors of college life</u>, James allowed his grades to drop.**

10. Regina returned the dress to the store, <u>which was torn at one of the seams</u>.

which was … the seams: INCORRECT. This modifier is misplaced. It seems to describe *store*, the adjacent noun; however, the modifier should modify *dress*. Thus, move the modifier next to *dress*. Since the modifier is relatively short, simply insert it and set it off with commas.

Correction: **Regina returned the dress, <u>which was torn at one of the seams</u>, to the store.**

11. Last night our air conditioner broke, <u>which caused great consternation</u>.

which caused great consternation: INCORRECT. This modifier is dangling, since the sentence contains no noun correctly modified by the clause *which caused great consternation*. The author's intent is to comment on the event (the breakdown of the air conditioner), but the main clause does not name the event with a noun. Therefore, change the modifier to a verb modifier, either a participle (*causing …*) or an absolute phrase (*an event that caused …*).

Correction: **Last night our air conditioner broke, <u>causing great consternation</u>.**

12. **The negotiations AMONG the company, the union, and the city government were initially contentious but ultimately amicable.**

The word *between* can only be used with two things. You must use the word *among* to describe relationships of three or more things. *Ultimately* is an adverb, and correctly modifies the adjective *amicable*.

13. **Jim is trying to reduce the AMOUNT of soda that he drinks; at last night's party, however, his resolve to drink LESS soda was sorely tested, AND he found himself quaffing A NUMBER of sodas.**

Number should be *amount* or *quantity*. Here *soda* is an uncountable substance—otherwise, *soda* would be *sodas*.

The comma after *drinks* should be a semicolon, which would appropriately separate two independent clauses: *Jim is trying … that he drinks* and *at last night's party … sorely tested*.

Fewer should be *less*. Once again, regard *soda* as an uncountable substance.

An *and* should be inserted after the comma after *tested*. This placement of *and* appropriately separates two main clauses: *his resolve … was sorely tested* and *he found … sodas*.

Many should be *a number*. Since there is an *-s* on the end of *sodas*, you know that *sodas* are now thought of as countable things—presumably servings of soda. *A number of* is an appropriate modifier for countable things.

14. **Between 1998 and 2003, there was heavy fighting in Parthia AMONG numerous armed factions; this conflict, so much more complicated than a conventional war between two states, involved no FEWER than eight countries and twenty-five militias.**

The first *between* is correct, since only two dates are mentioned.

The second *between* should be *among*, since the fighting involved more than two factions.

Yet should be a semicolon. *Yet* is illogical because the action in the second clause (*this conflict … militias*) did not happen <u>despite</u> the action in the first clause (*Between … factions*), as a word such as *yet* suggests.

The third *between* is correct, since only two states are mentioned.

Less should be *fewer*, because countries and militias are countable entities.

15. **Most legislators—including MANY in the governor's own party—realize that the governor's budget would imperil the state's finances; nonetheless, the budget is likely to be approved, because few legislators want to anger voters by cutting spending or raising taxes.**

Much should be *many*, because legislators are countable.

Nonetheless should be preceded by a semicolon. The clauses it connects are *Most legislators … state's finances* and *the budget is likely to be approved*.

The comma before *because* is correct. *Because* is a subordinating conjunction; therefore, it can be separated from a main clause by a comma.

Chapter 5 of

Sentence Correction

Parallelism

In This Chapter...

Chapter 5
Parallelism

According to the principle of parallelism, comparable sentence parts must be structurally and logically similar. What does this mean in practice? Here's an example:

> The employees were upset by the company's low pay, poor working conditions, and that they did not have enough outlets for their creativity.

This sentence has three comparable parts: the three things that upset the employees. The structure of the first two parts is similar; both parts consist of a noun phrase (centered on the nouns *pay* and *conditions*, respectively). However, the third part has a different structure altogether: it is a clause containing a subject, a verb, and an object. In order to make the sentence parallel, all three must either center on nouns or be clauses. In the sentence below, all three center on nouns:

> Right: The employees were upset by the company's low <u>pay</u>, poor working <u>conditions</u>, and <u>shortage</u> of outlets for employees' creativity.

It is *not* the case that every word has to be parallel within the three parallel phrases. However, the main word or words in each element must be parallel. In this case, the most important words in the three items in the list—*pay*, *conditions*, and *shortage*—are all nouns. As a result, the phrase *the company's* can now apply to each of the parallel parts:

> the company's   low <u>pay</u>
> the company's   poor working <u>conditions</u>
> the company's   <u>shortage</u> of outlets for employees' creativity

The portion before the list starts (*The employees were upset by the company's ...*) is called the **root phrase**. Each parallel element could finish the sentence started by the root phrase, so if you're not sure what the different elements are, try to plug each into the root phrase.

Parallelism Markers

How do you know when parts of a sentence need to be parallel to each other? Your clues will lie in parallelism markers that link or contrast items and that force those items to be parallel. Markers can be **open**, with a word or words between the two parallel elements, or **closed**, with a word or words between the two elements as well as before the first element. For example:

	Marker	**Structure**	**Example**
Open	And	X and Y	<u>Apples</u> AND <u>pears</u>
		X, Y, and Z	<u>Apples</u>, <u>pears</u>, AND <u>bananas</u>
	Or	X or Y	<u>Happy</u> OR <u>sad</u>
	Rather than	X rather than Y	<u>Play tennis</u> RATHER THAN <u>climb a mountain</u>
Closed	Both/And	Both X and Y	BOTH <u>men</u> AND <u>women</u>
	Either/Or	Either X or Y	EITHER <u>she works</u> OR <u>she plays</u>
	Not/But	Not X but Y	NOT <u>running</u> BUT <u>jogging</u>
	Not only/But also	Not only X but also Y	NOT ONLY <u>the manager</u> BUT ALSO <u>her team</u>
	From/To	From X to Y	FROM <u>the house</u> TO <u>the end of the driveway</u>

The most common parallel markers are the three conjunctions: *and*, *but*, and *or*. Of these, *and* is the most common. If you see any type of conjunction or *XY* idiom (such as *either X or Y*), ask yourself whether parallelism is an issue in the sentence.

Parallel Elements

Almost any part of a sentence can be made parallel to another part—though you only need to do so if a parallelism marker exists. The main word or clause in each element is required to be parallel, and each element has to connect to the root phrase of the sentence.

In the table below, the parallelism marker is capitalized and the main parallel elements are underlined.

Element	Example	Marker (open or closed)
Nouns	Her expression reflected BOTH <u>anger</u> AND <u>relief</u>.	both X and Y (closed)
Adjectives	The park was NEITHER <u>accessible</u> NOR <u>affordable</u>.	neither X nor Y (closed)
	We collected BOTH <u>second-</u> AND <u>third-grade</u> books.	both X and Y (closed)
Working Verbs	The custodian <u>cleaned</u> the basement AND <u>washed</u> the windows.	X and Y (open)

Element	Example	Marker (open or closed)
Infinitive Verbs	We would like NOT ONLY <u>to hear</u> your side of the story BUT ALSO <u>to provide</u> a response.	not only X but also Y (closed)
Participle Modifiers	The actor left quickly, <u>waving</u> to fans BUT <u>ducking</u> into a car.	X but Y (open)
Prepositional Phrases	It was important to leave the money <u>in the drawer</u> RATHER THAN <u>on the table</u>. (Note: the prepositions do *not* necessarily have to be the same.)	X rather than Y (open)
Subordinate Clauses	They contended <u>that the committee was biased</u> BUT <u>that it should not be disbanded</u>.	X but Y (open)

When open markers are used, it is not as easy to see where the *X* element begins, especially in longer sentences. Often, the two parallel phrases or clauses may begin with the same signal word in order to remove ambiguity about where the parallelism begins:

Wrong: I want to retire to a place <u>WHERE I can relax</u> AND <u>I pay low taxes</u>.
Right: I want to retire to a place <u>WHERE I can relax</u> AND <u>WHERE I pay low taxes</u>.

Without the repetition of the subordinator *where*, the first sentence could be read *I want to retire … and I pay low taxes*. Repeating the *where* eliminates ambiguity. The signal words do not have to be the same word. For example:

Right: There are many people <u>WHO speak English</u> BUT <u>WHOSE parents do not</u>.

When a closed marker is used, anything after the first portion of the marker applies only to the *X* element:

Wrong: Ralph likes BOTH <u>those who</u> are popular AND <u>who</u> are not as well-liked.
Right: Ralph likes BOTH <u>those who</u> are popular AND <u>those who</u> are not as well-liked.

Because parallelism starts with the marker word *both*, the *X* element is *those who are popular*. The main parallel words, *those who*, cannot carry over to the *Y* element; they have to be repeated.

Some verbs or forms derived from verbs have more than one word: *was opening, can lose, to increase*. If an open marker is used, the sentence can split apart these expressions, so that the first word or words count across all of the elements:

The division WAS <u>opening</u> offices, <u>hiring</u> staff, AND <u>investing</u> in equipment.

The railroad CAN <u>lose</u> more money OR <u>solve</u> its problems.

They wanted TO <u>increase</u> awareness, <u>spark</u> interest, AND <u>motivate</u> purchases.

In sum, when an open marker is used, check for ambiguity with respect to which words play the role of the *X* element; if ambiguity exists, eliminate that choice. When a closed marker is used, make sure that both the *X* and the *Y* elements contain the necessary starting words to form a structurally correct sentence.

Superficial Parallelism vs. Actual Parallelism

When people start learning how to use parallelism, they often mistakenly go overboard, assigning parallelism when no marker is present or without regard for the meaning of the sentence. Consider this example:

> Sal applied himself in his new job, arriving early every day, skipping lunch regularly, AND leaving late every night.

In the sentence above, the "*comma -ing*" modifiers *arriving early every day, skipping lunch regularly*, and *leaving late every night* are parallel. The main clause, *applied himself in his new job*, is not parallel to these participle phrases. This sentence is CORRECT. The *-ing* phrases provide additional information about how Sal applied himself in his new job. Changing the sentence to the superficially parallel version below would change the fundamental meaning of the sentence:

> Sal applied himself in his new job, arrived early every day, skipped lunch regularly, AND left late every night.

This version gives all the activities equal emphasis, instead of making the last three activities subordinate to the main activity (*applied himself in his new job*). At this level, the three latter activities do not have to have any connection to Sal's job. For example, the sentence could mean *Sal applied himself in his new job, arrived early every day at the gym, skipped lunch regularly on the weekend, AND left the bar late every Saturday night. The sentence is grammatically correct but it does not convey the same meaning as the original sentence above.*

As you learn to spot and fix parallelism errors, pay attention to the meaning of the sentence. This will help you avoid falling into the superficial parallelism trap.

The Importance of *And*

As mentioned earlier, the most common parallelism marker is the word *and*. This word always signals parallelism and can be used to connect any two similar structures, from independent clauses to individual words such as nouns or adjectives.

The most basic form is the marker *X and Y*, where *X* and *Y* are the two parallel elements. Some examples of correct usage are below; the parallelism marker is in capital letters and the main word or words in each element (that is the word or words that need to be made parallel) are underlined.

The <u>manager</u> AND her <u>team</u> were praised by the CEO.   → compound subject

In one terrible day, the account manager <u>lost</u> a client AND <u>greeted</u>
the CEO of her company by the wrong name.   → compound verb

New data indicate that, over the course of the past week, the <u>stock</u>
<u>market jumped</u> AND the <u>unemployment rate decreased</u>.   → two clauses

Parallelism can be part of the core sentence structure; in fact, all of the types of parallelism shown above were first introduced in Chapter 3 (*Sentence Structure*).

The *X and Y* structure can also be part of a modifying phrase or clause. For example:

A rapid improvement in <u>motor function</u> AND <u>vision</u> was
observed.   → prepositional phrase

Historians have uncovered new evidence, <u>confirming</u> several
theories AND <u>giving rise</u> to new hypotheses.   → adverbial modifier

When a parallel structure is part of a modifier, the sentence should work structurally and make sense logically using each parallel element individually. For example:

> A rapid improvement in <u>motor function</u> was observed.
> A rapid improvement in <u>vision</u> was observed.

The root phrase can be completed using just the *X* or the *Y* element (and dropping the parallelism marker). Here's the other sentence:

> Historians have uncovered new evidence, <u>confirming</u> several theories.
> Historians have uncovered new evidence, <u>giving rise</u> to new hypotheses.

If a parallel element does not work with the root phrase, then that element is incorrect:

Wrong: Historians have uncovered new evidence, <u>confirming</u> several theories AND <u>gave</u>
<u>rise to</u> new hypotheses.

The first element works in the overall sentence, but the second does not:

Wrong: Historians have uncovered new evidence, <u>gave rise to</u> new hypotheses.

Rather than check every sentence in this way, memorize these rules:

Element	Rule	Example
Nouns	Noun with noun	cat AND dog
	Action noun with action noun	eruption AND destruction
	Gerund with gerund	the rising AND the running
	Gerund with action noun	the uprising AND the escape

Element	Rule	Example
Verbs	Working verb with working verb Infinitive with infinitive	ran AND played eats AND drank* to run AND to play
Participles	Participle with participle	jumping AND yelling consulted AND advised fatigued AND dreaming**
Prepositions	Preposition with preposition	<u>in</u> the house AND <u>on</u> the roof
Clauses	Clause with clause	<u>I work</u> AND <u>she plays</u>. I think that <u>children learn</u> responsibility by taking care of pets AND that <u>cats make</u> the best pets.

* You can pair working verbs in different tenses, as long as the meaning of the sentence supports the different tenses. For example:

> She <u>eats</u> apples all the time AND <u>drank</u> some apple juice yesterday.

** Though not common on the GMAT, you can also pair present and past participles. For example:

> The cat slept in the sun, <u>fatigued</u> by play and <u>dreaming</u> of the mouse that got away.

In short, pair similar parts of speech together. When you're not sure, you can try completing the sentence with each parallel element separately. If the sentence doesn't work, that answer choice is incorrect.

3- or 4-Item Lists

The word *and* can also signal a list of three or four items.

List	Example
X, Y, and *Z*	apples, pears, <u>AND</u> bananas
X, Y, Z, and *W*	apples, pears, bananas, <u>AND</u> peaches

Correct lists obey these templates. No right answer omits *and* in a list just before the last item. Moreover, the GMAT always inserts a comma before the *and* anytime a list has at least three items:

Right: In today's news, technology stocks are up, while the <u>pharmaceutical</u>, <u>energy</u>, AND <u>retail</u> sectors are down.

Wrong: She argues that the agency acts with disregard for <u>human life</u> AND <u>property</u> AND <u>reckless abandon</u>.

MANHATTAN
PREP

The three underlined items, which are all connected by *and* right now, are not all at the same logical level. The agency acts *with disregard for human life* and the agency acts *with disregard for property*. It does not, however, act *with disregard for reckless abandon*; this is illogical. Presumably, the author wants to say that the agency acts *with reckless abandon*.

One way to fix these issues is as follows:

> Right: She argues THAT the agency acts <u>WITH reckless abandon</u> AND <u>WITH disregard</u> for <u>human life</u> AND <u>property</u>.

This diagram shows the different levels of parallelism within the sentence:

```
She argues  THAT the agency acts | WITH reckless abandon
                                 | AND
                                 | WITH disregard for | human life
                                 |                     | AND
                                 |                     | property
```

Idioms with Built-in Parallel Structure

Any idioms with *X* and *Y* elements require parallelism. One example is *both X and Y*: you are required to pair *both* with *and* (this is the idiom) and you are also required to make *X* and *Y* parallel.

A few examples are shown below; you can find others in Chapter 6, "Comparisons," and in Chapter 9, "Idioms":

Between X and Y	Distinguish X from Y	Think of X as Y
Consider X Y	Estimate X to be Y	View X as Y
In contrast to X, Y	Mistake X for Y	Whether X or Y

Parallel Meaning

A certain class of verb, the **linking verb**, is used to describe what a subject is or what condition the subject is in. These linking verbs are parallelism markers. For example:

> Right: <u>The bouquet</u> of flowers WAS <u>a gift</u> of love.

The subject, *bouquet*, and the object, *gift*, have to be parallel. In the sentence above, both are plain nouns, and therefore correctly parallel. Contrast that sentence with the sentence below:

> Wrong: <u>The bouquet</u> of flowers WAS <u>a giving</u> of love.

A giving is a gerund, or the noun form of a verb. Gerunds can be parallel to other gerunds or to action nouns, but they cannot be parallel to plain nouns, such as *bouquet*.

The two parallel elements also have to make logical sense:

> Wrong: Upon being nominated, <u>this politician</u> IS <u>a step forward</u> in urban–rural relations in this country.

According to this sentence, the *politician* himself or herself is *a step forward*, but this is illogical. Rather, the nomination (the event itself) is *a step forward*:

> Right: <u>The nomination</u> of this politician IS <u>a step forward</u> in urban–rural relations in this country.

The verb *to be* is the most common linking verb; other common linking verbs are in the table below.

To Be	Other Linking Verbs
is	appear
are	become
was	feel
were	grow
am	look
been	remain
be	represent
being	resemble
	seem
	smell
	sound
	stay
	taste
	turn

Problem Set

Each of the following sentences contains an error of parallelism in its underlined portion. For each sentence, begin by writing a correct version of the sentence.

Then, using your correct version of the sentence: (a) (circle) the parallelism markers, and (b) place [square brackets] around each set of parallel elements. In the solutions, key portions of the parallel elements will be capitalized.

1. Researchers have found a correlation between <u>exercise</u> and earning good grades.

2. Although we were sitting in the bleachers, the baseball game was as exciting to us <u>as the people</u> sitting behind home plate.

3. Many teachers choose to seek employment in the suburbs rather than <u>facing low salaries</u> in the city.

4. A good night's sleep not only gives your body a chance to rest, <u>but also energizing you</u> for the following day.

5. The joint business venture will increase employee satisfaction and <u>be improving relations</u> between upper management and staff.

6. The museum displays the work of a wide variety of artists, from those who are <u>world-renowned to who</u> are virtually unknown.

7. We were dismayed to learn that our neighbors were untidy, disagreeable, and <u>they were uninterested to make</u> new friends.

8. The students did poorly on the test more because they had not studied <u>than the material</u> was difficult.

9. The blizzard deposited more than a foot of snow on the train tracks, <u>prompted the transit authority to shut down service temporarily, and</u> causing discontent among commuters who were left stranded for hours.

10. The experiences we have <u>in childhood</u> influence our behavior as adults.

11. The band chosen for the annual spring concert appealed to both <u>the student body as well as to the administration.</u>

12. Tobacco companies, <u>shaken by a string</u> of legal setbacks in the United States, <u>but</u> which retain strong growth prospects in the developing world, face an uncertain future.

5

13. Voters want to elect a president who genuinely cares about health care, the <u>environment, the travails of ordinary men and women, has the experience, wisdom,</u> and strength of character required for the job.

14. The consultant is looking for a café <u>where there are comfortable chairs</u> and that provides free internet access.

15. Dr. Crock's claims <u>have been not corroborated</u> by other scientists nor published in a prestigious journal but have nonetheless garnered a great deal of attention from the public.

5

Solutions

1. Researchers have found a correlation [(between) EXERCISING (and) EARNING good grades].

2. (Although) we were sitting in the bleachers, the baseball game was [(as) exciting TO us (as) TO the people sitting behind home plate].

3. Many teachers choose to [SEEK employment in the suburbs (rather than) FACE low salaries in the city].

4. A good night's sleep [(not only) GIVES your body a chance to rest (, but also) ENERGIZES you for the following day].

5. The joint business venture will [INCREASE employee satisfaction (and) IMPROVE relations between upper management and staff].

6. The museum displays the work of a wide variety of artists, [(from) THOSE WHO are world-renowned (to) THOSE WHO are virtually unknown].

7. We were dismayed to learn that our neighbors were [UNTIDY(,) DISAGREEABLE (, and) UNINTERESTED in making new friends].

8. The students did poorly on the test [(more) BECAUSE they had not studied (than) BECAUSE the material was difficult].

9. The blizzard deposited more than a foot of snow on the train tracks, [PROMPTING the transit authority to shut down service temporarily (and) CAUSING discontent among commuters who were left stranded for hours]. (Note the removal of the comma after *temporarily*.)

10. The experiences we have AS CHILDREN influence our behavior AS ADULTS.

This sentence does not have any parallelism signals for you to circle. You know that *in childhood* should be parallel in structure to *in adulthood* because of logical considerations: the sentence is meant to highlight a connection between childhood and adulthood.

11. The band chosen for the annual spring concert appealed to [(both) the student BODY (and) the ADMINISTRATION].

It would normally be correct to write *The band ... appealed to the student body as well as to the administration*. However, the word both was not underlined in the original question, so you are forced to choose the *both X and Y* idiom as your parallelism structure.

12. Tobacco companies, [WHICH have been shaken by a string of legal setbacks in the United States (, but) WHICH retain strong growth prospects in the developing world], face an uncertain future.

13. Voters want to elect a president [WHO genuinely cares about [health care , the environment , and the travails of ordinary [men and women]] , and [WHO has the [experience , wisdom , and strength of character] required for the job]. (For clarity, several elements in lists have been left uncapitalized.)

14. The consultant is looking for a café [THAT has comfortable chairs and THAT provides free internet access].

15. Dr. Crock's claims [HAVE BEEN neither [CORROBORATED by other scientists nor PUBLISHED in a prestigious journal] but HAVE nonetheless GARNERED a great deal of attention from the public].

5

Chapter 6 _of_ Sentence Correction

Comparisons

In This Chapter...

Chapter 6

Comparisons

Comparisons are a subset of parallelism, but they get their own chapter because they require an additional check in order to ensure that they are valid.

For example, what's wrong with the sentence below?

> Wrong: Like Mary, Adam's car is green.

Poor Mary. She must be pretty sick if she's green, like Adam's car!

Comparison markers require parallelism between the two elements (nouns with nouns, for example), but they also require that the two compared items are fundamentally the same type of thing. These are called apples-to-apples comparisons:

> Right: LIKE Mary's car, Adam's car is green.

> Right: UNLIKE the architect's design for the new park, the mayor's plan kept most of the existing trees.

In short, comparisons follow the same general rules as parallelism, with one twist: it isn't enough to pair nouns and nouns (otherwise, Mary might really be green like the car!). The two elements have to be the same kind of thing: people to people, plans to plans, and so on.

Comparison Markers

There are different ways to write a logically parallel comparison. For example:

> Right: <u>Frank</u>, LIKE <u>his brother</u>, has a broad and muscular build.

This comparison has the structure *X, like Y*. A similar marker might be *Like X, Y*. The word *like* is the most common comparison marker. Here's another version:

> Right: <u>Frank's build</u>, LIKE <u>that of his brother</u>, is broad and muscular.

A comparison can also use a pronoun to stand in for the noun first mentioned; in the example above, the pronoun *that* refers to *build*. This is often considered preferable to repeating the same word—and it allows the GMAT to make the sentence a bit harder.

Some comparison structures can even omit the second main word of the comparison. In the example below, the two parallel structures *Frank's* and *brother's* imply that the same word follows both: *Frank's build* and *brother's build*:

> Right: <u>Frank's build</u>, LIKE <u>his brother's</u>, is broad and muscular.

What comparison is made in the sentence below?

> Beethoven's music, which broke a number of established rules with its structure and melodic form, is considered more revolutionary than Bach.

The comparison marker in this sentence is *X more than Y*. It is often easier to find the second element first, since it follows the comparison marker: *more revolutionary than <u>Bach</u>*. So, what is more revolutionary than Bach? The subject of the sentence: *Beethoven's <u>music</u>*. This comparison is not parallel.

In everyday speech, this sentence would likely sound fine, since people often talk about the music of Bach as "Bach" (e.g., *I like to listen to Bach on the radio)*. Grammar rules demand, however, that if the sentence has referred to Beethoven's music with the word *music*, then the sentence should do the same with Bach's music:

> Right: <u>Beethoven's music</u>, which broke a number of established rules with its structure and melodic form, is considered MORE revolutionary THAN <u>BACH'S</u>.

Note again that you do not have to repeat the word *music*, as long as the second element, *Bach's*, clearly refers back to music. The sentence could also use *that of Bach* as the second element.

The following comparison markers are common on the GMAT. Note that some comparisons are actually *contrasts*; that is, the two elements are dissimilar, not similar.

Marker	Sample Structure
Like	LIKE the <u>cat</u>, the <u>dog</u> is friendly.
	The <u>cat</u>, LIKE the <u>dog</u>, is friendly.
Unlike	UNLIKE her <u>parents</u>, <u>she</u> has green eyes.
	In <u>California</u>, UNLIKE <u>Florida</u>, the humidity is moderate.
As	<u>Divya</u> is smart, AS is <u>Abby</u>.

MANHATTAN
PREP

Marker	Sample Structure
Than	<u>You have earned</u> a BETTER score THAN <u>I have</u>. <u>Cisco's revenues</u> are considerably HIGHER THAN <u>Starbucks'</u>.
As (adjective) as	<u>Mira</u> is AS likely AS <u>Sam</u> to win the promotion.
Different from	My current <u>job</u> is quite DIFFERENT FROM my last <u>one</u>. (pronoun *one* refers to *job*)
In contrast to/with	Canada's <u>housing market</u> did not suffer many difficulties during the economic downturn, IN CONTRAST TO the <u>housing market</u> in the United States.

Comparisons also have to follow basic parallelism rules. As you learned in the previous chapter, parallelism requires the *X* and *Y* elements to have the same grammatical structure:

Wrong: The athlete enjoyed lifting weights more than to run around the track.

The *X* and *Y* elements of the comparison are *lifting weights* and *to run around the track*. These two elements are not parallel. Further, the second element would not work in the sentence by itself: *The athlete enjoyed to run around the track*. Below is the corrected sentence:

Right: The athlete enjoyed lifting weights more than running around the track.

Omitted Words

As shown earlier in this chapter, comparisons can sometimes omit words in the *Y* element and still be considered properly parallel. Both of the following sentences are correct:

Right: My car is bigger than Brian's [*car*].
Right: My house is smaller than the Smiths' [*house*].

Note that an *apostrophe-s* structure indicates a singular noun: Brian is one person. An *s-apostrophe* structure, on the other hand, indicates a plural noun: the entire Smith family, not just one Smith.

You can also omit units, verbs, and even whole clauses from the second term, as long as there is no ambiguity in the comparison:

Right: Whereas I drink two quarts of milk a day, my friend drinks three [*quarts of milk a day*].
Right: I walk faster than Brian [*walks*].
Right: I walk as fast now as [*I walked*] when I was younger.

In general, include the omitted words or appropriate helping verbs (such as *be*, *do*, and *have*) if the sentence would otherwise be ambiguous. For example:

Ambiguous: I like cheese more than Yvette.

Do you like cheese more than Yvette likes cheese? Or do you like cheese more than you like Yvette?

Right: I like cheese more than Yvette DOES. (*more than* Yvette *likes cheese*)
Right: I like cheese more than I DO Yvette. (*more than I like* Yvette)

The GMAT occasionally allows unnecessary helping verbs:

Right: Apples are more healthy to eat than caramels.
Right: Apples are more healthy to eat than caramels ARE.

The second sentence is not considered redundant or incorrect. If you see this on the test, ignore it and find some other difference on which to base your decision.

Like vs. As

Like and *as* are two very common comparison signals.

Like is used to compare nouns, pronouns, or noun phrases. Never put a clause or a prepositional phrase after *like*! (Remember, a clause contains a working verb, one that can be the main verb in a sentence.)

Consider the following example:

Right: LIKE her brother, Ava aced the test.

Here, *like* is followed by the noun phrase *her brother*. The whole phrase *Like her brother* indicates a comparison between *Ava* and *her brother* (two nouns). Note that *like* can be followed by gerunds (-*ing* forms used as nouns): *LIKE swimming, skiing is great exercise.*

On the other hand, *as* can be used to compare two clauses:

Wrong: LIKE her brother DID, Ava aced the test.
Right: AS her brother DID, Ava aced the test.

The words *her brother did* form a clause (*did* is a working verb). Therefore, use *as* to make the comparison between the two clauses *Ava aced the test* and *her brother did*, too.

According to the GMAT, there is no difference in meaning between *Like her brother, Ava aced the test* and *As her brother did, Ava aced the test*. You can compare *Ava* and *her brother* directly, or you can compare what they did, as long as you follow the appropriate grammar rules when writing the sentence.

Comparative and Superlative Forms

When comparing two things, use the comparative form of an adjective or adverb. When comparing more than two things, use the superlative form of an adjective or adverb.

> <u>Regular Forms</u>
> Comparative: She is SHORTER than her sister.
> Superlative: She is the SHORTEST of her five siblings.
> Comparative: You are MORE INTERESTING than he.
> Superlative: You are the MOST INTERESTING person here.

Do not compare an adverb that ends in -*ly* by changing the ending to -*er*. This error is common in speech. Instead, add *more*:

> Wrong: Adrian runs QUICKLY. He runs QUICKER than Jacob.
> Right: Adrian runs QUICKLY. He runs MORE QUICKLY than Jacob.

However, some adverbs that do not end in -*ly* are made into comparatives by adding -*er*:

> Right: Adrian runs FAST. He runs FASTER than Jacob.

Do not use a comparative adjective unless you have a *than* in the sentence:

> Wrong: With winter coming, I will have HIGHER energy bills.

The sentence <u>implies</u> the comparison *than now*. On the GMAT, however, you must make that comparison explicit, using the word *than*:

> Right: I will have HIGHER bills THAN last year.

6

Problem Set

In each of the following 15 sentences, underline all comparison signals and all comparative or superlative forms. If the sentence is fine, write CORRECT. If not, correct the errors in the sentence. For an ambiguous sentence, express each possible meaning of the sentence with a correct sentence of your own.

1. Like many other states, Virginia is technically a commonwealth.

2. I scored three goals in yesterday's game, as did Suzanne.

3. Juggling is a favorite pastime for me, like for you.

4. The rapid development of India in the twenty-first century is like England in the eighteenth century.

5. Law students learn to think like a lawyer does.

6. A leopard cannot run as fast as a cheetah.

7. A leopard cannot catch a wildebeest as fast as a cheetah.

8. A leopard's skill in catching a wildebeest is as impressive as a cheetah.

9. In contrast to the trapeze artists, who fumbled their routine, the antics of the circus clowns kept the audience entertained for hours.

10. The clothes looked more appealing inside the store than on the racks outside.

11. The clothes inside the store looked more appealing than on the racks outside.

12. Thomas is more interested in video games than his girlfriend.

13. Although the towers appear identical, the west tower is the tallest, standing 16 feet taller than the east tower.

14. Hugo is widely acknowledged to be our best employee, because he works harder and more creatively than anyone else in the company.

15. Courtney's experiences at Haleford, a large research university with renowned professors, affluent students, and imposing buildings, were unlike her high school on the reservation.

6

Solutions

1. **Like many other states, Virginia is technically a commonwealth.**

CORRECT. The noun phrase *many other states* follows the comparison signal like. This noun phrase is being compared to the noun *Virginia*, which is the subject of the sentence.

2. **I scored three goals in yesterday's game, as did Suzanne.**

CORRECT. The word <u>as</u> sets up a comparison between two clauses: *I scored three goals in yesterday's game* and *did Suzanne*. The verb *did* in the second clause stands for the entire verb phrase *scored three goals in yesterday's game*, which thus does not need to be repeated.

3. Juggling is a favorite pastime for me, like for you.

In this sentence, *like* is incorrectly followed by the prepositional phrase *for you*. *Like* can only be followed by a noun or noun phrase.

Change the second term of the comparison to a clause. Notice the parallelism in the verb *is*:

Correction: **Juggling is a favorite pastime for me, <u>as</u> it is for you.**

It would <u>not</u> be correct to drop the preposition *for* and simply write *Juggling is a favorite pastime for me, <u>like</u> you*. The comparison would then be ambiguous: do you mean to say that *juggling is a favorite pastime for you* or that *you are a favorite pastime for me*? In general, *like* does not form good comparisons with nouns or pronouns in prepositional phrases (e.g., *for <u>me</u>*), even if the preposition is correctly omitted after *like*.

4. The rapid development of India in the twenty-first century is like England in the eighteenth century.

This sentence incorrectly compares the *rapid development of India* to *England*. The easiest way to fix the sentence is to include the phrase *that of* to make it clear that the comparison is between the rapid developments of both companies.

Correction: **The rapid development of India in the twenty-first century is <u>like</u> that of England in the eighteenth century.**

5. Law students learn to think like a lawyer does.

This comparison can be made using either *like* or as. If you use *like*, however, you can't use the verb *does*, because like can't compare clauses.

Correction: **Law students learn to think <u>as</u> a lawyer does.**
        OR   **Law students learn to think like a lawyer.**

6. A leopard cannot run <u>as fast as</u> a cheetah.

CORRECT. The sentence is an abridgement of the longer sentence *A leopard cannot run* as fast as *a cheetah can run*. In the long version of the sentence, the clause *A leopard cannot run* is parallel to *a cheetah can run*. In the shortened version, which the GMAT would prefer for the sake of concision, the omitted words, *can run*, are understood.

Another acceptable version of this sentence is *A leopard cannot run as fast as a cheetah can*. Here the helping verb *can* stands for the full verb phrase *can run*.

7. A leopard cannot catch a wildebeest <u>as fast as</u> a cheetah.

This sentence is ambiguous because it's unclear what is being compared to what. Does it mean that the wildebeest is as fast as a cheetah?

Correction (a):   **A leopard cannot catch a wildebeest that runs <u>as fast as</u> a cheetah.**

Or does it mean that the leopard catches the cheetah?

Correction (b):   **A leopard cannot catch a wildebeest <u>as fast as</u> it can a cheetah.**

Or does it mean that the cheetah catches the wildebeest?

Correction (c):   **A leopard cannot catch a wildebeest <u>as fast as</u> a cheetah can.**

In this last version *can* stands for *can catch a wildebeest*, and the sentence compares the two clauses *A leopard cannot catch a wildebeest* and *a cheetah can (catch a wildebeest)*. For the sake of concision, it is better to say *can* rather than the full *can catch a wildebeest*. Likewise, in correction (b), you can omit the verb *catch*.

8. A leopard's skill in catching a wildebeest is <u>as impressive as a</u> cheetah.

This sentence makes an illogical comparison between a *skill* and a *cheetah*. A more logical comparison would be between a *skill* (that of the leopard) and another *skill* (that of the cheetah):

Correction: **A leopard's skill in catching a wildebeest is <u>as impressive as</u> a cheetah's.**
         OR   **A leopard's skill in catching a wildebeest is <u>as impressive as</u> that of a cheetah.**

9. <u>In contrast to</u> the trapeze artists, who fumbled their routine, the antics of the circus clowns kept the audience entertained for hours.

This sentence makes an illogical comparison between *trapeze artists* and *antics*. A more logical comparison would be between *trapeze artists* and *circus clowns*.

Correction: **<u>In contrast to</u> the trapeze artists, who fumbled their routine, the circus clowns kept the audience entertained for hours with their antics.**

10. The clothes looked <u>more appealing</u> inside the store <u>than</u> on the racks outside.

CORRECT. This sentence compares how some clothes looked *inside the store* with how the same clothes looked *on the racks outside*. A less concise, but acceptable, version of this sentence would be *The clothes looked more appealing inside the store than **they did** on the racks outside*. There are no logical or grammatical problems with either version of this comparison.

11. The clothes inside the store looked <u>more appealing than</u> on the racks outside.

This sentence seems to compare some <u>clothes</u> (*The clothes inside the store*) to a <u>location</u> (*on the racks outside*). It is hard to tell whether the author wants to compare two separate sets of clothes or one set of clothes in two display locations.

One way to correct the sentence would be to rewrite it as the sentence in problem 10.

Correction (a):   **The clothes looked <u>more appealing</u> inside the store <u>than</u> on the racks outside.**

This version makes sense because it puts the phrase *inside the store* <u>after</u> the comparison signal *more appealing*, thus making that phrase available for a comparison with *on the racks outside*. In this version, there is one set of clothes, and the comparison is between how these same clothes looked *inside the store* and how they looked *on the racks outside*. (Perhaps a customer brought the clothes into the store and is describing the different appearance of the same clothes before and after the move.)

Correction (b):   **The clothes inside the store looked <u>more appealing than</u> (did) those on the racks outside.**

This version compares <u>two</u> sets of clothes: *the clothes inside the store* and *those on the racks outside*. The word *did* is optional.

12. Thomas is <u>more interested</u> in video games <u>than</u> his girlfriend.

This sentence is ambiguous.

Correction (a):   **Thomas is <u>more interested</u> in video games <u>than</u> his girlfriend is.**

Correction (b):   **Thomas is <u>more interested</u> in video games <u>than</u> (he is) in his girlfriend.**

In the latter version, the words *he is* are optional because the parallelism between i*n video games* and *in his girlfriend* makes the meaning clear.

6

13. Although the towers appear identical, the west tower is the <u>tallest</u>, standing 16 feet <u>taller than</u> the east tower.

Since this sentence compares only two items—the west tower and the east tower—use the <u>comparative</u> *taller* rather than the superlative *tallest*. You could make the sentence grammatically correct by simply changing *tallest* to *taller*. To avoid possible redundancy, however, it would be better to avoid using the word *taller* twice.

Correction: **Although the towers appear identical, the west tower stands 16 feet <u>taller than</u> the east tower.**

14. **Hugo is widely acknowledged to be our <u>best</u> employee, because he works <u>harder</u> and <u>more creatively</u> than anyone else in the company.**

CORRECT. In the first clause, Hugo is being singled out from among a group (employees), so use a <u>superlative</u> (*best*) to modify *employee*.

In the second clause, there is a comparison between A and B, so use the <u>comparative</u> forms rather than the superlative forms. (The comparison is between how *he works* and how *anyone else in the company (works).*) The comparative form of the adverb creatively is <u>more creatively</u>. The comparative form of the adverb *harder* is simply *harder*, because *harder* is a short adverb that does not end in *–ly*.

15. Courtney's experiences at Haleford, a large research university with renowned professors, affluent students, and imposing buildings, were <u>unlike</u> her high school on the reservation.

This sentence makes an illogical comparison between <u>experiences</u> and *high school*. A more logical comparison would be between one set of <u>experiences</u> (those at *Haleford*) and another set of <u>experiences</u> (those at *her high school*).

Correction: **Courtney's experiences at Haleford, a large research university with renowned professors, affluent students, and imposing buildings, were <u>unlike</u> her experiences in high school on the reservation.**

6

Chapter 7 _of_
Sentence Correction

Pronouns

In This Chapter...

The Antecedent Must Exist and Be Sensible

The Antecedent and Pronoun Must Agree in Number

The Deadly Five: It, Its, They, Them, Their

This, That, These, and Those

Some Ambiguity Is Acceptable

Chapter 7

Pronouns

A pronoun is a word that takes the place of a noun, so that you do not have to repeat that noun elsewhere in the sentence. For example:

> GASOLINE has become so expensive that it now consumes as much as 16% of personal income in some rural areas.

In the sentence above, the pronoun *it* takes the place of the noun *gasoline*. In other words, *it* refers to *gasoline*. The noun *gasoline* is known as the **antecedent** of *it*.

On the GMAT, it is not unusual to think that a pronoun error exists, only to discover that the pronoun is correct after all. Use the answer choices to help guide you as to whether the problem is testing pronouns in the first place. If so, then you can apply the rules and possibly cross off some answers.

When you spot an underlined pronoun, check the answers first to see what other options are offered. Do the answers split between singular and plural? Between a pronoun and a regular noun? Occasionally, you may discover that the pronoun does not change in all five answers, in which case, look for some other issue to tackle instead!

If you think a non-underlined pronoun may be problematic, try to find the antecedent (you'll learn how in this chapter). If the antecedent is also not underlined, then the pronoun is fine; look for some other split. If the antecedent is underlined, check the answers to see what other options are offered.

These five pronoun markers are the most common on the GMAT:

it
its } singular

they
them } plural
their

The Antecedent Must Exist and Be Sensible

If the answer choices do offer different pronouns, then find the antecedent:

> The park rangers discussed measures to prevent severe wildfires, which would be devastating to <u>it</u>.

What noun does *it* refer to? Logically, it should refer to the *park*. However, in this sentence, *park* is not a noun. Rather, *park* is acting as an adjective in the phrase *the park rangers*. As a result, *park* cannot be the antecedent of *it*. Moreover, there is no other possible antecedent in the sentence, so this answer choice would be incorrect on a Sentence Correction question.

Watch out for adjectives! They cannot be antecedents of pronouns. The antecedent to which you want to refer must actually exist in the sentence as a noun.

Be careful not to gloss over the meaning. For example:

> Although the term "supercomputer" may sound fanciful or exaggerated, <u>it</u> is simply an extremely fast mainframe that can execute trillions of calculations every second.

The antecedent appears to be *the term "supercomputer."* Look what happens when the pronoun is replaced with this noun:

> … the TERM "supercomputer" is simply an extremely fast mainframe …

The term is not a *mainframe*; rather, the term *refers to* a mainframe. Therefore, you must change the verb or make some other edit:

> Right: Although the TERM "supercomputer" may sound fanciful or exaggerated, <u>it</u> simply REFERS TO an extremely fast mainframe that can execute trillions of calculations every second.

These issues are aspects of the *principle of meaning*. The GMAT tries to trick you into "assuming away" little wrinkles in meaning. Try replacing the pronoun with the antecedent to make sure that the sentence still makes sense.

The Antecedent and Pronoun Must Agree in Number

If the answers switch between singular and plural pronouns, then check the antecedent to see whether it is singular or plural. If the answers switch between singular and plural nouns, check either for pronouns or for verbs to help you decide whether the noun should be singular or plural. Consider this example:

Confronted by radical changes in production and distribution, modern Hollywood studios are attempting various experiments in an effort to retain its status
as the primary arbiter of movie consumption.

The antecedent of *its* is intended to be *studios*. However, *its* is singular, while *studios* is plural. Either the noun or the pronoun has to change (depending upon which portion is underlined in the problem):

Right: Confronted by radical changes in production and distribution, modern
Hollywood STUDIOS are attempting various experiments in an effort to retain
their status as the primary arbiters of movie consumption.

Right: Confronted by radical changes in production and distribution, the modern
Hollywood STUDIO is attempting various experiments in an effort to retain
its status as the primary arbiter of movie consumption.

The GMAT tends to test number agreement when you can easily express the relevant concepts either in singular or in plural form (*studio* or *studios*). Use the underline placement and the differences in the answers as your guide.

As you learned in Chapter 3, the GMAT can hide the match between a subject and its verb in various ways (e.g., by including middlemen to separate the two). The same disguises apply to pronoun anteced-ents.

The Deadly Five: *It, Its, They, Them, Their*

7

The most common pronoun mistakes involve the singular *it* and *its*, and the plural *they*, *them*, and *their*. Whenever you see one of these five pronouns, check the answers; if differences exist, find the anteced-ent and check its viability.

Be careful with *their*, which is often used in everyday speech to refer to singular subjects:

Wrong: Whenever a STUDENT calls, take down their information.
Right: Whenever a STUDENT calls, take down his or her information.
Right: Whenever STUDENTS call, take down their information.

This, That, These, and Those

This, *that*, *these*, and *those* can be used as adjectives in front of nouns:

New "NANO-PAPERS" incorporate fibers that give these materials strength.

You may also use *that* or *those* to indicate a "**new copy**" or copies of the antecedent:

> The MONEY spent by her parents is less than <u>that</u> spent by her children.

In this example, *that spent by her children* means *the money spent by her children*. Note that the two pots of money are NOT the same. One pot of money is spent by the parents; another pot of money, spent by the children, is the new copy. In contrast, when you use *it, they,* or other personal pronouns, you mean the same actual thing as the antecedent. Consider this example:

> The MONEY SPENT BY HER PARENTS is more than <u>it</u> was expected to be.

That or *those* indicating a new copy or copies must be modified. In other words, you have to add a description to indicate how the new copy is different from the previous version. For example:

> The MONEY spent by her parents is less than <u>that spent by her children</u>.
> Her COMPANY is outperforming <u>that of her competitor</u>.

Past GMAT questions have required that any new copy *that* or *those* agree in number with the previous version. If you must change number, repeat the noun:

> Wrong: Her COMPANY is outperforming <u>those of her competitors</u>.
> Right: Her COMPANY is outperforming <u>the companies of her competitors</u>.

Finally, on the GMAT, do not use *this* or *these* in place of nouns. A sentence such as *This is great* is unacceptably vague to the GMAT. Also, do not use *that* or *those* in place of nouns, unless you modify *that* or *those* to make them new copies. Instead, use *it, they,* or *them*:

> Wrong: Her PRODUCTS are unusual; many consider <u>these</u> unique.
> Right: Her PRODUCTS are unusual; many consider <u>them</u> unique.

Some Ambiguity Is Acceptable

In theory, every pronoun in a well-written sentence should clearly refer to one antecedent. If a sentence uses the same pronoun multiple times, every instance must refer to the same antecedent. If the first *it* refers to one noun and the second *it* refers to another, unacceptable confusion reigns.

It is also preferable to have pronouns of the same class refer to the same noun. *It* and *its* are one class, and *they, them,* and *their* are another class. This is a preference, however, not a rule; some correct GMAT sentences do use different pronouns of the same class to refer to different nouns. For example:

> Researchers claim to have developed new "nano-papers" incorporating tiny cellulose fibers, which <u>THEY</u> allege give <u>THEM</u> the strength of cast iron.

What nouns do *they* and *them* refer to? Logically, *they* refers to *researchers* (who *claim* something) and *them* refers to *new "nano-papers."* If another grammatically correct option exists without this mild ambiguity, choose the other option. If, however, the other four choices all contain errors, then this choice would be correct.

An answer choice could avoid potential ambiguity by not using a pronoun in the first place:

> Right: Researchers claim to have developed <u>new "nano-papers"</u> incorporating
>   tiny cellulose fibers, which give <u>THESE MATERIALS</u> the strength of cast
>   iron, according to the researchers.

If you spot a split between a pronoun and a regular noun, chances are good that the correct answer will use the regular noun, since that usage will prevent any possible misreading of a pronoun.

What if the sentence contains only one pronoun but more than one possible antecedent?

Sometimes, these answers are wrong; sometimes, the GMAT accepts a mild ambiguity. In general, if you run up against this issue, ignore it and use some other split to decide. If you are really gunning for a top score, Chapter 12 provides an advanced pronoun lesson on this topic.

7

Problem Set

Circle all the pronouns in the following sentences. Underline the antecedent, if there is one, of each pronoun. If you notice any pronoun errors in a sentence, correct the sentence by altering the pronoun(s). Explain what rules are violated by the incorrect sentences. If a sentence is correct, mark it with the word CORRECT.

1. When the guests finished their soup, they were brought plates of salad.

2. All students need his or her own copy of the textbook in order to take the class.

3. When tetrapods developed lungs, they became the first amphibians capable of surviving on land.

4. Meg left all her class notes at school because she decided that she could do her homework without it.

5. Some people believe that the benefits of a healthy diet outweigh that of regular exercise.

6. Oil traders have profited handsomely from the recent increase in its price.

7. The players' helmets need to be repainted before they are used in Sunday's game.

8. A few Shakespearean scholars maintain that he borrowed some of his most memorable lines from Christopher Marlowe.

9. The Smiths avoid the Browns because they dislike their children.

10. Our cat is cuter than those in the shelter.

11. Samantha took her laptop and her books with her on the airplane because she thought she could use these to get some work done.

7

Solutions

1. **When the guests finished (their) soup, (they) were brought plates of salad.**

    CORRECT.   *Guests* is the antecedent of *their* and *they*.

2. <u>All students</u> need (their) own copy of the textbook in order to take the class.

    All students is the antecedent of *their* (*his or her* is incorrect because *all students* is plural).

3. **When tetrapods developed lungs, (they) became the first amphibians capable of surviving on land.**

    CORRECT. Though the pronoun may technically be ambiguous because there are two possible antecedents (*tetrapods* and *lungs*), the GMAT would be very unlikely to consider this pronoun ambiguous, as it is illogical that *lungs* would become the first animals capable of surviving on land. In this type of situation, don't forget to compare answer choices; if every choice uses a pronoun, it is not ambiguous.

4. <u>Meg</u> left all (her) class <u>notes</u> at school because (she) decided that (she) could do (her) homework without (them.)

    Meg is the antecedent of *her* and *she*.
    Notes is the antecedent of *them*. (*It* is incorrect because *notes* is plural.)

5. Some people believe that the <u>benefits</u> of a healthy diet outweigh (those) of regular exercise.
    Benefits is the antecedent of *those*. (*That* is incorrect, because *benefits* is plural.)

6. Oil traders have profited handsomely from the recent increase in the price of oil.

    This new, correct version of the sentence contains no pronouns.

    The original sentence is incorrect because *its* has no antecedent. *Oil* is an adjective in the expression *oil traders*, and therefore cannot be the antecedent of *its*.

7. **The players' helmets need to be repainted before (they) are used in Sunday's game.**

    CORRECT. *Helmets* is the antecedent of *they*. You need not worry that *they* could refer to *players'*, because 1) *helmets* is the subject, and 2) *players'* is a possessive noun and is therefore not a good antecedent for a pronoun.

8.   A few Shakespearean scholars maintain that <u>Shakespeare</u> borrowed some of (his) most memorable lines from Christopher Marlowe.

Shakespeare is the antecedent of *his*.

The original sentence is incorrect because *he* has no antecedent. *Shakespearean* is an adjective and therefore cannot be the antecedent. Consequently, *he* needs to be replaced with *Shakespeare* in the correct sentence.

9.   The original sentence is far too ambiguous. The antecedent of *they* is almost certainly not meant to be the same as the antecedent of *their*, a confusing state of affairs. Either family is a reasonable antecedent for either pronoun. To correct this sentence, you could get rid of the pronouns. One possible version: *The Smiths avoid the Browns because the Browns dislike the Smiths' children.* It's not clear that this version accurately represents what the author intended, which may have been *The Smiths avoid the Browns because the Smiths dislike the Browns' children.*

10.   (Our) cat is cuter than the cats in the shelter.

This new, correct version of the sentence contains no third-person pronouns. (*Our* is a pronoun, but first-person pronouns such as *our* never have antecedents in the sentence.)

The original sentence is incorrect because *those* has no antecedent. *Those* is plural, and therefore cannot refer to *cat*.

11.   (Samantha) took (her) laptop and (her) books with (her) on the airplane because (she) thought (she) could use (them) to get some work done.

Samantha is the antecedent of all three *her's* and both *she's*.

Her laptop and her books is the antecedent of *them*. (The original *these* is incorrect because *these* is never used as a stand-alone pronoun without a noun following.)

Chapter 8 *of* Sentence Correction

Verbs

In This Chapter...

Chapter 8
Verbs

The **verb tense** of a working verb indicates when the action of the verb takes place. In addition, certain modifiers will pick up the time frame of the verb in the main clause of the sentence.

In sentences with one action, verb tense is relatively easy. Knowing this, the GMAT tries to complicate sentences by incorporating more than one action. As a result, you will need to pay close attention to the sequence of actions in GMAT sentences. This sequence will be driven by meaning; as you work through this chapter, pay close attention to the meaning that various constructions can convey.

The GMAT also sometimes tests **voice**, which you'll learn about later in this chapter, and on occasion **mood**, which you can learn about in Chapter 12 if you are aiming for an especially high Verbal score.

If you are a native speaker of American English, your ear may already be well-attuned to the right use of tense. Incorrect uses of tense (e.g., *He has gone to France last year*) will (correctly) sound funny to you; your instinctual correction (*He went to France last year*) will be correct. As you review this chapter, don't let any newly conscious knowledge mess up your instincts. Use this knowledge to reinforce those instincts.

However, if you are not a native speaker of American English, you may need to learn these rules consciously. Patterns of verb tense vary drastically among languages, even those related to English. For instance, *He is gone to France last year* is correct in French, German, and Italian, but it is 100% wrong in English.

Simple Tenses

The three simple tenses express three basic times:

1. Simple present: Sandy PLAYS well with her friends.
2. Simple past: Sandy PLAYED well with her friends yesterday.
3. Simple future: Sandy WILL PLAY well with her friends tomorrow.

The **simple present** tense is often used to express "eternal" states or frequent events. In the first example above, the sentence does not mean that Sandy is playing right now, but rather that, as a general rule, Sandy plays well with her friends.

The GMAT typically prefers the simple tenses, unless the sentence clearly requires one of the more complex tenses discussed below. The more complex tenses each have particular circumstances in which they can be used; if those circumstances do not exist, then don't use a complex tense.

Make Tenses Reflect Meaning

Sometimes, all the tenses in a sentence are the same, because all the actions take place in the same time frame:

> Right: She WALKED to school in the morning and RAN home in the afternoon.
> Right: She WALKS to school in the morning and RUNS home in the afternoon.
> Right: She WILL WALK to school in the morning and RUN home in the afternoon.

In each sentence, the verbs are in the same tense: simple past in the first, simple present in the second, and simple future in the third. (Note that *run* is understood as *will run*; parallelism allows the *will* to apply to both verbs.) In these examples, changing tense midstream would be confusing and incorrect.

However, in some sentences, the author clearly wants to talk about different periods of time. The tense should change to reflect that intention:

> Right: He IS thinner now because he WENT on a strict diet six months ago.
>
> Simple Present   Simple Past

The switch from present to past is logical, given the clear indications of time (*now* and *six months ago*).

You could also switch the order of the sentence:

> Right: Because he WENT on a strict diet six months ago, he IS thinner now.

Look what happens in this example:

> Wrong: Because he IS STARTING a strict diet, he LOST weight.

Even without the time markers (*six months ago, now*) that require certain tenses, this sentence can't be right. Logically, if he LOST the weight in the past, then STARTING his diet today is not the reason.

The GMAT might toss in so many modifiers that this tense mismatch is lost:

> Wrong: Because he IS STARTING a strict diet, as well as an exercise regimen that he BEGAN more than a year ago, he LOST weight.

Notice that the sentence does include another past tense verb, *began*. In addition to the logic problem already present, the introduction of *began* creates another. Logically, he can't currently be *starting ... an exercise regimen that he began more than a year ago.*

The Perfect Tenses: An Introduction

The two most commonly tested complex tenses on the GMAT are the perfect tenses: past perfect and present perfect.

Past Perfect: The Earlier Action

If two actions in a sentence occurred at *different* times in the past, you can use the **past perfect** tense for the earlier action and simple past for the later action. The past perfect is the "past of the past." For example:

Right: The film HAD STARTED by the time we ARRIVED at the theater.

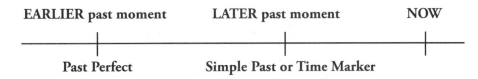

The past perfect tense is formed as follows:

$$\boxed{\textbf{Past Perfect} = \textbf{HAD} + \textbf{Past Participle}}$$

In order to use past perfect, the sentence must also contain either a verb in the simple past tense or a time marker that occurred in the past but later than the past perfect action. For example:

Right: BY 1945, the United States HAD BEEN at war for several years.
Right: The teacher THOUGHT that Jimmy HAD CHEATED on the exam.

In the first sentence, the United States went to war sometime before 1945 (a past time marker). In the second sentence, the earlier past action, *had cheated*, pairs with a simple past action, *thought*: first, Jimmy took the exam (and possibly cheated on it!) and, later, the teacher began to suspect Jimmy.

Even when the circumstances allow past perfect to be used, the sentence is not necessarily required to employ this more complex tense. Some sentences will still make sense even using simple tenses:

Right: Laura LOCKED the deadbolt <u>before</u> she LEFT for work.

The word *before* indicates the sequence of events clearly; it is not necessary to use past perfect to convey the proper meaning. When the meaning of a sentence is already clear, the correct answer may not use past perfect to indicate an earlier action. In this case, do not cross off answers that use simple past.

Instead, look for a different split to help you decide which answer to choose. The words *before* and *after* indicate the sequence of events clearly and emphatically enough to make the use of the past perfect unnecessary.

On hard questions, the GMAT may make a tricky sentence in which the past perfect verb is not the earliest action in the sentence:

> Right: The band U2 WAS just one of many new groups on the rock music scene in the early 1980s, but less than ten years later, U2 HAD fully ECLIPSED its early rivals in the pantheon of popular music.

The first independent clause uses simple past. The second independent clause (after the word *but*) contains a time marker (*ten years later*) and then mentions another action (*had eclipsed*) that occurs before that time marker. Even though *had eclipsed* is not the *earliest* action in the entire sentence, it is the earlier of the two actions in its independent clause. This complex construction is correct.

Present Perfect: Bridging Past and Present

The **present perfect** tense is used for actions that started in the past but continue into the present, or remain true in the present. The present Perfect tense has one foot in the past and one foot in the present.

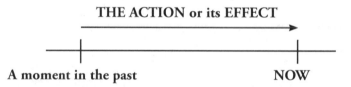

Consider this example:

> Right: The Millers HAVE LIVED in a hut for three days.

The Millers began living in the hut three days ago and they are still living in that hut. In comparison, a sentence in the simple past has a different meaning:

> Right: The Millers LIVED in a hut for three days.

At some point in the past, the Millers lived in a hut, but they no longer live in the hut now. The present perfect tense is formed as follows:

> **Present Perfect = HAVE/HAS + Past Participle**

The past participle of a regular verb, such as *walk* or *live*, is the *-ed* form of the verb: *walked*, *lived*. Irregular verbs, such as *go* or *see*, have unique past participles (*gone*, *seen*). If you are a native English speaker, you likely already know the irregular forms. Otherwise, study the list of irregular past participles in Appendix B.

Here are some examples of actions in the present perfect tense:

Right: This country HAS ENFORCED strict immigration laws <u>for thirty years</u>.
Right: They HAVE KNOWN each other <u>since 1987</u>.

Each example involves an action that began in the past and continues into the present. This country enforced strict immigration laws in the past and still enforces them today. They knew each other in the past and still know each other today. In each case, the idea of a continuing action is reinforced by a time phrase, such as *for thirty years* or *since 1987*, that states how long the action has been occurring or for how long the information has been true.

Sometimes, the present perfect tense means that the action is definitely over, but its *effect* is still relevant to the present moment. For example:

Right: The child HAS DRAWN a square in the sand.

In this example, the child is no longer in the act of drawing a square. However, the square is still there. If the square has disappeared, use simple past.

Right: The child DREW a square in the sand, but the ocean ERASED it.
Right: The child DREW a square in the sand, but the ocean HAS ERASED it.
Wrong: The child HAS DRAWN a square in the sand, but the ocean HAS ERASED it.

The present perfect indicates either *continued action* or *continued effect* of a *completed action* up to the present.

With *since*, use the present perfect to indicate an action or effect that continues to the present time:

Wrong: <u>Since 1986</u>, no one BROKE that world record.
Wrong: <u>Since 1986</u>, no one BREAKS that world record.
Right: <u>Since 1986</u>, no one HAS BROKEN that world record.

For the same reasons, use the present perfect with *within the past ...* or *in the last ...* phrases, such as *within the past five minutes* or *in the last ten days*. In contrast, a time phrase that does <u>not</u> include the present (*last month, in 2007,* etc.) should not be used with the present perfect. Use the simple past instead:

Wrong: Veronica HAS TRAVELED all over the world <u>in 2007</u>.
Right: Veronica TRAVELED all over the world <u>in 2007</u>.

You could also write *Veronica has traveled all over the world* and omit any specific time reference. In this case, you are making a statement about Veronica today (it is true today that she *has traveled all over the world*).

Finally, the present perfect can be used in certain circumstances to clarify an ambiguous sequence in time. For instance, the word *when* can mean either "at the same time" or "after." The use of present perfect resolves the meaning. Consider these examples:

Right:　　She WILL PAY you *when* you ASK her.　(No present perfect)
　　　　　　　= She will pay you <u>at the same time</u> as you ask her, or maybe just after.

Right:　　She WILL PAY you *when* you HAVE TAKEN out the garbage.　(present perfect)
　　　　　　　= She will pay you <u>after</u> you take out the garbage.

-ing Modifiers: Follow the Main Verb

If you haven't already studied Chapter 4, "Modifiers," or if you have forgotten about "*comma –ing*" modifiers, you may wish to review that section before proceeding here.

"*Comma –ing*" modifiers follow on from the tense of the main working verb to which they are attached. For example:

Right:　<u>Peering</u> out of the window, she WATCHED her dog frolic on the lawn.

The main verb, *watched*, is in past tense. The woman is not currently *peering* out of her window; rather, she peered out of her window while she watched the dog. The modifier *peering* picks up the time frame of the main verb.

Here's another example:

Right:　She WILL SIGN the contract tomorrow, <u>barring</u> any unforeseen disruptions.

If any unforeseen disruptions occur *in the future*—between now and when she plans to sign the contract—then she might not sign after all.

Which of the two sentences below is correct?

The country's economy is unstable, the result of a stock market crash occurring ten years ago.

The country's economy is unstable, the result of a stock market crash that occurred ten years ago.

In the first sentence, the word *occurring* seems to indicate that the crash is happening now, since the main verb is in present tense—but the sentence clearly states that the crash occurred ten years ago. This sentence is incorrect.

The second sentence correctly changes the modifier form to indicate that the crash occurred in the past.

Present to Future or Past to Conditional

Consider the following sentence:

> The scientist ANNOUNCED that the <u>supercollider WAS ready</u>, that <u>it HAD not COST too much to build</u>, and that <u>it WOULD PROVIDE new insights</u> into the workings of the universe.

The sentence uses multiple tenses:

> The scientist announced that…

> …*the supercollider WAS ready.* (simple past)
> …*that it HAD not COST too much to build.* (past perfect)
> …*that it WOULD PROVIDE new insights.* (conditional)

The **conditional tense** is formed by combining *would* with the base form of the verb: *would provide*. This construction expresses the future from the point of view of the past.

The typical sequences for these types of sentences are either Present + Future or Past + Conditional:

Right: The scientist <u>BELIEVES</u> that the machine <u>WILL BE</u> wonderful.
                        Present   Future

Wrong: The scientist <u>BELIEVES</u> that the machine <u>WOULD BE</u> wonderful.
                        Present   Conditional

Right: The scientist <u>BELIEVED</u> that the machine <u>WOULD BE</u> wonderful.
                        Past   Conditional

Wrong: The scientist <u>BELIEVED</u> that the machine <u>WILL BE </u>wonderful.
                        Past   Future

Active and Passive Voice

Verbs are written in either **active voice** or **passive voice**. In the active voice, the subject of the sentence performs the action. In the passive voice, the subject of the sentence has an action performed on it by someone or something else. For example,

Active: The hungry students ATE the pizza.
Passive: The pizza WAS EATEN by the hungry students.

The passive voice is formed with a form of the verb *to be* (in this case, *was*), followed by the past participle (*eaten*).

Though passive voice has a reputation for sounding awkward, it is still a grammatically valid construction:

Passive: It HAS BEEN DECIDED by Jason that he will not attend college.
Active: Jason HAS DECIDED not to attend college.

The active version may sound better than the passive one, but both are right. People often think that the passive voice is inherently wrong. The GMAT sometimes exploits this incorrect thinking by making the awkward, passive answer *correct*. Meanwhile, there's a great-sounding active answer with a subtle error somewhere else. Consider the following example:

Passive: It HAS BEEN DECIDED by Jason that he will not attend college next fall.
Active: Jason HAS DECIDED next fall not to attend college.

The active voice example says that Jason *decided next fall*. This is illogical! He either already *decided*, in the past, or he *will decide next fall* (in the future). Meanwhile, the passive sentence is correct, though it sounds awkward.

Don't be biased against the passive. Make sure that the structure of the non-underlined portion matches what you choose as your answer, whether that requires active or passive voice.

As a final note, you do not have to make active or passive voice parallel throughout a sentence. For example:

Right: The shuttle launch TOOK place flawlessly and WAS SEEN on television.

Both parallel elements work with the subject of the sentence: *The shuttle launch took place* and *the shuttle launch was seen on television*.

8

Problem Set

Each of the following sentences contains one or more underlined sections. If an underlined section contains no errors, mark it as CORRECT. Otherwise, write down a correct version of the underlined section. For extra credit, explain your decisions with respect to the tense, mood, and voice of the relevant verbs, and with respect to the nature of the relevant verbals.

1. Mozart, who died in 1791, <u>has lived</u> in Salzburg for most of his life.

2. The local government <u>has built</u> the school that was destroyed by the earthquake.

3. The editor of our local newspaper, who has earned much acclaim in her long career, <u>has been awarded</u> a Pulitzer Prize yesterday.

4. She already <u>woke up</u> when the phone rang.

5. Last Monday, Mary realized that she <u>will have</u> to spend all of that night rewriting her application because she <u>did not back up</u> her files.

6. By the end of the Apollo program, twelve Americans <u>have walked</u> on the moon.

7. Water freezes if it <u>were</u> cooled to zero degrees Celsius.

8. In the Fischer–Tropsch process, which <u>developed</u> in Germany by Franz Fischer and Hans Tropsch, coal <u>is converted</u> into a liquid fuel similar to petroleum.

9. <u>The dealer was asked to sell a painting by Picasso.</u>

8

Solutions

1. Mozart, who died in 1791, <u>has lived</u> in Salzburg for most of his life.

Has lived (present perfect tense) should be *lived* (simple past tense) or possibly *had lived* (past perfect). One possible reason to use the present perfect (*has lived*) is to indicate that an action or state of affairs is still in progress. Mozart is dead, so this reason does not apply here.

The other possible reason to use the present perfect is to indicate that an action, though completed in the past, still has some continuing effect on the subject of the verb. Since Mozart is dead, this reason does not apply either.

Since neither reason for using the present perfect applies to this sentence, use the simple past. There is no real need to use the past perfect (*had lived*), because the sequence of past events (Mozart's life and death) is obvious. Moreover, the actions are not contrasted (for instance, if he *lived* one place but *died* somewhere else). That said, to emphasize the sequence of events, you could choose to use the past perfect in this sentence:

Correction: **Mozart, who died in 1791, <u>lived</u> in Salzburg for most of his life.**

    OR   **Mozart, who died in 1791, <u>had lived</u> in Salzburg for most of his life.**

2. The local government <u>has built</u> the school that was destroyed by the earthquake.

Has built (present perfect tense) should be *built* (simple past tense) OR *had built* (past perfect). Sometimes, the present perfect is used to indicate that an action or state of affairs is still in progress. However, the original process of building the school cannot be continuing now, because the school was destroyed by the earthquake. The government might be rebuilding the school now, but that is not the same as building the school. The other possible reason to use the present perfect is to indicate that an action, though completed in the past, still has some continuing effect on the subject and object of the verb. The effects of the action of building were essentially wiped out by the earthquake, because the earthquake destroyed the school. Since neither possible reason for using the present perfect applies to this sentence, you cannot use the present perfect.

Either the simple past or the past perfect is possible. In the simple past version, the writer's mental time frame is concurrent with *built*. The following clause (*that was destroyed by the earthquake*) just serves to identify the school, and the writer might go on to discuss the building process. However, the past perfect emphasizes the sequence of events more than the simple past does. In the past perfect version, the writer's mental time frame is concurrent with *was destroyed*. The use of *had built* indicates that the writer is dipping back in time only for a moment to the building process. In fact, the writer might proceed to write more about the destruction (perhaps the consequences of shoddy construction methods).

Correction: **The local government <u>built</u> the school that was destroyed by the earthquake.**

    OR   **The local government <u>had built</u> the school that was destroyed by the earthquake.**

8

3. The editor of our local newspaper, who has earned much acclaim in her long career, <u>has been award-</u><u>ed</u> a Pulitzer Prize yesterday.

Has been awarded (present perfect tense) should be *was awarded* (simple past tense). The verb has to be in the simple past because you are told that the action occurred at a specific time in the past (*yesterday*).

Correction: **The editor of our local newspaper, who has earned much acclaim in her long career, <u>was awarded</u> a Pulitzer Prize yesterday.**

4. She already <u>woke up</u> when the phone rang.

Already woke up (simple past) should be *had already woken up* (past perfect). You need to use the past perfect here because the word *already* requires this use for a momentary action such as *wake up*, when placed prior to another past action. It would be fine to say *She was already awake when the phone rang*, because *was awake* is a state and thus takes up time. In that case, *already* would indicate that this state was in effect before the phone rang. However, when you use *already* with the simple past of a momentary action, you convey a present perfect meaning. As your spouse shakes you out of bed, you might say *I already woke up*, but in proper English, you should say *I HAVE already woken up*. In other words, the action is complete AND the effect (your wakefulness) continues to the present. In the sample sentence, since you want the subject's wakefulness to continue up through some point <u>in the past</u> (*when the phone rang*), you must use the past perfect of *wake up*:

Correction: **She <u>had</u> already <u>woken up</u> when the phone rang.**

5. Last Monday, Mary realized that she <u>will have</u> to spend all of that night rewriting her application because she <u>did not back up</u> her files.

Will have (simple future tense) should be *would have* (conditional tense). Mary made her realization on Monday. At that time, her sleepless night spent rewriting the application was in the <u>future</u>. However, last Monday night is now in the <u>past</u>. An action that was in the future (relative to the time of the main verb, *realized*), but is now in the past, must be rendered in <u>the conditional tense</u>. This tense is formed by replacing *will* with *would*.

Did not back up (simple past tense) should be *had not backed up* (past perfect tense). The past perfect tense is required here because Mary's failure to back up her files must logically have occurred <u>before</u> Mary became aware of (*realized*) this failure:

Correction: **Last Monday Mary realized that she <u>would have</u> to spend all of that night rewriting her application because she <u>had not backed up</u> her files.**

6. By the end of the Apollo program, twelve Americans <u>have walked</u> on the moon.

Have walked (present perfect tense) should be *had walked* (past perfect tense). The past perfect is required because the twelve Americans did their walking before the end of the Apollo program. Here, the phrase *end of the Apollo program* functions much like a specific date in the past.

Correction: **By the end of the Apollo program, twelve Americans <u>had walked</u> on the moon.**

7. Water freezes if it <u>were</u> cooled to zero degrees Celsius.

Were (simple past tense) should be *is* (present tense). This sentence is stating a general truth or rule. You can also omit a tensed verb altogether from the *if*-clause: *Water freezes if cooled to zero degrees Celsius.*

Correction: **Water freezes if it <u>is</u> cooled to zero degrees Celsius.**

8. In the Fischer–Tropsch process, which <u>developed</u> in Germany by Franz Fischer and Hans Tropsch, coal is converted into a liquid fuel similar to petroleum.

Developed (active voice) should be *was developed* (passive voice). The passive voice is required because the people who developed the process appear in the non-underlined phrase *by Franz Fischer and Hans Tropsch.*

Is converted (passive voice) is correct. The passive voice is required because unnamed agent(s), rather than the coal itself, cause the conversion of the coal into a liquid fuel. Supposing that the whole sentence were underlined and that you were therefore free to rewrite it completely, should you change it into the active voice? No, because the passive voice is ideally suited to the purposes of this sentence. The author wants to tell you about the Fischer–Tropsch process, not to list the various parties who happen to use that process. It is therefore fitting for the words *Fischer–Tropsch process* to be in the subject position. To put *Fischer–Tropsch* in the subject position, the verb *to develop* must be in the passive voice.

Correction: **In the Fischer–Tropsch process, which <u>was developed</u> in Germany by Franz Fischer and Hans Tropsch, coal <u>is converted</u> into a liquid fuel similar to petroleum.**

9. <u>The dealer was asked to sell a painting by Picasso.</u>

The words *by Picasso* are ambiguous. Because *was asked* is in the passive voice, *by Picasso* could be meant to tell you who asked the dealer to sell the painting—in which case the sentence should read *Picasso asked the dealer to sell the painting.* Alternatively, *by Picasso* could simply be meant to identify the painting as a work by Picasso, in which case the sentence should read *The dealer was asked to sell a Picasso painting.*

Correction: **<u>Picasso asked the dealer to sell a painting.</u>**
    OR   **<u>The dealer was asked to sell a Picasso painting.</u>**

8

Chapter 9

of

Sentence Correction

Idioms

In This Chapter...

Spot – Extract – Replace

Idiom List

Chapter 9
Idioms

Idioms are expressions that have unique forms. There is no hard and fast rule for determining the form of an idiom; rather, it is just a form that you know or memorize. For example, *They tried to reach the summit and succeeded in doing so* is correct, but *They tried in reaching the summit and succeeded to do so* is not correct. The verb *to try* is followed by an infinitive, but the verb *to succeed* is followed by *in* and an *-ing* form of the verb. Why? There is no reason. *Try to do* and *succeed in doing* are the accepted English idioms.

If you are a native English speaker, most idiomatic expressions are already wired into your brain from years of hearing and speaking English. For non-native speakers, the task is more difficult. However, the GMAT does tend to focus on certain common idioms. Review the common idiom list in this chapter and memorize any that you do not know. If you want an especially high Verbal GMAT score, you can also spend some time learning some of the expressions listed in Appendix A of this guide (though there are enough that you may not want to try to memorize them all).

Spot – Extract – Replace

Your ear is your most valuable weapon as you try to figure out the proper form of an idiom. Here's how to use your ear well:

(A) Some historians attribute the eventual development of accurate methods for measuring longitude as the monetary prizes offered by various governments.

(B) Some historians attribute the eventual development of accurate methods for measuring longitude to the monetary prizes offered by various governments.

1. SPOT the suspect idiomatic expression. Compare answer choices to find the splits. In the choices above, the words that vary are *as* and *to*. What pairs with *as* or *to*? In this case, the idiom revolves around the use of the verb *attribute*.

2. <u>EXTRACT the various forms of the idiom</u> and put them into simpler sentences that you can easily compare. You can delete words, such as extraneous modifiers, or you can make up brand-new sentences. Either way, strip the sentence to a simple example:

(A)   Historians attribute the development AS the prizes.

(B)   Historians attribute the development TO the prizes.

If you know this idiom, then the correct version will sound better to your ear. *Attribute TO* is the correct idiom.

<u>(3) REPLACE the corrected idiom in the sentence</u> and confirm that it works:

(B)   Some historians <u>attribute</u> the eventual development of accurate methods for measuring longitude TO the monetary prizes offered by various governments.

The choice that your ear preferred should work in the entire GMAT sentence. If it does not work, check whether you spotted and extracted the idiom correctly.

Idiom List

The English language includes thousands of idioms. You can't possibly memorize them all. Certain idioms are more commonly tested, however; concentrate on these. This chapter contains the most commonly tested idioms, as seen on official GMAT test questions. Appendix A contains additional idioms that have appeared on real questions but are not as common as the ones in this chapter.

Label	Definition
RIGHT:	Expressions that the GMAT considers correct.
SUSPECT:	*Expressions that the GMAT seems to avoid if possible. These expressions are sometimes grammatically correct, but they may be wordy, controversial, or simply less preferred than other forms.*
WRONG:	*Expressions that the GMAT considers incorrect.*

ABILITY

RIGHT:	I value my ABILITY TO SING.
WRONG:	*I value my ABILITY OF SINGING.*
	I value my ABILITY FOR SINGING.
	I value the ABILITY FOR me TO SING.

ALLOW

RIGHT:	The holiday ALLOWS Maria TO WATCH the movie today. (= permits)
	Maria WAS ALLOWED TO WATCH the movie.

The demolition of the old building ALLOWS FOR new construction.
(= permits the existence of)

WRONG: *The holiday ALLOWED FOR Maria TO WATCH the movie.*
The holiday ALLOWED Maria the WATCHING OF the movie.
The holiday ALLOWS THAT homework BE done (or CAN BE done).
Homework is ALLOWED FOR DOING BY Maria.
The ALLOWING OF shopping TO DO (or TO BE DONE).

ALTHOUGH   See BUT.

AND

RIGHT: We are concerned about the forests AND the oceans.
We are concerned about the forests, the oceans, AND the mountains.
We work all night, AND we sleep all day. (note the comma before AND)

SUSPECT: *We are concerned about the forests AND ALSO the oceans.*

WRONG: *We are concerned about the forests, ALSO the oceans.*

AS

RIGHT: AS I walked, I became more nervous. (= during)
AS I had already paid, I was unconcerned. (= because, since)
AS we did last year, we will win this year. (= in the same way)
JUST AS we did last year, we will win this year. (= in the same way)
AS the president of the company, she works hard. (= in the role of)
AS a child, I delivered newspapers. (= in the stage of being)
My first job was an apprenticeship AS a sketch artist.
AS PART OF the arrangement, he received severance.

SUSPECT: *AS A PART OF the arrangement, he received severance.*

WRONG: *My first job was an apprenticeship OF a sketch artist.*
They worked AS a sketch artist. (Needs to agree in number.)
WHILE BEING a child, I delivered newspapers.
AS BEING a child, I delivered newspapers.
WHILE IN childhood, I delivered newspapers.

AS ... AS

RIGHT: Cheese is AS GREAT AS people say.
Cheese is NOT AS great AS people say.
We have AS MANY apples AS need to be cooked.
We have THREE TIMES AS MANY pears AS you.
We have AT LEAST AS MANY apples AS you.
We have 10 apples, ABOUT AS MANY AS we picked yesterday.
His knowledge springs AS MUCH from experience AS from schooling.

His knowledge springs NOT SO MUCH from experience AS from schooling.

He wins frequently, AS MUCH because he plays SO hard AS because he cheats.

SUSPECT: *Cheese is NOT SO great AS people say.*

We have AS MANY apples AS OR MORE apples THAN you.

We have AS MANY apples AS THERE need to be cooked.

He wins frequently, AS MUCH because he plays AS hard AS because he cheats.

WRONG: *Cheese is SO great AS people say.*

Cheese is SO great THAT people say.

Cheese is AS great THAT people say.

We have AS MANY apples THAN you.

We have SO MANY apples AS you.

We have AS MANY OR MORE apples THAN you.

We have THREE TIMES AS MANY MORE pears AS you.

We have 10 apples, ABOUT EQUIVALENT TO what we picked yesterday.

His knowledge springs NOT from experience AS from schooling.

BECUASE

RIGHT: BECAUSE the sun SHINES, plants grow.

Plants grow BECAUSE the sun SHINES.

BECAUSE OF the sun, plants grow.

BY SHINING, the sun makes plants grow.

Plants grow, FOR the sun shines. (grammatically correct but very formal)

SUSPECT: *Plants grow BECAUSE OF the sun, WHICH SHINES.*

Plants are amazing IN THAT they grow in the sun. (correct but wordy)

The growth of plants IS EXPLAINED BY THE FACT THAT the sun shines.

(correct but wordy)

WRONG: *Plants grow BECAUSE OF the sun SHINING.*

Plants grow AS A RESULT OF the sun SHINING.

BECAUSE OF SHINING, the sun makes plants grow.

ON ACCOUNT OF SHINING or ITS SHINING, the sun makes plants grow.

BECAUSE the sun SHINES IS the REASON that plants grow.

The ABILITY OF plants TO grow IS BECAUSE the sun shines.

BEING THAT the sun shines, plants grow.

The growth of plants IS EXPLAINED BECAUSE OF the shining of the sun.

The growth of plants IS EXPLAINED BECAUSE the sun shines.

BEING

RIGHT: BEING infected does not make you sick.

The judges saw the horses BEING led to the stables.

SUSPECT: *BEING an advocate of reform, I would like to make a different proposal.*

Note: The word BEING is <u>often</u> wordy or awkward. However, having caught on to the

"BEING is wrong" shortcut, the GMAT problem writers have created a few problems that force you to choose BEING. BEING appears in many more wrong answers than right ones. The word can, however, be used correctly as a gerund or as a participle.

BELIEVE

RIGHT:	She BELIEVES THAT Gary IS right.
	She BELIEVES Gary TO BE right.
	IT IS BELIEVED THAT Gary IS right.
	Gary IS BELIEVED TO BE right.
SUSPECT:	*Gary IS BELIEVED BY her TO BE right.*

BOTH … AND

RIGHT:	She was interested BOTH in plants AND in animals.
	She was interested in BOTH plants AND animals.
WRONG:	*She was interested BOTH in plants AND animals.*
	She was interested BOTH in plants AS WELL AS in animals.
	She was interested BOTH in plants BUT ALSO in animals.

BUT

RIGHT:	I STUDY hard BUT TAKE breaks.
	I STUDY hard, BUT I TAKE breaks.
	ALTHOUGH I TAKE frequent naps, I STUDY effectively.
	DESPITE TAKING frequent naps, I STUDY effectively.
	I TAKE frequent naps, YET I STUDY effectively.
SUSPECT:	*DESPITE THE FACT THAT I TAKE frequent naps, I STUDY effectively.*
	ALTHOUGH a frequent napper, I STUDY effectively.
	(ALTHOUGH should generally be followed by a clause.)
WRONG:	*I STUDY effectively ALTHOUGH TAKING frequent naps.*
	ALTHOUGH I TAKE frequent naps, YET I STUDY effectively.
	ALTHOUGH I TAKE frequent naps, AND I STUDY effectively.
	DESPITE TAKING frequent naps, YET I STUDY effectively.

CAN

RIGHT:	The manager CAN RUN the plant.
	The plant CAN CAUSE damage.
SUSPECT:	*It is POSSIBLE FOR the plant TO CAUSE damage.*
	The plant POSSIBLY CAUSES damage.
WRONG:	*The manager HAS THE CAPABILITY OF RUNNING the plant.*
	The plant HAS THE POSSIBILITY OF CAUSING damage.

9

CONSIDER

RIGHT: I CONSIDER her a friend. I CONSIDER her intelligent.

                 Note: You can switch the order of the two objects, if one is long.

                 I CONSIDER illegal the law passed last week by the new regime.

                 The law IS CONSIDERED illegal.

SUSPECT: *The judge CONSIDERS the law TO BE illegal.*

WRONG: *The judge CONSIDERS the law AS illegal (or AS BEING illegal).*

                 The judge CONSIDERS the law SHOULD BE illegal.

                 The judge CONSIDERS the law AS IF IT WERE illegal.

EITHER ... OR

RIGHT: I will take EITHER the subway OR the bus.

WRONG: *I will take EITHER the subway AND the bus.*

EXPECT

RIGHT: We EXPECT the price TO FALL. The price IS EXPECTED TO FALL.

                 We EXPECT THAT the price WILL FALL.

                 IT IS EXPECTED THAT the price WILL FALL.

                 Inflation rose more than we EXPECTED.

                 There IS an EXPECTATION THAT the price will fall.

SUSPECT: *There IS an EXPECTATION the price WILL FALL.*

                 There IS an EXPECTATION OF the price FALLING.

WRONG: *The price IS EXPECTED FOR IT TO FALL.*

                 IT IS EXPECTED THAT the price SHOULD FALL.

FOR (conjunction)   See BECAUSE.

FROM ... TO

RIGHT: The price fell FROM 10 euros TO 3 euros.

                 The price fell TO 3 euros FROM 10 euros.

WRONG: *The price fell FROM 10 euros DOWN TO 3 euros.*

                 The price rose FROM 3 euros UP TO 10 euros.

IN ORDER TO

RIGHT: She drank coffee IN ORDER TO STAY awake.

                 She drank coffee TO STAY awake. (Infinitive TO STAY indicates purpose.)

SUSPECT: *She drank coffee IN ORDER THAT (or SO THAT) she MIGHT stay awake.*

                 She drank coffee SO AS TO STAY awake.

WRONG: *She drank coffee FOR STAYING awake.*

             Coffee was drunk by her TO STAY awake (or IN ORDER TO STAY awake).

             Note: The subject COFFEE is not trying TO STAY awake.

INDICATE

RIGHT: A report INDICATES THAT unique bacteria LIVE on our skin.

....

SUSPECT: *A report IS INDICATIVE OF the presence of unique bacteria on our skin.*

....

WRONG: *A report INDICATES unique bacteria LIVE on our skin. (THAT is needed.)*

             A report IS INDICATIVE THAT unique bacteria LIVE on our skin.

             A report INDICATES unique bacteria AS present on our skin.

             A report INDICATES unique bacteria TO LIVE on our skin.

INSTEAD OF   See RATHER THAN.

LIKE   See also SUCH AS.

RIGHT: LIKE his sister, Matt drives fast cars. (= both drive fast cars)

             Matt drives fast cars LIKE his sister's.

             (= both drive <u>similar</u> cars OR, less optimally, one of the cars he drives is his sister's)

....

WRONG: *Matt drives fast cars LIKE his sister does.*

             LIKE his sister, SO Matt drives fast cars.

NOT ... BUT

RIGHT: She DID NOT EAT mangoes BUT ATE other kinds of fruit.

             She DID NOT EAT mangoes BUT LIKED other kinds of fruit AND later BEGAN
             to like kiwis, too.

             A tomato is NOT a vegetable BUT a fruit.

             A tomato is NOT a vegetable BUT RATHER a fruit.

....

WRONG: *She DID NOT EAT mangoes BUT other kinds of fruit.*

NOT ONLY ... BUT ALSO

RIGHT: We wore NOT ONLY boots BUT ALSO sandals.

             We wore NOT ONLY boots, BUT ALSO sandals. (Comma is optional.)

             We wore NOT JUST boots BUT ALSO sandals.

             We wore NOT ONLY boots BUT sandals.

....

SUSPECT: *We wore NOT ONLY boots BUT sandals AS WELL.*

             We wore boots AND ALSO sandals.

....

WRONG: *We wore NOT ONLY boots AND ALSO sandals.*

             We wore NOT ONLY boots BUT, AS WELL, sandals.

RATHER THAN

RIGHT: He wrote with pencils RATHER THAN with pens.

SUSPECT: *He wrote with pencils, BUT NOT pens.*

WRONG: *He wrote with pencils INSTEAD OF with pens.* (*Of with* is incorrect.)

SO … AS TO

SUSPECT: *The sauce was SO hot AS TO burn my mouth.*

Note: The GMAT has an inconsistent position on this idiom. Question #39 in *The Official Guide for GMAT Review (2015)* claims that this idiom is "incorrect" with no further explanation. However, a problem in GMATPrep® has this idiom in a correct answer choice. Other authorities consider this idiom correct, and we agree. Nevertheless, you should be wary of its use.

WRONG: *The sauce had SUCH heat AS TO burn my mouth.*
           The sauce had SO MUCH heat AS TO burn my mouth.

SO … THAT   See also ENOUGH.

RIGHT: The book was SO SHORT THAT I could read it in one night.
           The book was SHORT ENOUGH FOR me TO READ in one night.
           Note: These two expressions have slightly different emphases, but it is unlikely that you will need to choose an answer solely on this basis.

SUSPECT: *The book was SO SHORT I could read it. (THAT is preferred.)*
           The book was OF SUCH SHORTNESS THAT I could read it.
           SUCH was the SHORTNESS of the book THAT I could read it.

WRONG: *The book had SO MUCH SHORTNESS THAT I could read it.*
           The book was OF SUCH SHORTNESS, I could read it.
           The book was SHORT TO SUCH A DEGREE AS TO ALLOW me to read it.

SO THAT

RIGHT: She gave money SO THAT the school could offer scholarships. (= purpose)

SUSPECT: *She gave money, SO the school was grateful.* (= result)

WRONG: *She gave money SO the school could offer scholarships.*

SUCH AS

RIGHT: Matt drives fast cars, SUCH AS Ferraris. (= example)
           Matt enjoys driving SUCH cars AS Ferraris.
           Matt enjoys intense activities, SUCH AS DRIVING fast cars.

SUSPECT: *Matt drives fast cars LIKE Ferraris.* (= similar to, but "example" is implied)
           Note: The GMAT has backed off from claiming that *like* cannot introduce examples, but it is probable that the use of *like* with examples will continue to be avoided.

WRONG: *Matt drives Ferraris AND THE LIKE.*
               Matt drives Ferraris AND OTHER cars SUCH AS THESE.
               Matt trains in many ways SUCH AS BY DRIVING on racetracks.
               Matt enjoys intense activities, SUCH AS TO DRIVE fast cars.

THAN
RIGHT: His books are MORE impressive THAN those of other writers.
               This paper is LESS impressive THAN that one.
               This paper is NO LESS impressive THAN that one.
               This newspaper cost 50 cents MORE THAN that one.
               MORE THAN 250 newspapers are published here.
               Sales are HIGHER this year THAN last year.

WRONG: *His books are MORE impressive AS those of other writers.*
               This paper is MORE impressive RATHER THAN that one.
               This paper is MORE impressive INSTEAD OF that one.
               This paper is NO LESS impressive AS that one.
               This paper is NONE THE LESS impressive THAN that one.
               This newspaper cost 50 cents AS MUCH AS that one.
               AS MANY AS OR MORE THAN 250 newspapers are published here.
               Sales are HIGHER this year OVER last years.

UNLIKE   See also CONTRAST.
RIGHT: UNLIKE the spiny anteater, the aardvark is docile.

WRONG: *UNLIKE WITH the spiny anteater, the aardvark is docile.*

WHETHER
RIGHT: I do not know WHETHER I will go.

SUSPECT: *I do not know WHETHER OR NOT I will go.*

WRONG: *I do not know IF I will go. (IF requires a consequence)*

WHETHER ... OR
RIGHT: I decided to eat the food, WHETHER it was tasty OR NOT.
               WHETHER trash OR treasure, the recyclables must be picked up.

WRONG: *WHETHER trash OR ALSO treasure, the recyclables must be picked up.*
               WHETHER THEY BE trash OR treasure, the recyclables must go.

YET   See BUT.

Problem Set

In each of the following problems, there will be multiple versions of a sentence. These versions will differ by the form of an idiom. <u>Underline</u> the idiom in each version. For idioms that are split up, be sure to <u>underline</u> both parts. Then evaluate each idiom using the Spot–Extract–Replace method. Label each version as RIGHT, SUSPECT, or WRONG.

1. (a) The conflict started both because of ethnic tensions as well as because of economic dislocations.
   (b) The conflict started both because of ethnic tensions and because of economic dislocations.
   (c) The conflict started both because of ethnic tensions but also because of economic dislocations.

2. (a) These results indicate the health of the marsh's ecosystem has seriously declined.
   (b) These results are indicative that the health of the marsh's ecosystem has seriously declined.
   (c) These results indicate that the health of the marsh's ecosystem has seriously declined.
   (d) These results indicate the health of the marsh's ecosystem to have seriously declined.

3. (a) The ring-tailed squirrel is more adept at surviving harsh winter conditions as its cousin, the golden-mantled squirrel.
   (b) The ring-tailed squirrel is more adept at surviving harsh winter conditions rather than its cousin, the golden-mantled squirrel.
   (c) The ring-tailed squirrel is more adept at surviving harsh winter conditions instead of its cousin, the golden-mantled squirrel.
   (d) The ring-tailed squirrel is more adept at surviving harsh winter conditions than its cousin, the golden-mantled squirrel.

4. (a) Unlike humans and guinea pigs, most mammals have the ability of synthesizing Vitamin C from glucose, a simple sugar.
   (b) Unlike humans and guinea pigs, most mammals have the capability of synthesizing Vitamin C from glucose, a simple sugar.
   (c) Unlike humans and guinea pigs, most mammals can synthesize Vitamin C from glucose, a simple sugar.

5. (a) Advances in the production of high-temperature superconductors are expected to increase the viability of so-called "maglev" trains that float on magnetic fields.

    (b) It is expected that advances in the production of high-temperature supercon-ductors should increase the viability of so-called "maglev" trains that float on magnetic fields.

    (c) It is expected that advances in the production of high-temperature supercon-ductors will increase the viability of so-called "maglev" trains that float on mag-netic fields.

    (d) Advances in the production of high-temperature superconductors are expected for them to increase the viability of so-called "maglev" trains that float on mag-netic fields.

6. (a) Faced with the recurrence of natural disasters, such as floods and wildfires, many state governments have imposed significant taxes on their citizens in order to raise funds in advance of the next calamity.

    (b) Faced with the recurrence of natural disasters, such as floods and wildfires, many state governments have imposed significant taxes on their citizens for raising funds in advance of the next calamity.

    (c) Faced with the recurrence of natural disasters, such as floods and wildfires, many state governments have imposed significant taxes on their citizens so as to raise funds in advance of the next calamity.

    (d) Faced with the recurrence of natural disasters, such as floods and wildfires, many state governments have imposed significant taxes on their citizens in order that the governments might raise funds in advance of the next calamity.

    (e) Faced with the recurrence of natural disasters, such as floods and wildfires, many state governments have imposed significant taxes on their citizens to raise funds in advance of the next calamity.

7. (a) Many places are called Naples—not only the cities in Italy and in Florida, and also a town in Clark County, South Dakota (population 25).

    (b) Many places are called Naples—not only the cities in Italy and in Florida, but a town in Clark County, South Dakota (population 25) as well.

    (c) Many places are called Naples—not only the cities in Italy and in Florida, but also a town in Clark County, South Dakota (population 25).

    (d) Many places are called Naples—the cities in Italy and in Florida, and also a town in Clark County, South Dakota (population 25).

    (e) Many places are called Naples—not only the cities in Italy and in Florida but a town in Clark County, South Dakota (population 25).

    (f) Many places are called Naples—not only the cities in Italy and in Florida but, as well, a town in Clark County, South Dakota (population 25).

9

8. (a) The Caucasus region has several times as many indigenous languages per square
         mile than most other areas of the world.
    (b) The Caucasus region has several times as many indigenous languages per square
         mile as most other areas of the world.
    (c) The Caucasus region has several times so many indigenous languages per square
         mile as most other areas of the world.
    (d) The Caucasus region has several times more indigenous languages per square
         mile that most other areas of the world.
    (e) The Caucasus region has several times as many more indigenous languages per
         square mile as most other areas of the world.

9

Solutions

1. (a) The conflict started <u>both</u> because of ethnic tensions <u>as well as</u> because of economic dislocations. (both … as well as …) **WRONG**

   (b) The conflict started <u>both</u> because of ethnic tensions <u>and</u> because of economic dislocations. (both … and …) **RIGHT**

   (c) The conflict started <u>both</u> because of ethnic tensions <u>but also</u> because of economic dislocations. (both … but also …) **WRONG**

2. (a) These results <u>indicate</u> the health of the marsh's ecosystem has seriously declined. (indicate + clause) **WRONG**

   (b) These results <u>are indicative that</u> the health of the marsh's ecosystem has seriously declined. (are indicative that + clause) **WRONG**

   (c) These results <u>indicate that</u> the health of the marsh's ecosystem has seriously declined. (indicate that + clause) **RIGHT**

   (d) These results <u>indicate</u> the health of the marsh's ecosystem to have seriously declined. (indicate + noun + to do) **WRONG**

   Note: The use of <u>decline</u> is also idiomatic. Both forms in this problem are correct (a decline in the health OR the health has declined).

3. (a) The ring-tailed squirrel is <u>more</u> adept at surviving harsh winter conditions <u>as</u> its cousin, the golden-mantled squirrel. (more … as …) **WRONG**

   (b) The ring-tailed squirrel is <u>more</u> adept at surviving harsh winter conditions <u>rather than</u> its cousin, the golden-mantled squirrel. (more … rather than …) **WRONG**

   (c) The ring-tailed squirrel is <u>more</u> adept at surviving harsh winter conditions <u>instead of</u> its cousin, the golden-mantled squirrel. (more … instead of …) **WRONG**

   (d) The ring-tailed squirrel is <u>more</u> adept at surviving harsh winter conditions <u>than</u> its cousin, the golden-mantled squirrel. (more … than …) **RIGHT**

4. (a) Unlike humans and guinea pigs, most mammals <u>have the ability of synthesizing</u> Vitamin C from glucose, a simple sugar. (have the ability of doing) **WRONG**

   (b) Unlike humans and guinea pigs, most mammals <u>have the capability of synthesizing</u> Vitamin C from glucose, a simple sugar. (have the capability of doing) **WRONG**

   (c) Unlike humans and guinea pigs, most mammals <u>can synthesize</u> Vitamin C from glucose, a simple sugar. (can do) **RIGHT**

5. (a) Advances in the production of high-temperature superconductors <u>are expected to increase</u> the viability of so-called "maglev" trains that float on magnetic fields. (are expected to do) **RIGHT**

   (b) <u>It is expected that</u> advances in the production of high-temperature superconductors <u>should increase</u> the viability of so-called "maglev" trains that float on magnetic fields. (it is expected that + should do) **WRONG**

   (c) <u>It is expected that</u> advances in the production of high-temperature superconductors <u>will</u>

increase the viability of so-called "maglev" trains that float on magnetic fields. (it is expected that + will do) **RIGHT**

(d) Advances in the production of high-temperature superconductors <u>are expected for them to increase</u> the viability of so-called "maglev" trains that float on magnetic fields. (are expected for them to do) **WRONG**

6. (a) Faced with the recurrence of natural disasters, such as floods and wildfires, many state governments have imposed significant taxes on their citizens <u>in order to raise</u> funds in advance of the next calamity. (in order to do) **RIGHT**

(b) Faced with the recurrence of natural disasters, such as floods and wildfires, many state governments have imposed significant taxes on their citizens <u>for raising</u> funds in advance of the next calamity. (for doing) **WRONG**

(c) Faced with the recurrence of natural disasters, such as floods and wildfires, many state governments have imposed significant taxes on their citizens <u>so as to raise</u> funds in advance of the next calamity. (so as to do) **WRONG**

(d) Faced with the recurrence of natural disasters, such as floods and wildfires, many state governments have imposed significant taxes on their citizens <u>in order that</u> the governments <u>might raise</u> funds in advance of the next calamity. (in order that + might do) **SUSPECT**

(e) Faced with the recurrence of natural disasters, such as floods and wildfires, many state governments have imposed significant taxes on their citizens <u>to raise</u> funds in advance of the next calamity. (to do) **RIGHT**

7. (a) Many places are called Naples—<u>not only</u> the cities in Italy and in Florida, <u>and also</u> a town in Clark County, South Dakota (population 25). (not only … and also …) **WRONG**

(b) Many places are called Naples—<u>not only</u> the cities in Italy and in Florida, <u>but</u> a town in Clark County, South Dakota (population 25) <u>as well</u>. (not only … but … as well) **SUSPECT**

(c) Many places are called Naples—<u>not only</u> the cities in Italy and in Florida, <u>but also</u> a town in Clark County, South Dakota (population 25). (not only … but also …) **RIGHT**

(d) Many places are called Naples—the cities in Italy and in Florida, <u>and also</u> a town in Clark County, South Dakota (population 25). (… and also …) **WRONG**

(e) Many places are called Naples—<u>not only</u> the cities in Italy and in Florida <u>but</u> a town in Clark County, South Dakota (population 25). (not only … but …) **RIGHT**

(f) Many places are called Naples—<u>not only</u> the cities in Italy and in Florida <u>but, as well,</u> a town in Clark County, South Dakota (population 25). (not only … but, as well, …) **WRONG**

8. (a) The Caucasus region has <u>several times as many</u> indigenous languages per square mile <u>than</u> most other areas of the world. (several times as many ... than) **WRONG**

   (b) The Caucasus region has <u>several times as many</u> indigenous languages per square mile <u>as</u> most other areas of the world. (several times as many ... as) **RIGHT**

   (c) The Caucasus region has <u>several times so many</u> indigenous languages per square mile <u>as</u> most other areas of the world. (several times so many ... as) **WRONG**

   (d) The Caucasus region has <u>several times more</u> indigenous languages per square mile <u>that</u> most other areas of the world. (several times more ... that) **WRONG**

   (e) The Caucasus region has <u>several times as many more</u> indigenous languages per square mile <u>as</u> most other areas of the world. (several times as many more ... as) **WRONG**

9

Chapter 10
of
Sentence Correction

Meaning, Structure, & Modifiers: Extra

In This Chapter...

Chapter 10
Meaning, Structure, & Modifiers: Extra

The previous chapters address the core rules of grammar and meaning tested on the GMAT. In contrast, the next three chapters provide <u>extra</u> material: nuances, exceptions, and rules of thumb. Only approach this material after you have mastered the core concepts of Sentence Correction (and assuming that you want a 90th percentile or higher score on the GMAT).

In this chapter, you will cover further applications of overall meaning, structure, and modifier issues.

Concision: Don't Make It Too Short

As you eliminate redundant wording, be careful not to cut too much out of the sentence! Avoid creating awkward phrasings or introducing new errors.

The GMAT sometimes tries to trick you with **false concision**: tempting expressions that are too short for their own good. Some patterns are listed below.

<u>"Too Short" Pattern 1: Keep the prepositional phrase if you need to.</u>

> Too Short: I talked to the BOSTON SOLDIER.
> Better: I talked to the SOLDIER FROM BOSTON.

It is possible to turn something like *soldier from Boston* into the more concise *Boston soldier*. In this case, however, *Boston soldier* seems to refer to a type of soldier, not a soldier who happens to be *from* a particular city.

This process works the best when the preposition is *of*, the simplest and most common preposition in English.

> Right: A wall <u>OF stone</u>   OR   A <u>stone</u> wall
>   (*stone* is a noun-adjective here)

Whenever you have a time period, quantity, or other measurement as the first word, however, keep the prepositional phrase with *of*. Never modify a measurement using a noun-adjective. Also, you should generally avoid using a possessive (*'s* or *s'*) to modify a measurement. Study the examples below:

Too Short	**Better**
Memorial Day week	the week OF Memorial Day
OR Memorial Day's week	
the merger year	the year OF the merger
the oxygen amount	the amount OF oxygen
the honeybee population density	the density OF the honeybee population
OR the honeybee population's density	

<u>"Too Short" Pattern 2: Keep *that of* or *those of* if you need to.</u>

Too Short: <u>The face</u> I see in ads every day is <u>a famous actor</u>.

Better: <u>The face</u> I see in ads every day is <u>THAT OF a famous actor</u>.

As you trim words, you can wind up creating an illogical sentence if you are not careful. The first sentence above seems nice and short, until you check the meaning. Can a *face* be an *actor*? No. *The face I see …* must be *THE FACE OF a famous actor*. The word *that* stands for *face*, so the second sentence is correct.

Note that the GMAT sometimes inserts an unnecessary *that of* or *those of*, which you do have to remove:

Wordy: <u>The fields</u> I most enjoy studying are <u>THOSE OF physics and chemistry</u>.

Better: <u>The fields</u> I most enjoy studying are <u>physics and chemistry</u>.

Physics and chemistry are in fact *fields* (of study), so say *The fields … are physics and chemistry*.

Compound Subjects

In Chapter 3, you learned that the word *and* can create a compound subject but other conjunctions do not. If you use *or* to connect two potential subjects, here's what happens:

Right: Lin or Guy has a black car.
Wrong: Lin or Guy have a black car.

MANHATTAN
PREP

In this case, only one of the two people has a black car; they cannot both count as the subject. If the two nouns disagree in number, use the noun closest to the verb to determine agreement. For example:

Right: Either the manager or the EMPLOYEES TAKE a break.

Right: Either the employees or the MANAGER TAKES a break.

One or both of those sentences may sound awkward to your ear, but they are both correct. In each case, the verb matches the noun that is closest to it, because the conjunction *or* allows you to pick only one noun to be the subject. This is also true for the constructions *either … or*, *nor*, and *neither … nor*.

More Connecting Punctuation

Colon

The colon (:) provides further explanation for what comes before it. What comes before the colon must be able to stand alone as a sentence. What comes after the colon does not have to be able to stand alone. For example:

Wrong: I love listening to: classical, rock, rap, and pop music.

In this example, the words preceding the colon (*I love listening to*) do not form a complete sentence.

Right: I love listening to many kinds of music: classical, rock, rap, and pop.

In the corrected version, the words preceding the colon can stand alone as a sentence. Moreover, the words following the colon (*classical, rock, rap,* and *pop*) give further explanation of the *many kinds of music* mentioned. Note that you can insert *namely* or *that is* after the colon, and the result would still make sense; most correct usages of the colon on the GMAT will work this way:

Right: I love listening to many kinds of music: namely, classical, rock, rap, and
            pop.

Whatever needs explanation should be placed as close to the colon as possible. For example:

Worse: Three factors affect the rate of a reaction: concentration, surface area, and
            temperature.

Better: The rate of a reaction is affected by three factors: concentration, surface
            area, and temperature.

You can put a main clause after a colon as well. The key is that this clause must explain what precedes the colon—perhaps the entire preceding clause. Consider this example:

10

Right: On January 1, 2000, the national mood was completely different from what it would become just a few years later: at the turn of the century, given a seemingly unstoppable stock market and a seemingly peaceful world, the country was content.

The words after the colon, *at the turn of the century ... was content*, can stand alone as a sentence. They serve to explain the entire clause that comes before the colon (a clause that asserts an upcoming change in the national mood, as of the first of the year 2000).

Do not confuse the semicolon (;) with the colon (:). The semicolon connects two related independent clauses, but the second does not necessarily explain the first. In contrast, the colon always connects a sentence with examples or a further explanation.

Dash

The dash (—) is a flexible punctuation mark that the GMAT occasionally employs. You can use a dash as an emphatic comma, semicolon, or colon. For example:

Right: By January 2, 2000, the so-called "Y2K problem" was already widely considered a joke — although the reason for the non-event was the prior corporate and governmental investment in countermeasures.

In the case above, either a comma or a dash would be correct. Sometimes, a dash helps to maintain an unambiguous meaning. For instance, compare these two sentences:

Wrong: My three best friends, Danny, Enrico, and Joey, and I went skiing.

Right: My three best friends — Danny, Enrico, and Joey — and I went skiing.

If you used commas in this sentence, the reader might think that seven people were going skiing (you, your three best friends, and Danny, Enrico, and Joey) rather than four.

You can also use the dash to restate or explain an earlier part of the sentence. Unlike the colon, the dash does not need to be immediately preceded by the part needing explanation:

Right: Post-MBA compensation for investment bankers tends to surge far ahead of that for management consultants—by tens, if not hundreds, of thousands of dollars a year.

The phrase after the dash (*by tens ... a year*) explains the word *far* in the phrase *far ahead*. In comparison, a colon would not work so well here.

Collective Nouns: Find the Clue

A **collective noun** is a noun that looks singular (it usually does not end with an -s) but can refer to a group of people or objects. Some examples include the following:

People: agency, army, audience, class, committee, crowd, orchestra, team
Items: baggage, citrus, equipment, fleet, fruit, furniture

In American English, such nouns are considered singular, though in British English, they are considered plural. On the GMAT, the sentence will contain a clue that tells you which is which. For instance, a sentence might read:

Wrong: The wildfire division, comprising more than thirty firefighters, is stationed on the outskirts of the town <u>and include wildfire management and first responder teams</u>.

The sentence has a compound verb structure: *The division is stationed ... and include.* The first verb is not underlined, so division is intended to be singular in this sentence. The second verb, then, must change to the singular *includes*.

Some words can be either singular or plural depending upon context. For example:

Wrong: The data collected by the researchers confirm <u>that heart disease is congenital; it also indicates that certain genes are sex-linked.</u>

In this case, *data* is matched with the plural (and non-underlined) verb *confirm*, but the second half of the sentence incorrectly refers back to *data* using the singular *it ... indicates*.

Indefinite Pronouns: Usually Singular

Pronouns are words that replace other nouns or pronouns. An **indefinite pronoun** is not specific about the thing to which it refers. *Anyone* is an example of an indefinite pronoun. The following indefinite pronouns are considered singular and require singular verb forms. Note that all the pronouns that end in *-one, -body,* or *-thing* fall into this category.

Anyone, anybody, anything	No one, nobody, nothing
Each, every *(as pronouns)*	Someone, somebody, something
Everyone, everybody, everything	Whatever, whoever
Either, neither *(may require a plural verb if paired with or/nor)*	

10

There are, however, five indefinite pronouns that can be either singular or plural depending on the context of the sentence. You can remember these five by the acronym SANAM:

THE SANAM PRONOUNS: **S**ome, **A**ny, **N**one, **A**ll, **M**ore/**M**ost

How can you tell whether these pronouns are singular or plural? Think about meaning, and look at the *Of*-phrase that usually follows the pronoun. You may recall that you are usually supposed to ignore *Of*-prepositional phrases (since they are misleading middlemen). But with the SANAM pronouns, the noun object of the *Of*-phrase can help you determine the number of the subject:

Right: Some of the <u>money WAS stolen</u> from my wallet. (*Money* is singular.)
Right: Some of the <u>documents WERE stolen</u> from the bank. (*Documents* is plural.)

Don't apply the *Of*-phrase mechanically. *None of* and *any of* followed by a plural noun can be singular:

Right: Any of these women <u>IS</u> a suitable candidate for marriage to my son.

Any *one* of the women is suitable. Since the usage of these pronouns is hotly contested among experts, the GMAT is unlikely to test controversial cases.

Note that *not one* is always singular: NOT ONE of my friends IS here this weekend.

Each and *Every*: Singular Sensations

You have just learned that as the subject of a sentence, *each* or *every* requires a singular verb form. The same is true for any subject preceded by the word *each* or *every*:

Right: EVERY dog HAS paws.
Right: EVERY dog and cat HAS paws.
Right: EACH of these shirts IS pretty.

You may think that the subjects of the second and third sentences are plural. However, in each case, the subject is preceded by *each* or *every*. Therefore, the subject is considered singular.

Quantity Words and Phrases

The phrase *THE number of* takes a singular verb, but *A number of* takes a plural verb:

THE NUMBER of hardworking students in this class IS quite large.

This sentence follows the normal rule: eliminate the middlemen (*of hardworking students in this class*). The subject is *the number* (singular), which agrees with the singular verb *is*. Now consier this example:

A number of STUDENTS in this class ARE hard workers.

On the other hand, *a number of* is an idiomatic expression. In modern English, it has become equivalent to *some* or *many*. As a result, *students* is considered the subject.

In some expressions that designate quantities or parts, such as *half of*, whether the subject is plural is determined by the noun in the prepositional phrase. The SANAM pronouns are examples of this phenomenon. Other examples include fractions and percents:

> Half of the <u>pie</u> <u>IS</u> blueberry, and half of the <u>slices</u> <u>ARE</u> already gone.

The words *majority*, *minority*, and *plurality* are either singular or plural, depending on their context. If you want to indicate the many individual parts of the totality, use a plural verb. If you want to indicate the totality itself, then use a singular verb form:

> The majority of the <u>students</u> in this class <u>ARE</u> hard workers.
> In the Senate, the <u>majority</u> <u>HAS coalesced</u> into a unified voting block.

Treat quantity phrases in the same way as SANAM pronouns: the noun in the *Of*-prepositional phrase will indicate whether the verb is singular or plural.

Subject Phrases and Clauses: Always Singular

Sometimes the subject of a sentence is an *-ing* phrase or even a whole clause. This sort of subject is always singular and requires a singular verb form:

> <u>Having good friends</u> <u>IS</u> a wonderful thing.

The subject is the singular phrase *having good friends*, <u>not</u> the plural noun *friends*. Now consider this example:

> <u>Whatever they want to do</u> <u>IS</u> fine with me.

The subject is the clause *whatever they want to do*, which is considered singular.

Flip It!

In most English sentences the subject precedes the verb. However, the GMAT occasionally attempts to confuse you by inverting this order and placing the subject after the verb. In sentences in which the subject follows the verb, flip the word order of the sentence so that the subject precedes the verb. This way, you will identify the subject much more readily. For example:

> Wrong: Near those buildings SIT a lonely house, inhabited by squatters.
> Flip it!   A lonely <u>house</u>, inhabited by squatters, <u>SITS</u> near those buildings.
> Right: Near those buildings <u>SITS</u> a lonely <u>house</u>, inhabited by squatters.

10

In the original sentence, the singular subject *house* follows the verb. The verb form *sit* is mistakenly plural, but your ear may not catch this error because the verb is near the plural word *buildings*. Consider this example:

Wrong: There IS a young man and an older woman at the bus stop.

Flip it!   <u>A young man and an older woman</u> <u>ARE</u> there at the bus stop.

Right: There <u>ARE</u> <u>a young man and an older woman</u> at the bus stop.

By flipping the sentence so that the subject precedes the verb, you can see more easily that the compound subject *a young man and an older woman* is plural. In spoken English, *there is* is often used incorrectly with plural subjects. The subject of a *there is* or *there are* expression follows the verb.

Look for flipped subjects and verbs in subordinate clauses as well:

Uncertain: *Pong* is a classic game from which have/has descended many current computer pastimes.

Flip it!   *Pong* is a classic game from which many current computer <u>pastimes</u> <u>HAVE descended</u>.

Right: *Pong* is a classic game from which <u>HAVE descended</u> many current computer <u>pastimes</u>.

When in Doubt, Think Singular

You may have noticed that confusing subjects are more often singular than plural.

Singular subjects dominate the chart. Thus, if you cannot remember a particular rule for determining the number of a subject, place your bet that the subject is singular!

Singular Subjects	Plural Subjects	It Depends
A singular subject linked to other nouns by something other than *and*	Subjects joined by *and*	Subjects joined by *or* or *nor*
		Collective nouns
Most indefinite pronouns		SANAM pronouns
Subjects preceded by *each* or *every*		
Subjects preceded by *the number of*	Subjects preceded by *a number of*	Other numerical words and phrases
Subject phrases or clauses		

Noun Modifier Placement

In general, noun modifiers must be as close as possible to the nouns they modify. As you saw in Chapter 4, an essential modifier is allowed to come between a noun and a nonessential modifier. There are also some other, more rare exceptions.

1. A very short predicate falls between, shifting a very long modifier back:

Right: A new CEO has been hired <u>who will transform the company by decentralizing authority to various division heads while increasing their accountability through the use of public scorecards.</u>

The alternative construction is confusing, because the modifier is extremely lengthy:

Awkward: A new CEO <u>who will transform the company by decentralizing authority to various division heads while increasing their accountability through the use of public scorecards</u> has been hired.

2. A short, nonessential phrase intervenes and is set off by commas:

Right: Our system of Presidential elections favors STATES, <u>such as Delaware, that by population are over-represented in the Electoral College</u>.

The short phrase *such as Delaware* sneaks between the noun *states* and its essential modifier *that by population are over-represented in the Electoral College*. There is no other logical place to put the phrase *such as Delaware*. Because this phrase is short, its insertion is acceptable.

3. The modifier is part of a series of parallel modifiers, one of which touches the noun:

Right: In heraldry, the term "tincture" refers to a COLOR <u>emblazoned on a coat of arms</u> and <u>labeled with a special French word</u>.

The second modifier, *labeled with a special French word,* is not positioned right next to the noun it modifies, namely *color*. However, this modifier is in a parallel construction with another modifier, *emblazoned on a coat of arms*, that is positioned right next to the noun *color*. Thus, the second modifier is considered well-placed.

10

Possessive Nuances

Do not choose *Y OF X's* to indicate that *Y* belongs to *X*. Choose either the form *Y OF X* or the form *X's Y*. Other grammar authorities allow *Y OF X's*, but this construction is considered redundant by the GMAT. For example:

> Wrong: The orca, a RELATIVE <u>of the blue whale's</u>, is found throughout the globe.
>
> Right: The orca, a RELATIVE <u>of the blue whale</u>, is found throughout the globe.

Also, as a guessing rule of thumb, try to steer clear of the plural possessive form (*-s'*) in answer choices. In roughly 80–90% of publicly released problems that contain the plural possessive in the underlined portion, the GMAT avoids the plural possessive answer choice or choices for several reasons:

1. You cannot easily modify the noun that is in the possessive.

2. With a possessive, you cannot express a relationship other than *of*.

3. The plural possessive can be easily misread, especially within a prepositional phrase. For one thing, it sounds the same as the singular possessive, and you can easily miss the added-on apostrophe after the final *-s*.

> Wrong: Certain <u>humans'</u> parasites have been shown to provide bacterial resistance and protection against auto-immune disorders.
>
> Right: Certain parasites <u>in humans</u> have been shown to provide bacterial resistance and protection against auto-immune disorders.

The correct version clears up the ambiguity as to what the adjective *certain* modifies (does the sentence mean *certain humans* or *certain parasites*?). The correct version also properly identifies the relationship between *parasites* and *humans* (it is more precise to say *parasites IN humans* than *parasites OF humans*).

The GMAT may force you to choose a plural possessive in the right answer. If you have to guess, though, avoid the plural possessive option.

Subgroup Modifiers

When you want to describe a part of a larger group with a modifier, use one of the following three subgroup modifier constructions:

> Right: This model explains all known subatomic particles, <u>SOME OF WHICH WERE only recently discovered</u>.
>
> Right: This model explains all known subatomic particles, <u>SOME OF THEM only recently discovered</u>.
>
> Right: This model explains all known subatomic particles, <u>SOME only recently discovered</u>.

Notice that only the *which* construction has a working verb (*were*) in it. In contrast, wrong answer choices often include the following three <u>incorrect</u> constructions, which scramble the correct forms:

Wrong: This model explains all known subatomic particles, <u>OF WHICH SOME WERE only recently discovered.</u>

Wrong: This model explains all known subatomic particles, <u>SOME OF THEM WHICH WERE only recently discovered.</u>

Wrong: This model explains all known subatomic particles, <u>SOME OF WHICH only recently discovered.</u>

In place of *some*, you can substitute the other SANAM pronouns (*any, none, all, more/most*), as well as *many, each, either, neither, half, one*, and any other number or pronoun that picks out a subgroup.

More on Relative Clauses vs. Participles

In many cases, a relative clause (a clause headed by a relative pronoun) and a present participle modifier are practically interchangeable. For example:

Right: The man <u>WHO IS CLEANING the steps</u> is my uncle.
Right: The man <u>CLEANING the steps</u> is my uncle.

However, consider these examples:

(A)   The rate of language extinction is accelerating, a tendency ultimately culminating in the survival of just a few languages, according to some.

(B)   The rate of language extinction is accelerating, a tendency that will ultimately culminate in the survival of just a few languages, according to some.

Which sentence is correct? The adverb *ultimately* indicates that the action of *culminate* or *culminating* is meant to happen in the future. However, *culminating* by itself, in the context of choice (A), indicates the present time frame because the main verb of the sentence, *is accelerating*, is in the present tense. In contrast, through the use of the word *will*, choice (B) correctly establishes that the action is meant to occur in the future. The correct answer is (**B**).

10

Absolute Phrases

A few GMAT sentences use a sophisticated modifier called an **absolute phrase**. Absolute phrases are composed of a noun plus a noun modifier. These phrases do not have to modify what they touch; rather, they modify the main clause in some way. For example:

Right: <u>His head held high</u>, Owen walked out of the store.

The absolute phrase *His head held high* is composed of a noun (*His head*) and a noun modifier (*held high*) that describes the noun. The phrase *His head held high* describes <u>how</u> Owen walked out of the store. Thus, this absolute phrase acts as an adverbial modifier.

You might argue that the noun *Owen* is directly described by *His head held high*, especially since the pronoun *His* refers to *Owen*. Note, though, that you could move the modifier to the end of the sentence; you cannot do so with normal noun modifiers:

> Right: Owen walked out of the store, <u>his head held high</u>.
> Right: Owen walked out of the store <u>with his head held high</u>.

Consider another example:

> Right: Scientists have found high levels of iridium in certain geological formations around the world, <u>results that suggest the cataclysmic impact of a meteor millions of years ago.</u>

The absolute phrase in this sentence, *results that suggest the cataclysmic impact of a meteor millions of years ago*, is composed of the noun *results* and the noun modifier *that suggest … years ago*. Notice that the noun *results* does not modify *world*, the closest noun in the main clause. The noun *results* refers to either *high levels of iridium* or the act of finding these levels. The absolute phrase construction provides a way to link a second part of the sentence to the first. Consider this example:

> Right: Scientists have found high levels of iridium in certain geological formations around the world. <u>These results suggest the cataclysmic impact of a meteor millions of years ago.</u>

You will never see two separate sentences in a Sentence Correction problem. However, the example illustrates how an absolute phrase at the end of a sentence gives you a legitimate way to tack on a second thought. Remember, never use *which* to do so!

> Wrong: Scientists have found high levels of iridium in certain geological formations around the world, <u>which suggests the cataclysmic impact of a meteor millions of years ago.</u>

Again, the relative pronoun *which* must refer to the main noun closest to the *which*. In speech, you might say something like the next example, although it would be wrong on the GMAT:

> Wrong: Scientists have found high levels of iridium in certain geological formations around the world, <u>AND THIS suggests the cataclysmic impact of a meteor millions of years ago.</u>

The GMAT does not like *this* or *that* by themselves, since these pronouns have vague antecedents unless they are attached to a noun (e.g., *these results*). If you find yourself wanting to say *and this …* or *and that* … to add a second thought, then you need an absolute phrase or another legitimate way to refer to the previous thought.

In fact, you do have one more legal way to refer to the whole previous clause and indicate the result of that clause: an *-ing* form placed after a comma. Consider this example:

> Right: Scientists have found high levels of iridium in certain geological forma-tions around the world, <u>SUGGESTING the cataclysmic impact of a meteor millions of years ago</u>.

In some cases, you can use an *-ing* form (with a comma) in place of an absolute phrase. At the end of a sentence, either an *-ing* form or an absolute phrase can indicate a result of the preceding clause.

An absolute phrase is typically separated from the rest of the sentence by a comma. However, for an absolute phrase at the end of a sentence, you may also use an em dash (—).

10

Problem Set

A.   Subject–Verb Agreement

In each of the following sentences, (a) circle the verb, and (b) underline the subject. Then (c) determine whether the subject and the verb make sense together, and (d) determine whether the subject agrees in number with the verb. If the subject is singular, the verb form must be singular. If the subject is plural, the verb form must be plural.

If the sentence is a fragment, or if the subject and verb do not make sense together, or if the subject and verb do not agree, (e) rewrite the sentence correcting the mistake. If the sentence is correct as it is, mark it with the word CORRECT.

1.   The young bride, as well as her husband, were amazed by the generosity of the wedding guests.

2.   Neither she nor her parents understands the challenging math problem.

3.   A congressional majority is opposed to the current policy.

4.   Although progress is still difficult to measure, the researchers have found that the benefit of applying interdisciplinary approaches and of fostering cooperation across multiple teams and divisions outweigh any potential cost.

5.   She knows that despite the element of luck, the judgment and the wisdom displayed by each contestant evidently affects the outcome.

6.   The traveling salesman was dismayed to learn that neither his sons nor his daughter were interested in moving.

7.   I was so thirsty that either of the two drinks were fine with me.

8.   Planting all these seeds is more involved than I thought.

9.   Whoever rented these movies has to take them back before midnight.

10.   Tired of practicing, the orchestra decide to walk out on its astonished conductor.

10

B.   Modifiers

Each of the following sentences contains one or more underlined modifiers. For each of these modifiers, (1) identify the word or words, if any, that it modifies, and (2) indicate whether the modifier is correct. If the modifier is incorrect, suggest a way to correct the error.

1. Some critics <u>of the Olympian Party candidate Zeus Pater's</u> are pleased that he has chosen Artemis Rhodes, <u>the prefect of Alexandria,</u> to be his running mate; as many commentators have pointed out, her views on social issues are more in line with the Olympian Party platform than are <u>Pater's.</u>

2. The principal tried to calm the <u>worried</u> students' parents, as a result of those <u>students</u> fighting at the pep rally.

3. Kelp is a natural fertilizer <u>that has become popular among growers of heirloom tomatoes</u>, <u>who generally are willing to pay a premium for organic products</u>.

4. After many years of difficult negotiations, a deal has been reached <u>that will lower tariffs and end many subsidies</u>, potentially changing the lives of millions of people in both the developed and the developing world.

5. The houses <u>on Canal Street,</u> <u>of which many had been damaged in the storm</u>, looked <u>abandoned</u>.

6. The acquaintances <u>who we like most</u> are those <u>that flatter us best</u>.

Solutions

A. Subject–Verb Agreement

1. <u>The young bride</u>, as well as her husband, (was) amazed by the generosity of the wedding guests.

2. Neither she nor <u>her parents</u> (understand) the challenging math problem.

3. <u>A congressional majority</u> (is) opposed to the current policy. CORRECT

4. Although <u>progress</u> (is) still difficult to measure, <u>the researchers</u> (have found) that <u>the benefits</u> of applying interdisciplinary approaches and of fostering cooperation across multiple teams and divisions (outweigh) any potential costs. (or *the benefit outweighs the cost*)

5. <u>She</u> (knows) that despite the element of luck, <u>the judgment and the wisdom</u> displayed by each contestant evidently (affect) the outcome.

6. The traveling salesman (was) dismayed to learn that neither his sons nor <u>his daughter</u> (was) interested in moving.

7. <u>I</u> (was) so thirsty that <u>either</u> of the two drinks (was) fine with me. (*Either* as a pronoun is singular.)

8. <u>Planting all these seeds</u> (is) more involved than I thought. CORRECT (Subject phrases are singular.)

9. <u>Whoever rented these movies</u> (has) to take them back before midnight. CORRECT (Subject phrases are singular.)

10. Tired of practicing, <u>the orchestra</u> (decides) to walk out on *its* astonished conductor. (The singular pronoun *its* signals that the collective noun *orchestra* is singular in this sentence, so the verb must also be singular.)

B. Modifiers

1. Some critics <u>of the Olympian Party candidate Zeus Pater's</u> are pleased that he has chosen Artemis Rhodes, <u>the prefect of Alexandria</u>, to be his running mate; as many commentators have pointed out, her views on social issues are more in line with the Olympian Party platform than are <u>Pater's</u>.

Of the Olympian Party candidate Zeus Pater's: INCORRECT. This prepositional phrase modifies the noun *critics*. The phrase is incorrect, according to the GMAT, because it uses two possessives (*of* and *'s*) when only one is necessary. The GMAT claims that you must say either *critics of Zeus Pater* or *Zeus Pater's critics*.

the prefect of Alexandria: CORRECT. This noun phrase modifies another noun, *Artemis Rhodes*.

Pater's: CORRECT. *Pater's* is the possessive form of the noun *Pater*; therefore, it can be thought of as an adjective. What does it modify? The last clause can be seen as an abbreviation of *her views on social*

issues are more in line with the Olympian Party platform than are Pater's <u>views on social issues</u>. Thus, *Pater's* modifies the implied second occurrence of the noun phrase *views on social issues*.

Correction: **Some critics <u>of the Olympian Party candidate Zeus Pater</u> are pleased that he has chosen Artemis Rhodes, <u>the prefect of Alexandria</u>, to be his running mate; as many commentators have pointed out, her views on social issues are more in line with the Olympian Party platform than are <u>Pater's</u>.**

2. The principal tried to calm the <u>worried</u> students' parents, as a result of those <u>students</u> fighting at the pep rally.

Worried: INCORRECT. *Worried* is a past participle derived from the verb *to worry*. It is used here as an adjective, but its meaning is ambiguous. Its placement suggests that it modifies *students'*, but logic suggests that it should modify *parents*.

Students: INCORRECT. *Students*, in the phrase *those students fighting*, is a noun that seems intended to modify the gerund *fighting*. The reason is that what is worrying the adults is not the students themselves but their fight. A noun that modifies a gerund has to be in the possessive form, however, so *those students' fighting* would be better. *Those students' fight* would be even better, because possessive nouns before gerunds tend to sound awkward.

The best way to salvage this sentence would be to rewrite it completely.

Correction: **The principal tried to calm the <u>worried</u> parents of the students who had fought at the pep rally.**

3. **Kelp is a natural fertilizer <u>that has become popular among growers of heirloom tomatoes, who generally are willing to pay a premium for organic products</u>.**

that has ... heirloom tomatoes: CORRECT. This clause modifies *fertilizer*.

who generally ... organic products: CORRECT. Perhaps surprisingly, this clause correctly modifies *growers*, or more precisely the noun phrase *growers of heirloom tomatoes*. The prepositional phrase *of heirloom tomatoes* is a "mission-critical" modifier: it cannot be moved away from *growers*, the noun that is <u>defined</u> by the prepositional phrase. Moreover, *of heirloom tomatoes* is short, and the relative pronoun *who* cannot refer to objects such as *tomatoes*. For all these reasons, you are allowed to position the relative clause a few words away from *growers*.

4. **After many years of difficult negotiations, a deal has been reached <u>that will lower tariffs and end many subsidies</u>, potentially changing the lives of millions of people in both the developed and the developing world.**

that will lower tariffs and end many subsidies: CORRECT. This clause modifies *a deal*. Normally, a relative clause should touch its antecedent, but you are allowed to put a short verb phrase between a relative clause and its antecedent. In this sentence, the long participial phrase *potentially changing ... world*

MANHATTAN
PREP

needs to be close to the verbs that it modifies (*will lower … and end …*). The only alternative to the current configuration of the sentence would put *has been reached* at the end of the sentence, so far away from *a deal* that the sentence would be difficult to understand: *After many years of difficult negotiations, a deal that will lower tariffs and end many subsidies, potentially changing the lives of millions of people in both the developed and the developing world, has been reached.*

5. The houses <u>on Canal Street</u>, <u>of which many had been damaged in the storm</u>, looked <u>abandoned</u>.

on Canal Street: CORRECT. This phrase modifies *houses*.

of which many … storm: INCORRECT. This is a subgroup modifier because it makes a statement about a subgroup of the houses on Canal Street. The wording is wrong, however. One corrected version is *many of which had been damaged in the storm.*

abandoned: CORRECT. This past participle modifies *houses*, because *looked* is a linking verb.

Correction: **The houses <u>on Canal Street</u>, <u>many of which had been damaged in the storm</u>, looked <u>abandoned</u>.**

6. The acquaintances <u>who we like most</u> are those <u>that flatter us best</u>.

who we like most: INCORRECT. The relative pronoun *who* should be *whom*, because *whom* is the object of the verb *like*. The word *whom* is in fact optional in this circumstance. You can say either *The acquaintances whom we like most* or *The acquaintances we like most.*

that flatter us best: INCORRECT. *Who*, not *that*, should be used to refer to people (*acquaintances*).

Correction: **The acquaintances <u>whom we like most</u> are those <u>who flatter us best</u>.**

Chapter 11
of
Sentence Correction

Parallelism & Comparisons: Extra

In This Chapter...

Chapter 11

Parallelism & Comparisons: Extra

Parallelism: Concrete Nouns and Action Nouns

As you learned in Chapter 5, "Parallelism," make concrete nouns parallel to concrete nouns and action nouns parallel to action nouns.

Concrete nouns refer to things, people, places, and even time periods or certain events.

> rock, continent, electron, politician, region, holiday, week

Action nouns refer to actions, as their name implies. They are often formed from verbs:

> eruption, pollution, nomination, withdrawal, development, change, growth

Unfortunately, the distinctions do not end there! Gerunds, or *-ing* words functioning as nouns, are divided into two categories: simple and complex.

Simple gerund phrases do not have an article (*a* or *the*) at the beginning of the phrase:

> <u>Tracking satellites accurately</u> is important for the space agency.

Complex gerund phrases do start with an article:

> <u>The accurate tracking of satellites</u> is important for the space agency.

The GMAT will not make simple gerund phrases parallel to complex ones:

> Wrong: I enjoyed <u>drinking the water</u> AND <u>the wine tasting</u>.

Drinking the water is a simple gerund phrase, but *the wine tasting* is a complex gerund phrase:

> Right: I enjoyed <u>drinking the water</u> AND <u>tasting the wine</u>.

In addition, of the two types of gerund phrases, <u>only</u> complex ones can be parallel to action nouns. In a list of action nouns, a simple gerund phrase might be mistaken for something other than a noun:

Wrong: The rebels demanded the <u>withdrawal</u> of government forces from disputed regions, significant <u>reductions</u> in overall troop levels, <u>raising</u> the rebel flag on holidays, AND a general <u>pardon</u>.

Withdrawal, reductions, and *pardon* are all action nouns, so *raising* cannot be another parallel element in the list. Rather, the complex gerund *the raising of* is needed:

Right: The rebels demanded the <u>withdrawal</u> of government forces from disputed regions, significant <u>reductions</u> in overall troop levels, the <u>raising</u> of the rebel flag on holidays, AND a general <u>pardon</u>.

Also, if an appropriate action noun for a particular verb already exists in the English language, then avoid creating a complex gerund phrase. Instead, use the action noun:

Wrong: The rebels demanded the <u>withdrawal</u> of government forces from disputed regions AND <u>releasing</u> certain political prisoners.

Wrong: The rebels demanded the <u>withdrawing</u> of government forces from disputed regions AND the <u>releasing</u> of certain political prisoners.

Right: The rebels demanded the <u>withdrawal</u> of government forces from disputed regions AND the <u>release</u> of certain political prisoners.

In brief, there are three categories of nouns: 1) concrete nouns, 2) action nouns and complex gerunds, and 3) simple gerunds. When making nouns parallel, do not mix these categories.

Adjectives and Participles

In certain circumstances, adjectives can be parallel to present or past participles:

A mastodon carcass, <u>thawed</u> only once AND still <u>fresh</u>, is on display.

Both *thawed* and *fresh* describe *carcass*. *Thawed* is a past participle, whereas *fresh* is an adjective. However, they are parallel to each other, since they both function as adjectives to modify a noun. Consider this example:

Only a few feet <u>wide</u> BUT <u>spanning</u> a continent, the railroad changed history.

Both *wide* and *spanning* describe the railroad. *Wide* is an adjective, whereas *spanning* is a present participle. However, in this context, they are parallel to each other.

11

More on *Like* and *As*

Like can be used to modify a noun or a verb, creating a comparison. Remember, only nouns or pronouns can follow *like*.

Notice that the position of the *like* phrase can change the meaning slightly, as in *LIKE you, I danced last night* and *I danced LIKE you last night*. Also, note that a *like* comparison might be metaphorical, not literal. *He ran like the wind* does not imply that the wind "runs"—only that the wind moves fast, and that he runs fast as well.

Be careful about ambiguity with a *like* phrase at the end of a sentence:

> 1. Ambiguous: I want to coach divers LIKE Greg Louganis.
>   = I want to coach <u>divers</u> WHO ARE LIKE <u>Greg Louganis</u>.
>
> OR
>   = I want to <u>coach divers</u> IN THE SAME WAY AS Greg Louganis <u>coaches divers</u>.
>
> 2. Unambiguous: I want to coach divers, LIKE Greg Louganis. (note the comma before *like*)
>   = LIKE <u>Greg Louganis</u>, <u>I</u> want to coach divers. (He coaches divers; I want to do so.)

Unlike is also common on the GMAT:

> Right: UNLIKE <u>you</u>, I danced last night.   (You did not dance last night.)

Unlike can come at the end of a sentence (just as *like* can), as long as there is no ambiguity. In the latter situation, the noun following *unlike* will generally be compared to the subject:

> Right: <u>Most materials</u> under a wide range of conditions resist the flow of electric current to some degree, UNLIKE <u>superconductors</u>, which demonstrate zero electrical resistance.

The word *as* can be either a conjunction or a preposition, depending on the context.

Conjunction as: appears with a clause and has three uses:

> 1. Duration *as:*   AS I strolled to the store, I smelled the air. (= while, during)
> 2. Causation *as:*   I will not tell you, AS you already know. (= since, because)
> 3. Comparison *as:* You should walk AS she wants you to walk. (= in the same way)

Comparison *as* is the most important conjunction use of *as* on the GMAT. It sometimes appears together with *just*, *so*, or even *so too*:

> Right: JUST AS the trains were late yesterday, the buses are late today.
> Right: JUST AS the trains were late yesterday, SO TOO are they late today.

In rare cases, comparison *as* can also appear with a phrase, rather than a full clause:

Right: AS <u>in the previous case</u>, the judge took an early break.

Preposition as: used with a noun or noun phrase and has three uses:

1. Function *As*:   AS your leader, I am in charge. (= in the role of)
2. Equation *As*:   I think of you AS my friend. (= *you* are *my friend*)
3. Stage *As*:   AS a child, I thought I could fly. (= when I was)

In any of these prepositional senses, *as* does not mean *similar to* and is not used to make a comparison:

Right: I will jump up AS a clown. (= in a clown suit!)

To force the comparison *as* meaning, use a clause. To make a clause, include a verb:

Right: I will jump up AS a clown MIGHT. (= like a hypothetical clown)
Right: I will jump up AS clowns DO. (= like actual clowns)

In modern English, however, *like* is often misused to mean "for example." Even the *New York Times* endorses this faulty usage. On the GMAT, however, *such as* means *for example*:

Wrong: I enjoy fast food LIKE hamburgers. (= *fast food* SIMILAR TO *hamburgers*)
Right: I enjoy fast food SUCH AS hamburgers.

Do not use *like* to introduce examples. Instead, use the phrase *such as*. See the idiom list in Appendix A for more details.

Numbers in Comparisons

To indicate how much larger one quantity is than another, you have a few options.

If you want to relate the quantities by multiplication, use *times* and *as ... as* together:

Right: The man is FIVE TIMES AS OLD AS his grandson.
Wrong: The man is FIVE TIMES OLDER THAN his grandson.

The first sentence means that the man's age is equal to 5 × his grandson's age. In the second example, the author is technically saying that the man is *six* times as old as his grandson. This meaning is unlikely; the author probably meant "five times as old."

Use *times* without *as* or *than* to indicate direct multiplication (*twice* means *two times*):

Right: The cost of a ticket is $12, SIX TIMES <u>the cost ten years ago.</u>
Right: The concert was attended by 300 people, TWICE <u>the previous attendance.</u>

MANHATTAN
PREP

11

If you want to relate two quantities by addition or subtraction, use *more than* or *less than*. Consider the following:

Right:	I am TEN years OLDER THAN you.
Wrong:	I am TEN years AS OLD AS you.

The first sentence means that my age = your age + 10 years. The second sentence is nonsensical.

The words *more* and *less* are rather flexible. They can be used as nouns (or pronouns), adjectives, or adverbs:

Right:	I own MORE THAN I should.	(*more* = noun or pronoun)
Right:	I own MORE SHIRTS THAN I should.	(*more* = adjective)
Right:	I sleep MORE THAN I should.	(*more* = adverb)

In numerical comparisons, the words *high* and *low*, as well as *higher* and *lower*, should only be used as adjectives:

Right:	My bills are LOWER than they were last year.
Wrong:	I spend LOWER than I did last year.
Right:	I spend LESS than I did last year.

Other Comparison Constructions

Put *more* and *less* in the right positions. Watch out for ambiguity, especially when *more* comes before an adjective plus a noun:

> We have even MORE efficient engines than before.

Does this sentence mean that they have a greater quantity of efficient engines? Or do they have engines that are more efficient? The right answer will resolve the ambiguity:

Right:	We have even MORE engines that are efficient than before.
Right:	We have engines even MORE efficient than before.

Occasionally, a less common comparison signal appears in a GMAT sentence. For instance, some verbs, such as *exceed* or *surpass*, indicate comparisons. As always, make sure that the two items under comparison are parallel. Consider this example:

Wrong:	The incidence of the disease among men exceeds women.

An *incidence* cannot logically *exceed women*. In the construction *X exceeds Y*, the subject *X* and the object *Y* must be parallel. To fix the problem, you can repeat the noun *incidence* or use the pronoun *that*. In any case, you must repeat the preposition *among*:

Right: The incidence of the disease among men EXCEEDS the incidence among
women.

Right: The incidence of the disease among men EXCEEDS its incidence among
women.

Right: The incidence of the disease among men EXCEEDS that among women.

The phrase *in addition to* is worth mentioning. At the beginning of a sentence, you can use this construction to add another example to the subject. You can also use it to add another example to a different noun in the sentence, such as the object of the verb or some other noun:

Right: IN ADDITION TO taxes, death is inevitable.

Right: IN ADDITION TO Munster cheese, I like Swiss.

Problem Set

A.   Parallelism

Each of the following sentences contains an error of parallelism in its underlined portion. For each sentence, begin by writing a correct version of the sentence.

Then, using your correct version of the sentence: (a) (circle) the parallelism markers, and (b) place [square brackets] around each set of parallel elements. In the solutions, key portions of the parallel elements will be capitalized.

1.   Most employers agree that how a candidate dresses for a job interview and even <u>the way he positions himself</u> in his seat leave a lasting impression.

2.   Dr. King's "Letter from a Birmingham Jail" is <u>a condemning of racial injustice and a calling for</u> nonviolent resistance to that injustice.

3.   The network security team is responsible for <u>detecting new viruses</u> and the creation of software patches to block those viruses.

4.   He received a medal for <u>sinking an enemy ship</u> and the capture of its crew.

B.   Like vs. As

Each of the following sentences contains a blank space. Fill the blank space with either "like" or "as," depending on which you think is appropriate.

1.   The person in the recording sounds ___ a child.

2.   ___ a child has been injured, we must stop the party and call an ambulance.

3.   ___ a child, Rebecca lived in Bristol.

4.   My grandfather eats ___ a child, slurping loudly and helping himself to plenty of ketchup.

5.   Mrs. Jones watched ___ a child played with a stick.

6.   Frankie never went to law school, but he believes that years of watching *Law & Order* have taught him to think ___ a lawyer.

7.   Eyewitnesses describe the missing passenger ___ a lawyer in his late forties.

8.   ___ lawyers, doctors are bound by a code of professional ethics.

9.   Having passed the state bar exam, she is licensed to work ___ a lawyer in Illinois.

11

Solutions

A.   Parallelism

1. Most employers agree that [HOW a candidate dresses for a job interview (and) even <u>HOW he positions himself in his seat</u>] leave a lasting impression.

How a candidate dresses for a job interview and *how he positions himself in his seat* are **noun clauses**. You can tell that they are <u>clauses</u> because each of them contains a subject (*candidate*, *he*) and a verb (*dresses*, *positions*). You can tell that they are <u>noun</u> clauses because they do the work of nouns—in this case, acting as the subject of a verb (*leave*).

2. [Dr. King's "Letter from a Birmingham Jail" (is) [a CONDEMNATION of racial injustice (and) a CALL for nonviolent resistance to that injustice]].

The verb *is* equates the two parallel halves of this sentence, both of which are **action noun phrases**. In order to maximize parallelism between the latter half of the sentence and the first half, common action nouns (*condemnation, call*) are better than gerunds (*condemning, calling*).

Note that the latter half of the sentence is one noun phrase that contains within itself two parallel noun phrases, *a condemnation of racial injustice* and *a call for resistance to that injustice*.

3. The network security team is responsible for [the DETECTION of new viruses (and) the CREATION of software patches to block those viruses].

The detection of new viruses and *the creation of software patches to block those viruses* are **parallel noun phrases**. Both are centered on **action nouns** (*detection, creation*). The original sentence was incorrect because it attempted to put a **simple gerund phrase** (*detecting new viruses*) in parallel with an **action noun phrase**.

4. He received a medal for [the SINKING of an enemy ship and (the) CAPTURE of its crew].

The sinking of an enemy ship is a **complex gerund phrase**, and *the capture of its crew* is a **noun phrase** that centers on an **action noun** (*capture*). The original sentence was incorrect because it attempted to put a **simple gerund phrase** (*sinking an enemy ship*) in parallel with an **action noun phrase**.

[Why not use an **action noun phrase** instead of a **complex gerund phrase** in this answer? Simply because no appropriate **action noun** exists for the verb *to sink*. "Sinkage" is an English word, but it does NOT mean the <u>act</u> of causing something to sink.]

B.   Like vs. As

1. The person in the recording sounds LIKE a child.

Use *like*, not *as*, to make this comparison because *a child* is a noun, not a clause.

2. AS a child has been injured, we must stop the party and call an ambulance.

The logic of the sentence requires you to choose *as*, because the injury to the child is *why we must stop the party and call an ambulance.*

3. AS a child, Rebecca lived in Bristol.

4. My grandfather eats LIKE a child, slurping loudly and helping himself to plenty of ketchup.

Use *like*, not *as*, to make this comparison because *a child* is a noun, not a clause.

5. Mrs. Jones watched AS a child played with a stick.

6. Frankie never went to law school, but he believes that years of watching *Law & Order* have taught him to think LIKE a lawyer.

Use *like*, not *as*, to make this comparison because *a lawyer* is a noun, not a clause. Moreover, *like* indicates similarity, but *as* would indicate an actual ability to function as a lawyer. Whoever can *think AS a lawyer* is probably a lawyer.

7. Eyewitnesses describe the missing passenger AS a lawyer in his late forties.

The eyewitnesses are saying that the passenger is, or appears to be, *a lawyer in his late forties.*

8. LIKE lawyers, doctors are bound by a code of professional ethics.

Use *like*, not *as*, to make this comparison because *a lawyer* is a noun, not a clause.

9. Having passed the state bar exam, she is licensed to work AS a lawyer in Illinois.

Chapter 12

of

Sentence Correction

Pronouns & Verbs: Extra

In This Chapter...

Chapter 12
Pronouns & Verbs: Extra

Pronoun Ambiguity

If the pronoun points to the same noun both structurally and logically, then the sentence is probably acceptable, even if other possible antecedents exist. For example:

> Right: <u>Supernovas</u> destroy their immediate environments in vast explosions, but by synthesizing heavy chemical elements, <u>THEY</u> provide the universe with the possibility of biochemistry-based life as we know it.

The pronoun *they* is plural. There are three plural nouns in the sentence: *supernovas, explosions,* and *chemical elements.*

Logically, *they* cannot refer to the *chemical elements*, because those elements can't *synthesize* themselves. Further, logically, the *supernovas* provide the universe with the possibility of life, not the *explosions.*

Structurally, *they* most likely refers to *supernovas* because each functions as the subject of its respective clause.

Structurally and logically, then, *they* refers to *supernovas*, so the sentence is acceptable.

Note that the pronoun and noun are not *required* to play the same role in the sentence. For instance, the sentence below is correct even though a subject pronoun, *they*, does not refer to the subject of the previous clause, the *board*:

> Right: The board is investigating the compensation packages of several EXECUTIVES in order to determine how much <u>they</u> may have been improperly awarded.

If the sentence might be ambiguous, then check the structure, as a matching structure can reduce ambiguity. Otherwise, as additional examples show below, the noun and pronoun are not required to have the same structure.

In order to examine the structure, you'll need to know the **pronoun cases**, which are grammatical roles or functions for nouns and pronouns. There are three cases in English: subject, object, and possessive.

Subject pronouns can be the subjects of sentences:

I   you   he   she   it   we   they   who   *They arrived late.*

Object pronouns can be the objects of verbs or prepositions:

me   you   him   her   it   us   them   whom   *No one saw them or talked to them.*

Possessive pronouns indicate ownership or a similar relation:

my/mine   your/yours   his   her/hers   its
our/ours   their/theirs   whose   *Their presence went unnoticed.*

Any of the three cases can be used to refer to a noun anywhere in a sentence. For example:

MARY has a job that <u>she</u> loves. (subject case)
If you see MARY, could you please give this to <u>her</u>? (object case)
MARY drives <u>her</u> car every day. (possessive case)

In all three examples, Mary is a noun, so any pronoun form can refer to Mary.

One exception exists to the "antecedent must be a noun" rule. When the antecedent is in possessive noun form, a possessive pronoun can be used. For example:

Right: MARY'S job is in jeopardy because of her mistake. (possessive case)

In this sentence, MARY'S technically functions as an adjective, not a noun. The possessive pronoun also functions as an adjective: *Mary's job is in jeopardy because of Mary's mistake.* In this one circumstance, a pronoun can refer to a possessive noun instead of a regular noun.

Other Pronouns

As you learned in Chapter 7, the most important pronouns are the "Deadly Five" (*it, its, they, them, their*), as well as the demonstrative pronouns (*this, that, these,* and *those*). Other pronouns can also be tested on the GMAT.

There

Technically an adverb, *there* means "in that place." Thus, *there* acts a lot like a pronoun. The antecedent is often referred to in a prepositional phrase and should be a noun, not an adjective:

Wrong: At current prices, Antarctic oil may be worth drilling for, if wells can be
            dug <u>THERE</u> and environmental concerns addressed.

12

MANHATTAN
PREP

Right: At current prices, oil <u>in Antarctica</u> may be worth drilling for, if wells can be dug <u>THERE</u> and environmental concerns addressed.

Note that *there* can also be used as a "dummy" pronoun in expressions such as *There is a cat in a tree* or *There are roses on my doorstep*. In these cases, you do not need an antecedent.

Itself, Themselves, One Another, Each Other

The **reflexive pronouns** *itself* and *themselves* are used as objects to refer directly back to the subject: *The panda groomed <u>itself</u>*. You must use a reflexive pronoun to indicate when the subject acts upon itself. Consider this example:

Right: After the AGREEMENT surfaced, the commission dissolved <u>it</u>.

It must refer to t*he agreement*, because *it* cannot refer to the subject *the commission*. If you wish to refer to the commission, you must use *itself*. Note the difference in meaning below:

Right: After the agreement surfaced, the COMMISSION dissolved <u>itself</u>.

Itself and *themselves* are also used to intensify a noun: *The commission <u>itself</u> was wrong*.

The **reciprocal pronouns** *one another* and *each other* are used to indicate interaction between parties. These pronouns are not interchangeable with *themselves*:

Wrong: The <u>guests</u> at the party interacted with <u>THEMSELVES</u>.
Right: The <u>guests</u> at the party interacted with <u>ONE ANOTHER</u>.

Such and *Other/Another*

The words *such* and *other/another* often combine with a general noun to indicate an antecedent. *Such* means "like the antecedent." For example:

After the LAND-USE AGREEMENT surfaced, the commission decided to subject any <u>such</u> CONTRACTS to debate in the future.

In this example, *the land-use agreement* is a type of *contract*. Similarly, *other* and *another* mean "additional thing of the same type," though not necessarily "exactly alike":

After the LAND-USE AGREEMENT surfaced, the commission decided to subject any <u>other</u> CONTRACTS to debate in the future.

One

One indicates an indefinite copy or a single, indefinite part of a collection:

After walking by the CHOCOLATES so many times, Roger finally had to eat <u>one</u>.

The particular chocolate was not delineated ahead of time. In contrast, the personal pronouns *it* and *they/them* indicate definite selection of an entire object or collection:

12

> After walking by the CHOCOLATES so many times, Roger finally had to eat <u>them</u>.

In this case, Roger ate *all* the chocolates! Notice that after Roger has selected a chocolate, you now refer to that particular chocolate using the definite pronoun *it*:

> After walking by the CHOCOLATES so many times, Roger finally had to eat <u>one</u>.
> <u>It</u> was delicious, but HE could eat only half of <u>it</u>.

Do So versus *Do It*

Do so can refer to an entire action, including a verb, its objects, and its modifiers. For example:

> Quinn DID NOT eat dinner quickly, but her brother <u>did so</u>:

Quinn's brother *ate dinner quickly*. In referring to an earlier part of the sentence, the expression *do so* functions like a pronoun. (Technically, *do so* is called a "pro-verb," since it stands for a verb or even an entire predicate.)

Alternatively, you can repeat the helping verb without *so*.

> Quinn DID NOT eat dinner quickly, but her brother <u>did</u>.

On the other hand, in the phrase *do it*, the pronoun *it* must refer to a noun, not a verb:

> Quinn failed to do the HOMEWORK, but her brother did <u>it</u>.

It refers specifically to *the homework*. Of course, the verb does not have to be *do*:

> Quinn did not eat the SOUP, but her brother ate <u>it</u>.

Placeholder *It*

Some sentences use what is called a **placeholder it**, also known as a **dummy pronoun**. For example, when you say, "It's cold outside," that *it* doesn't stand for any noun. Therefore, a placeholder *it* doesn't have to have an antecedent.

Here are the three situations in which you might want to use placeholder *it* on the GMAT:

1. Postpone Infinitive Subjects

> Awkward: <u>TO RESIST temptation</u> is futile.

The subject of the sentence is the infinitive phrase *to resist temptation*. Although this sentence is grammatically correct, the GMAT usually avoids similar sentences on stylistic grounds.

> Better: <u>It</u> is futile to resist temptation.

12

2. Postpone *That*-Clause Subjects

Awkward: <u>THAT we scored at all</u> gave us encouragement.

The subject of the sentence is a *that*-clause, namely, *That we scored at all*. Again, this sentence is grammatically correct, since *that*-clauses containing full subjects and verbs can function as nouns. However, the position is awkward. Try to postpone a *that*-clause in subject position with a placeholder *it*:

Better: <u>It</u> gave us encouragement that we scored at all.

3. Postpone Infinitive or *That*-Clause Objects

Right: She made <u>it</u> possible for us to attend the movie.

You cannot say this sentence any other way, unless you change the infinitive phrase *to attend* into the action noun *attendance*. Then you should drop the placeholder *it*:

Right: She made possible our attendance at the movie.
Right: She made our attendance at the movie possible.

If you come across a sentence that uses *it* in the same way as the sentence *it is cold outside*, then you do not have to find an antecedent for the pronoun *it*.

Avoiding Pronouns Altogether

Sometimes, the best way to deal with a pronoun problem is to eliminate the pronoun altogether. For instance, at the end of a long sentence, a pronoun such as *it* or *them* might inevitably have ambiguous antecedents, no matter how you try to recast the sentence. For example:

Suspect: After roasting the potato, the camper extinguished the fire and then searched for a fork with which to eat it.

Repeating the antecedent noun is always an option, if not necessarily the most elegant:

Right: After roasting the potato, the camper extinguished the fire and then searched for a fork with which to eat the potato.

It is often smoother—and much more GMAT-like—to use a generic synonym for the antecedent than to repeat the noun exactly. Such a synonym stands in for the antecedent and functions just like a pronoun, but with none of the drawbacks. The synonym is often more general than the antecedent, which refers to an example of the generic synonym. Recall this example:

Right: New "NANO-PAPERS" incorporate fibers that give <u>these materials</u> strength.

12

The generic synonym *materials* refers to "*nano-papers*," which are types of *materials*. Consider this example:

Right: After roasting the POTATO, the camper extinguished the fire and then
           searched for a fork with which to eat <u>the tuber</u>.

The generic synonym *tuber* refers to *the potato*.

Progressive Tenses

The **progressive tenses** emphasize the ongoing nature of an action: it takes place over some period of time. These tenses are formed using the verb *to be* and the present participle (*-ing*) form of the desired verb:

PRESENT PROGRESSIVE: Sandy IS PLAYING soccer.
PAST PROGRESSIVE: Sandy WAS PLAYING soccer yesterday.
FUTURE PROGRESSIVE: Sandy WILL BE PLAYING soccer tomorrow.

The present progressive indicates action happening right now, whether the sentence contains words such as *right now* or not. Sandy is actually playing soccer at the present moment. In contrast, the simple present version, *Sandy plays soccer*, means that she frequently plays, or that she knows how to play, but she may not necessarily be playing right now.

Do not use the present progressive for general definitions. Instead, use the simple present:

Wrong: Cherenkov radiation is light that particles ARE EMITTING when they ARE TRAV-
           ELING faster than the effective speed of light in any medium.
Right: Cherenkov radiation is light that particles EMIT when they TRAVEL faster than
           the effective speed of light in any medium.

In GMAT sentences, do not use the present progressive to indicate future actions. This usage is considered too colloquial. Instead, use the simple future:

Wrong: Quentin IS MEETING Harvey for lunch tomorrow.
Right: Quentin WILL MEET Harvey for lunch tomorrow.

Verbs that express general states do not normally take progressive forms. Such **state verbs** include *know* or *signify*:

Wrong: This inscription IS SIGNIFYING the emperor's birth.
Right: This inscription SIGNIFIES the emperor's birth.

If . . . Then Constructions

Sentences with an *if* condition and a *then* outcome can follow several tense/mood patterns:

> Right: IF you study diligently, [THEN] you will score highly.
> Right: You will score highly IF you study diligently.

Note that the actual word *then* is frequently omitted. Also, the *if* clause does not have to appear first in the sentence. Here are the five common patterns of *if . . . then* sentences.

1. General Rule with Certainty

> IF Sophie EATS pizza, THEN she BECOMES ill.
> IF present, THEN present.

This pattern is equivalent to *whenever: WHENEVER Sophie EATS pizza, she BECOMES ill.*

2. General Rule with Some Uncertainty

> IF Sophie EATS pizza, THEN she MAY BECOME ill.
> IF present, THEN *can* or *may*.

Here, the helping verbs *can* or *may* can be used to allow for a somewhat uncertain outcome.

3. Particular Case (in the future) with Certainty

> IF Sophie EATS pizza tomorrow, THEN she WILL BECOME ill.
> IF present, THEN future.

Another possibility for the particular case (in the present) is present perfect: *If Sophie HAS EATEN pizza, then she WILL BECOME ill.*

4. Unlikely Case (in the future)

> IF Sophie ATE pizza tomorrow, THEN she WOULD BECOME ill.
> IF hypothetical subjunctive*, THEN conditional.

Here, the writer thinks that Sophie is unlikely to eat pizza tomorrow. The conditional tense (*would*) shows the hypothetical result of an unlikely or untrue condition. In place of *would*, the form *could* can be used to indicate improbability as well.

* The hypothetical subjunctive is identical to the past tense form of the desired verb, with the exception of the verb *to be*. For *to be*, always use *were*, not *was*. For example:

> If Sophie were to eat pizza, she would become ill.

5. Case That Never Happened (in the past)

> IF Sophie HAD EATEN pizza yesterday, THEN she WOULD HAVE BECOME ill.
> IF past perfect, THEN conditional perfect.

12

To form the conditional perfect, use *would have* + *past participle*.

Other patterns are possible, but the *if ... then* sentences that you encounter on the GMAT should con-form to one of these five patterns.

The helping verbs *would* and *should* should NEVER go in the *if* part of the sentence, according to the GMAT! Be careful, as this construction is common in some regional forms of English.

The Command Subjunctive

The command subjunctive is used with certain bossy verbs, such as *require* or *propose*. Bossy verbs tell people to do things. For example:

> The agency REQUIRED that Gary BE ready before noon.
> We PROPOSE that the school board DISBAND.

In these examples, the verbs *be* and *disband* are in the command subjunctive mood. The form of the command subjunctive is the form you would use to command Gary or the school board directly:

> BE ready before noon, Gary!
> DISBAND, school board!

This form is also known as the bare form of the verb: the infinitive (*to be, to disband*) without the *to*.

The subjunctive construction with a bossy verb is always as follows:

> Bossy Verb + *THAT* + subject + Command Subjunctive

> We PROPOSE THAT the school board DISBAND.

Take note of the following **incorrect** constructions:

> Wrong: We PROPOSE the school board DISBAND. (You must use the word *that*.)
> Wrong: We PROPOSE THAT the school board DISBANDS.
> Wrong: We PROPOSE THAT the school board SHOULD DISBAND.

Complicating matters, not every bossy verb uses the command subjunctive. In fact, with some of the most common bossy verbs, such as *want*, you cannot use the command subjunctive; instead, you must use an infinitive (*to* + the bare form):

> Wrong: The vice-president WANTS THAT she GO to the retreat.
> Right: The vice-president WANTS her TO GO to the retreat.

Which bossy verbs take which construction: subjunctive or infinitive? Unfortunately, this issue is idi-omatic. In other words, there is no rule. You simply have to memorize which verbs take which. If you are a native English speaker, your ear will guide you. See the idiom lists in Chapter 9 and Appendix A for more details on each verb.

<u>These verbs take ONLY the command subjunctive when indicating desire:</u>
demand, dictate, insist, mandate, propose, recommend, request, stipulate, suggest

> We <u>demand</u> THAT HE BE here.

Note that *propose* <u>can</u> take an infinitive when there's no second subject: *The attorneys <u>proposed to meet</u> the following day.*

<u>These verbs take ONLY the infinitive:</u>
advise, allow, forbid, persuade, want

> We <u>allow</u> HIM TO BE here.

<u>These verbs take EITHER the command subjunctive OR the infinitive:</u>
ask, beg, intend, order, prefer, urge, require (pay particular attention to *require*)

> We <u>require</u> THAT HE BE here.   OR   We <u>require</u> HIM TO BE here.

A few bossy verbs, most notably *prohibit*, take other constructions altogether:

> Right: The agency PROHIBITED Gary FROM WORKING on weekends.

The command subjunctive can also be used with nouns derived from bossy verbs, such as *a demand* or *a request*:

> Right: His <u>demand</u> THAT he BE paid full severance was not met.

By the way, a few bossy verbs can be used in non-bossy ways: *Her presence <u>suggests</u> that she <u>is</u> happy.* In this context, *suggests* means "probably means"; it is not acting bossy. As always, pay close attention to the meaning!

Helping Verbs

The three primary helping verbs are *BE, DO,* and *HAVE.* The verb *be* generates the progressive tenses and the passive voice, while *have* generates the perfect tenses. *Do* is used with simple present or past to negate verbs (*I DO not like eggs*), emphasize verbs (*He DOES like eggs*), or ask questions (*DO you like eggs?*).

You can use helping verbs to stand for longer verbs or verb phrases:

> Wordy: I have never seen an aardvark, but my father <u>has seen an aardvark.</u>
> Better: I <u>have</u> never <u>seen</u> an aardvark, but my father HAS.

12

The first instance of the verb should usually match the helping verb in tense. If you need to change tenses, repeat the whole verb in the new tense:

Wrong: I <u>have</u> never <u>seen</u> an aardvark, but last year my father DID.
Right: I <u>have</u> never <u>seen</u> an aardvark, but last year my father <u>SAW</u> one.

In the rare cases in which the tenses do not need to match, the exact verb form missing after the helping verb should be present elsewhere in the sentence:

Wrong: Our cars were designed to inspire envy, and they ARE.
Right: Our cars were designed to inspire envy, and they DO. (= *do inspire envy*)

They DO inspire is acceptable, but *they ARE inspire* is not grammatical. For *they ARE* to work, the form *inspiring* would need to be present in the sentence.

Note that the helping verbs *be*, *do*, and *have* stand for the positive form of a verb phrase, even if the full verb phrase expressed elsewhere in the sentence is negative:

Right: Some people <u>do not eat soup</u>, but others DO. (= *do eat soup*)
Right: Some people <u>do not eat soup</u> as others DO. (= *do eat soup*)

Use *be*, *do*, and *have* in this way only if you mean the positive form of the verb.

In addition to these three primary helping verbs, there are several **modal helping verbs**. The principal modal helping verbs are *can*, *could*, *may*, *might*, *must*, *shall*, *should*, *will*, and *would*.

Sometimes, the GMAT uses modal verbs (or their substitutes, such as *have to* for *must*) in a redundant or awkward manner. The idea of obligation or advisability may already be expressed elsewhere, or the modal verb may be placed in the wrong part of the sentence:

Wrong: This plan <u>ensures</u> that action MUST be taken.
Right: This plan <u>ensures</u> that action WILL be taken.

Wrong: Our division spent significant funds on HAVING TO build facilities.
Right: Our division HAD TO spend significant funds on building facilities.

Finally, express a condition by using the word *if*, not by inverting the subject and adding a modal verb such as *should*. This inverted construction is considered awkward by the GMAT:

Awkward: SHOULD he PASS the test, he will graduate.
Right: IF he PASSES the test, he will graduate.

Verbals: An Overview

The term **verbals** refers to verb forms used as adjectives, adverbs, or nouns; you've already learned about these earlier in the book:

1. Infinitives: *to watch, to throw, to see*
2. Gerunds: *watching, throwing, seeing* (used as nouns)
3. Participles:
    (a) Present participles: *watching, throwing, seeing* (used as adjectives or adverbs)
    (b) Past participles: *watched, thrown, seen* (used as adjectives)

You don't need to memorize the grammar terms, but you do need to know how each type works if you're going to earn a top Verbal score.

Infinitives

Infinitives, such as *to watch, to throw,* or *to see,* are considered the "dictionary" form of the verb: the most basic version. Infinitives may serve as nouns, adjectives, or adverbs. For example:

Noun:	I love TO SWIM.	*To swim* is the object of the verb *love.*
Adjective:	The person TO MEET is here.	*To meet* modifies the noun *person.*
Adverb:	Sue paused TO EAT lunch.	*To eat* modifies the verb *paused.*

In the last example, the infinitive expresses purpose: <u>why</u> *she paused* or <u>for what end</u>. You can also write *Sue paused <u>in order to eat</u> lunch*. The *in order to* construction is not automatically too wordy, as some people mistakenly think.

Whether you use *in order to* or not, pay attention to infinitives of purpose. Consider this example:

Right: The contractors <u>DEMOLISHED</u> the building <u>to keep</u> it from falling down accidentally.

The subject of the main verb *demolished* is the noun *contractors,* which is also the implied subject of the infinitive *to keep,* which expresses the purpose of the demolition. The object *it* refers to *the building.*

Wrong: The building WAS DEMOLISHED <u>to avoid</u> falling down accidentally.

In the above example, the subject of the main verb *was demolished* is the noun *building,* which is also the implied subject of the infinitive *to avoid.* However, a building cannot avoid something intentionally. Thus, the sentence above is nonsensical. Now consider this example:

Right: The building WAS DEMOLISHED <u>to keep it</u> from falling down accidentally.

The subject *building* would normally be the implied subject of the infinitive *to keep*. However, *it* refers to *building*. Since *building* is the object of the infinitive, the version above is fine as written. (Assume that the same unnamed people who demolished the building wanted to keep it from falling down accidentally.)

Note that infinitives can be used as nouns, but they are not very noun-like structures. Infinitives can be used as subjects of verbs, but in general you should postpone an infinitive subject using the placeholder *it* discussed earlier in this chapter.

Gerunds

Gerunds are *-ing* forms used as nouns. The *-ing* forms are much more noun-like than infinitives. You can easily use them not only as objects of verbs, but also as subjects of verbs and objects of prepositions:

Subject of verb:	SWIMMING is fun.	*Swimming* is the subject of *is*.
Object of verb:	I love SWIMMING.	*Swimming* is the object of *love*.
Object of preposition:	I dream of SWIMMING.	*Swimming* is the object of *of*.

As discussed in Chapter 11, you can classify gerund phrases as simple or complex, depending on whether the gerund is preceded by an article:

Simple gerund:	EATING apples quickly	(more verb-like)
Complex gerund:	The quick EATING of apples	(more noun-like)

Remember that you should not make a simple gerund and a complex gerund parallel to each other. Also, do not create a complex gerund if the corresponding action noun exists in the answers: *the quick consumption of apples* is better than *the quick eating of apples*.

A noun preceding a gerund must be in the possessive case if the noun is the doer of the action described by the gerund:

Wrong:	Mike SWIMMING is the product of new coaching techniques.
Right:	Mike's SWIMMING is the product of new coaching techniques.

Before applying this rule, make sure that the *-ing* form does indeed function as a noun rather than as a noun modifier. Sometimes either interpretation may be possible:

Suspect:	I like Mike SWIMMING. (= I like *Mike* only as he swims, not as he runs? OR I like for him to be swimming rather than lifting weights?)
Right:	I like Mike's SWIMMING. (= I like his *swimming* itself.)
Right:	Mike SWIMMING is a sight to behold. (*Mike* himself can be the *sight*.)
Right:	Mike's SWIMMING is a sight to behold. (The *swimming* can be the *sight*.)

Participles

As discussed in Chapter 4, "Modifiers," both present participles and past participles may be used as modifiers.

Present participles are *-ing* forms used to modify nouns, verbs, or even whole clauses. There are four members of the "*-ing* Dynasty," representing four key uses of the *-ing* form:

Verb (progressive tense)	She is FIXING the faucet.
Noun (gerund)	FIXING the faucet is not fun.
Adjective (present participle)	The person FIXING the faucet is tired.
Adverb (present participle)	She crouched under the sink, FIXING the faucet.

In contrast, the past participle is typically used as part of a perfect-tense verb or as an adjective:

Verb (perfect tense)	She has BROKEN the lamp.
Adjective (present participle)	The BROKEN lamp is on the stairs.

When to Use Which Verbal or Verb

Switching from a present participle to an infinitive can change the meaning of the sentence:

Present participle:	Investors sold the stock rapidly, CAUSING panic.
Infinitive:	Investors sold the stock rapidly TO CAUSE panic.

In the first example, the present participle expresses a <u>result</u>: the rapid sale of the stock caused panic. However, with the present participle, you know nothing about intention. The investors may have wanted to cause panic or panic may simply have occurred unintentionally.

In contrast, the infinitive example expresses <u>intention</u>: the investors wanted to cause panic. However, with the infinitive, you know nothing about result. Panic may or may not have actually occurred.

Problem Set

A. Pronouns

(Circle) all the pronouns in the following sentences. <u>Underline</u> the antecedent, if there is one, of each pronoun. If you notice any pronoun errors in a sentence, correct the sentence by altering the pronoun(s). Explain what rules are violated by the incorrect sentences. If a sentence is correct, mark it with the word CORRECT.

1.   The police have significantly reduced violent crime and are pleased with them for doing it.

2.   When Norma and her husband read an article about Florida's adorable manatees, they promised each other that they would one day go there and see one.

3.   Most European countries—including those of Bulgaria and Romania—have joined the European Union; Norway and Switzerland, however, have steadfastly refused to do it.

4.   It would hardly be fair for the meatpacking industry to blame regulators for the harm that it has inflicted upon itself in the sub-prime meat sector.

5.   Jim may not be elected CEO by the board because he does not meet their standards.

6.   Caroline receives email from friends who she knows well, from acquaintances who's names are only vaguely familiar, and from strangers about who she knows nothing at all.

B. Verb Tense, Mood, & Voice

Each of the following sentences contains one or more underlined sections. If an underlined section contains no errors, mark it as CORRECT. Otherwise, write down a correct version of the underlined section. For extra credit, explain your decisions with respect to the tense, mood, and voice of the relevant verbs, and with respect to the nature of the relevant verbals.

1.   <u>Having been shown</u> into the office, Julia waited for the dentist to arrive.

2.   When he <u>swam</u> across the lake, he lay down on the far shore and relaxed in the sunshine until he was thoroughly dry.

3.   Helen would feel better if she <u>was</u> my daughter.

4.   Helen may feel better if she <u>would swallow</u> this pill.

5.   If the supplier <u>has signed</u> a binding contract, he will deliver the goods.

6. If the supplier <u>has signed</u> a binding contract, he would have delivered the goods.

7. If Abraham Lincoln <u>were born</u> in Livonia, he <u>cannot become</u> the President of the United States.

8. <u>Brokered</u> by the President of Silonia, the ceasefire agreement mandates <u>Carpathian forces will cease</u> their advance into Zapadnia, but allows <u>them to engage</u> in limited operations in areas already captured.

9. Because epidemiological evidence suggests that some tomatoes <u>are</u> contaminated with bacteria, Rachel suggested that Patrick <u>make</u> a salad without tomatoes.

10. It is necessary that our condominium association <u>must comply</u> with the new ordinance, which requires homeowners <u>clear</u> the snow from the sidewalks in front of their property.

11. A <u>frightening</u> storm <u>has been lashing</u> South Padre Island, <u>forcing</u> Natalie and Todd to postpone their wedding.

12. Sitting at the kitchen table, <u>a decision to bake a cake got made by Eric</u>.

13. Louise wanted <u>to buy</u> something <u>to eat</u>, so she stopped at the ATM <u>to withdraw</u> some cash.

14. The <u>athlete's wearing </u>the Brand X logo is a famous Olympian; <u>his swimming</u> has led to a lucrative endorsement contract.

15. Although Bernard normally <u>is eating</u> inexpensive foods, and indeed <u>is eating</u> a hot dog right now, he <u>is eating</u> lobster and steak at tomorrow's party.

16. Because Cole <u>wears</u> a helmet when he <u>struck</u> on the head by a falling coconut ten years ago, he <u>has escaped</u> serious injury in that episode.

17. Helen would feel better if she <u>swallowed</u> this pill.

18. Ethan is unsure what to do tonight: his boss wants <u>that he stay</u> at the office, but his wife insists <u>that he come</u> home for dinner.

19. New regulations require that every cyclist in the Tour de France <u>has to be tested</u> for performance-enhancing substances.

Solutions

A.   Pronouns

1.   The <u>police</u> have significantly reduced violent crime and are pleased with (themselves) for doing so.

     Police is the antecedent of *themselves*. (*Them* is <u>incorrect</u> here because you need a <u>reflexive</u> pronoun here.)

     It in the original sentence is <u>incorrect</u>. Its only possible antecedent, *violent crime*, does not make logical sense. The author's intention is to refer to the verb phrase *have significantly reduced violent crime*, but a pronoun cannot have such an antecedent. To solve this problem, you can write *doing so* instead of *doing it*. Alternatively, you can replace *doing it* with an appropriate noun, such as *this achievement*.

2.   When <u>Norma and (her) husband</u> read an article about Florida's adorable manatees, (they) promised (each other) that (they) would one day go to Florida and see (one.)

     Norma is the antecedent of *her*.

     Norma and her husband is the antecedent of the first *they* and of *each other*. *Manatees* is a closer antecedent, but *they* and Norma and her husband are in parallel positions in the two clauses. As for the second <u>they</u>, you can presume that the antecedent of this <u>they</u> is the people, not the manatees.

     Manatees is the antecedent of *one*. Recall that *one*, although singular, can take either a singular or a plural antecedent.

     There in the original sentence is <u>incorrect</u>. *There* is an adverb that behaves much like a pronoun. The problem with *there* in the original sentence is that it cannot refer to Florida, because *Florida's* is in the possessive case.

3.   Most European countries—including Bulgaria and Romania—have joined the European Union; Norway and Switzerland, however, have steadfastly refused to do so.

     This new, correct version of the sentence contains no pronouns, although *do so* acts somewhat like a pronoun by referring to something else in the sentence (the verb phrase *have joined the European Union*).

     The original sentence is <u>incorrect</u> for three reasons: 1) *those* has no antecedent, 2) *those of* is redundant, since Bulgaria and Romania <u>are</u> European countries, and 3) the sentence attempts to use the pronoun *it* to refer to the verb phrase *joined the European Union*.

12

4. It would hardly be fair for the meatpacking industry to blame regulators for the harm that it has inflicted upon itself in the sub-prime meat sector.

CORRECT.

The antecedent of the first *it* (which is a placeholder *it*) is the long infinitive phrase *to blame … meat sector.*

The antecedent of the second *it* and of *itself* is *industry.*

5. Jim may not be elected CEO by the board because he does not meet its standards.

Board is the antecedent of *its. Their* is incorrect, because *board* is a singular collective noun.

6. Caroline receives email from friends whom she knows well, from acquaintances whose names are only vaguely familiar, and from strangers about whom she knows nothing at all.

Caroline is the antecedent of both *she's.*

Friends is the antecedent of the first *whom. Who* is incorrect because the objective case is required here. *Whom* is the direct object of the verb *knows*; you would say that *she knows them.*

Acquaintances is the antecedent of *whose. Who's* is incorrect, because *who's* means "*who is.*" You need the possessive pronoun *whose* to indicate that the *names* belong to the acquaintances.

Strangers is the antecedent of *whom. Who* is incorrect because you need the objective case here. *Whom* is the object of the preposition *about.*

B. Verb Tense, Mood, & Voice

1. **Having been shown into the office, Julia waited for the dentist to arrive.**

CORRECT. The words *having been shown* are considered a participle, not a working verb. The whole phrase that precedes the comma (*Having been shown into the office*) functions as a participial phrase modifying the verb *waited.*

Nonetheless, the words *having been shown* have verb-like features, and they are strongly analogous to a verb in the past perfect tense and in the passive voice.

The presence of the helping verb *to be*, here in the form *been*, puts this in the passive voice. The use of the verb *to have*, here in the form *having*, indicates that the action of being shown into the office occurred before Julia waited for the dentist. Since this meaning is perfectly logical, the participle *having been shown* is correct.

2. When he swam across the lake, he lay down on the far shore and relaxed in the sunshine until he was thoroughly dry.

12

Swam (simple past tense) should be *had swum* (past perfect tense). The verbs *lay* and *relaxed* are in the simple past tense. Because the swimming must have happened before the lying and relaxing *on the far shore*, the past perfect *had swum* is more appropriate than the simple past *swam*.

Correction: **When he <u>had swum</u> across the lake, he lay down on the far shore and relaxed in the sunshine until he was thoroughly dry.**

3.   Helen would feel better if she was <u>my</u> daughter.

Was (<u>past</u> tense of the <u>indicative</u> mood) should be were (<u>present</u> tense of the hypothetical <u>subjunctive</u> mood). The presence of *would* in the clause *Helen would feel better* requires the *if*-clause to be in the hypothetical subjunctive mood. In other words, the verb in the *if*-clause takes the hypothetical subjunctive mood because *would* indicates that Helen is not, or is unlikely to be, my daughter.

Correction: **Helen would feel better if she <u>were</u> my daughter.**

4.   Helen may feel better if she <u>would swallow</u> this pill.

Would swallow should be *swallows*. *Would swallow* is incorrect because it uses *would* in an *if*-clause. Never use *would* in an *if*-clause! *Swallows* is in the <u>present</u> tense of the <u>indicative</u> mood. The presence of *may* in the clause *She may feel better* requires that the *if*-clause be in the indicative mood. In other words, the verb in the *if*-clause takes the indicative mood because, as the use of *may* demonstrates, the author is at least neutral in his or her beliefs about Helen's chances of swallowing the pill.

Correction: **Helen may feel better if she <u>swallows</u> this pill.**

5.   **If the supplier <u>has signed</u> a binding contract, he will deliver the goods.**

CORRECT. *Has signed* is in the <u>present perfect</u> tense of the <u>indicative</u> mood. The presence of *will* in the clause *he will deliver the goods* requires the *if*-clause to be in the indicative mood. In other words, the author is at least neutral in his or her beliefs about the supplier's likelihood of having signed the contract.

Notice that the use of the <u>present perfect</u> tense here indicates that the author is referring to a possible signing at an unspecified time in the <u>past</u>. This is equivalent to saying *If it is NOW true that the supplier has signed… .*In contrast, the sentence *If the supplier signs a binding contract, he will deliver the goods* is also correct, but it refers to a possible signing in the <u>future</u>.

6.   If the supplier <u>has signed</u> a binding contract, he would have delivered the goods.

Has signed (present perfect tense of the indicative mood) should be *had signed* (past tense of the hypothetical subjunctive mood).

The presence of *would* in the clause *he would have delivered the goods* requires the *if*-clause to be in the hypothetical <u>subjunctive</u> mood. In other words, the supplier did not actually sign, or is unlikely to have signed, a binding contract. You need to use the <u>past</u> tense of the hypothetical subjunctive here because the presence of *have* in *would have delivered* makes clear that the delivery of the goods would have happened in the past.

Correction:　　　**If the supplier <u>had signed</u> a binding contract, he would have delivered the goods.**

7.　　　If Abraham Lincoln <u>were born</u> in Livonia, he <u>cannot become</u> the President of the United States.

Was born (simple past tense of the indicative mood) should be *had been born* (past tense of the hypothetical subjunctive mood). The birth of Abraham Lincoln in Livonia is an unreal past event. Therefore, it must be rendered in the past hypothetical subjunctive.

Cannot become should be *could not have become*. The second clause of this sentence is the *then*-clause of an *if… then* sentence. Since the *if*-clause describes something that never happened, the *then*-clause must contain a helping verb such as *would*, *could*, or *might*. *Could* is closest in meaning to *can*, so *could* is the best option here. The reason you need to say *could not HAVE become*, rather than simply *could not become*, is that Abraham Lincoln actually became President of the United States in the past.

Correction:　　　**If Abraham Lincoln <u>had been born</u> in Livonia, he <u>could not have become</u> the President of the United States.**

8.　　　<u>Brokered</u> by the President of Silonia, the ceasefire agreement mandates <u>Carpathian forces will cease</u> their advance into Zapadnia, but allows <u>them to engage</u> in limited operations in areas already captured.

Brokered is correct. In this sentence it functions as a modifier, not a working verb. The participial phrase *Brokered by the President of Silonia* modifies *the ceasefire agreement. Carpathian forces will cease* should be *that Carpathian forces cease*, because *mandate* is a verb that must be followed by *that* and by a verb in the command subjunctive (*cease*, not *will cease*).

Them to engage is correct, because *allow* is a verb that takes only the infinitive.

Correction:　　　**<u>Brokered</u> by the President of Silonia, the ceasefire agreement mandates <u>that Carpathian forces cease</u> their advance into Zapadnia, but allows <u>them to engage</u> in limited operations in areas already captured.**

9.　　　**Because epidemiological evidence suggests that some tomatoes <u>are</u> contaminated with bacteria, Rachel suggested that Patrick <u>make</u> a salad without tomatoes.**

CORRECT. Use *are* (indicative mood), not *be* (command subjunctive mood), even though the verb is in a *that*-clause following the verb *suggests*. This usage is correct because *suggests* in the first clause of this sentence is <u>not</u> being used as a bossy verb. The *epidemiological evidence* is not really telling anybody what to do, so *epidemiological evidence suggests* is not a signal for you to use the command subjunctive. In contrast, *suggested* in the second clause does count as a bossy verb, because Rachel is definitely telling

Patrick what to do. When *suggest* is used as a bossy verb, it must be followed by the command subjunctive (*make*).

10.   It is necessary that our condominium association <u>must comply</u> with the new ordinance, which requires homeowners <u>clear</u> the snow from the sidewalks in front of their property.

Must comply should be *comply* (command subjunctive). *It is necessary* is an expression that functions like a bossy verb. In general, it can be followed by either an infinitive or a command subjunctive. In this sentence, however, you have to choose the command subjunctive because *it is necessary* is followed by *that*.

Clear (command subjunctive) should be *to clear* (infinitive). *Require* is a verb that can take either the command subjunctive or the infinitive. In this sentence, however, you have to choose the infinitive because *requires* is not followed by *that*. Never use the command subjunctive without a *that* in front of the clause containing the command subjunctive.

Correction: **It is necessary that our condominium association <u>comply</u> with the new ordinance, which requires homeowners <u>to clear</u> the snow from the sidewalks in front of their property.**

11.   **A <u>frightening</u> storm <u>has been lashing</u> South Padre Island, <u>forcing</u> Natalie and Todd to postpone their <u>wedding</u>.**

CORRECT. This sentence correctly uses all four members of the *-ing* Dynasty. The participle *frightening* is an adjective modifying *storm*. *Has been lashing* is a <u>working verb</u> in the present perfect progressive tense. It is <u>present perfect</u> because the first helping verb is *has*. It is the <u>progressive</u> version of the present perfect tense because it also includes *to be* as a helping verb (*been*). Remember that an *-ing* word is never a working verb <u>unless</u> it is immediately preceded by a form of *to be*. The participle *forcing* works as an <u>adverb</u> modifying the verb in the first clause (*has been lashing*). The full adverb here is actually the <u>whole</u> participial phrase *forcing Natalie and Todd to postpone their wedding*. Like many participial adverbs, it describes a <u>consequence</u> of the action in the clause that it modifies. Finally, *wedding* is a gerund. In other words, it is an *-ing* noun derived from a verb (*to wed*).

12.   Sitting at the kitchen table, <u>a decision to bake a cake got made by Eric.</u>

The underlined words are the main clause of this sentence. There are a number of reasons to reject and restructure the original version of the clause:

1. The active voice makes the sentence more direct and concise.
2. The use of the passive voice, which results in a *decision* being at the start of the clause, makes it seem as if *a decision* had been *sitting at the kitchen table*.
3. The original version uses the wrong helping verb (*got*) in the verb *got made*. Always use *to be* as the helping verb in the passive voice.

Correction: **Sitting at the kitchen table, <u>Eric decided to bake a cake.</u>**

13. **Louise wanted <u>to buy</u> something <u>to eat</u>, so she stopped at the ATM <u>to withdraw</u> some cash.**

CORRECT. Infinitives can function as nouns, adjectives, and adverbs. Each of the three infinitives in this sentence correctly fulfills one of these roles. *To buy* serves as a noun. More precisely, the full phrase *to buy something to eat* serves as a noun. The phrase acts as a noun because it is the object of the verb *wanted*, much as *a snack* is the object of *wanted* in the sentence *Louise wanted a snack*. *To eat* serves as an adjective. It modifies the pronoun *something*, much as *edible* modifies *something* in the phrase *something edible*. Finally, *to withdraw* serves as an adverb. More precisely, the full phrase *to withdraw some cash* modifies the verb *stopped*, telling you the purpose for which Louise stopped.

14. The <u>athlete's wearing</u> the Brand X logo is a famous Olympian; <u>his swimming</u> has led to a lucrative endorsement contract.

Athlete's wearing should be *athlete wearing*. In *athlete's wearing the ... logo*, the word *athlete's* is an adjective modifying the gerund phrase *wearing the ... logo*. In *athlete wearing the ... logo*, however, *wearing the ... logo* is a participial phrase that acts as an adjective modifying the noun *athlete*. To see which version is correct, you need to look at the rest of the clause. Who or what *is a famous Olympian*—the *wearing* or the *athlete*? Clearly it must be the *athlete*, so choose the version in which *athlete* is a noun. This means choosing *athlete wearing*, not *athlete's wearing*. In the second clause, *his swimming* is correct. Here *his* acts as an adjective, modifying the gerund *swimming*. Since the *swimming* itself has plausibly *led to a lucrative endorsement contract*, the second clause is correct.

Correction: **The <u>athlete wearing</u> the Brand X logo is a famous Olympian; <u>his swimming</u> has led to a lucrative endorsement contract.**

15. Although Bernard normally <u>is eating</u> inexpensive foods, and indeed <u>is eating</u> a hot dog right now, he <u>is eating</u> lobster and steak at tomorrow's party.

Is eating is in the present progressive tense. The first *is eating* should be *eats* (simple present tense). The word *normally* makes clear that this is a habitual action. Use the simple present for habitual actions. The second *is eating* is CORRECT. The present progressive is used for an action that is happening right now. The third is eating should be <u>will eat</u> (simple future tense). The simple future tense is preferred for a future action. You know the action is future because the party is tomorrow.

Correction: **Although Bernard normally <u>eats</u> inexpensive foods, and indeed <u>is eating</u> a hot dog right now, he will eat lobster and steak at tomorrow's party.**

16. Because <u>Cole</u> wears a helmet when he <u>struck</u> on the head by a falling coconut ten years ago, he <u>has escaped</u> serious injury in that episode.

Wears (present tense) should be *was wearing* (past progressive tense). The verb needs to be in the past progressive because the action of wearing the helmet is a background state of affairs that was happening when the foreground event (the fall of the coconut) occurred.

Struck (active voice) should be *was struck* (passive voice). The verb has to be in the passive voice because the phrase *by a falling coconut* tells you that the coconut hit Cole.

Has escaped (present perfect tense) should be *escaped* (simple past tense). The verb has to be in the simple past because you are told that the escape occurred at a specific time in the past (*ten years ago*, in *that episode*).

Correction: **Because Cole <u>was wearing</u> a helmet when he <u>was struck</u> on the head by a falling coconut ten years ago, he <u>escaped</u> serious injury in that episode.**

17.   **Helen would feel better if she <u>swallowed</u> this pill.**

CORRECT. *Swallowed* is in the <u>present</u> tense of the hypothetical <u>subjunctive</u> mood. The presence of *would* in the clause *Helen would feel better* requires that the *if*-clause be in the hypothetical subjunctive mood. In other words, the verb in the *if*-clause takes the hypothetical subjunctive mood because *would* indicates that Helen is unlikely to take the pill.

18.   Ethan is unsure what to do tonight: his boss wants <u>that he stay</u> at the office, but his wife insists <u>that he come</u> home for dinner.

That he stay (command subjunctive) should be *him to stay* (infinitive), because *want* is a verb that requires the infinitive. *That he come* (command subjunctive) is correct because *insist* is a verb that requires the command subjunctive.

Correction: **Ethan is unsure what to do tonight: his boss wants <u>him to stay</u> at the office, but his wife insists <u>that he come</u> home for dinner.**

19.   New regulations require that every cyclist in the Tour de France <u>has to be tested</u> for performance-enhancing substances.

Has to be tested should be *be tested* (command subjunctive). *Has to be tested* is redundant because *has to* unnecessarily repeats the idea, already expressed by the verb *require*, that the testing is obligatory. *Be tested* is correct because *require*, when followed immediately by the conjunction *that*, takes the command subjunctive.

Correction: **New regulations require that every cyclist in the Tour de France <u>be tested</u> for performance-enhancing substances.**

Appendix A

of

Sentence Correction

Idioms

Appendix A
Idioms

This appendix contains idioms that have been tested on the GMAT in the past but that are not among the most commonly tested idioms. The list is quite long; we don't recommend memorizing every idiom here.

Rather, use this appendix as a reference. If you miss a problem that uses one of these idioms, check the entry to learn the acceptable uses of the idiom.

ACT

RIGHT:	The bay ACTED AS a funnel for the tide. (= functioned as)
	My friend ACTED LIKE a fool. (= behaved in a similar manner)

SUSPECT:	*The bay ACTED LIKE a funnel for the tide.*
	Note: #66 in *The Official Guide for GMAT Review, 2015* tests this idiom. The explanation claims that ACT LIKE must be used only with people. This claim is contradicted by other published problems. The way to resolve this issue is to ask whether the author intends <u>metaphorical comparison</u> (= LIKE) or <u>actual function</u> (= AS). If "actual function" is possible, use AS.

AFFECT / EFFECT

RIGHT:	The new rules will AFFECT our performance.
WRONG:	*The new rules will CAUSE AN EFFECT ON our performance.*

AFTER

RIGHT:	AFTER the gold rush, the mining town collapsed.
SUSPECT:	*FOLLOWING the gold rush, the mining town collapsed.* (ambiguous)

AGGRAVATE

RIGHT:	His behavior AGGRAVATED the problem. (= made worse)
WRONG:	*His behavior WAS AGGRAVATING TO the problem.* (= was annoying to)

AGREE

RIGHT:
They AGREE THAT electrons EXIST.

Electrons are particles THAT physicists AGREE EXIST.

SUSPECT:
They AGREE electrons EXIST. (AGREE THAT is preferred)

WRONG:
There is AGREEMENT AMONG them TO THE FACT THAT electrons exist.

Electrons are particles physicists AGREE THAT EXIST.

Electrons are particles physicists AGREE TO EXIST.

Electrons are particles THAT physicists AGREE ON AS EXISTING.

AID

RIGHT:
She AIDS her neighbor.

She provides AID TO victims. AID FOR victims is available.

Her AID IN WALKING the dog was appreciated.

WRONG:
Her AID TO WALK the dog was appreciated.

AIM

RIGHT:
We adopted new procedures AIMED AT REDUCING theft.

We adopted new procedures WITH THE AIM OF REDUCING theft.

WRONG:
We adopted new policies WITH THE AIM TO REDUCE theft.

AMONG   See BETWEEN.

ANXIETY

RIGHT:
His ANXIETY ABOUT his company's future is ill-founded.

His ANXIETY THAT his company MAY BE SOLD is ill-founded.

WRONG:
His ANXIETY ABOUT his company MAY BE SOLD is ill-founded.

APPEAR

RIGHT:
Imperfections APPEAR AS tiny cracks. (= show up as)

He APPEARS CONFUSED. (= seems)

The dinosaurs APPEAR TO HAVE BEEN relatively smart.

IT APPEARS THAT the dinosaurs WERE smart.

WRONG:
He APPEARS AS confused. The dinosaurs APPEARED AS smart.

APPLY

RIGHT:
The rules APPLY TO all of us.

WRONG:
All of us ARE SUBJECT TO THE APPLICABILITY OF the rules.

AS LONG AS

RIGHT:	I will leave, AS LONG AS it IS safe.
	I will leave, SO LONG AS it IS safe.
	I will leave, PROVIDED THAT it IS safe.
SUSPECT:	*I will leave, BUT it HAS TO BE safe.*
WRONG:	*I will leave, BUT it BE safe.*

AS ... SO

RIGHT:	AS you practice, SO shall you play. (= in the same way or manner)
	JUST AS you practice, SO shall you play. (= in the same way or manner)
	JUST AS you practice piano regularly, you should study regularly.
	(= in the same way; the situations are analogous)
WRONG:	*You practice, SO shall you play.*
	JUST LIKE you practice, SO shall you play.

ASK

RIGHT:	I ASKED FOR his AID.
	He ASKED her TO GO to the store.
	He ASKED THAT she GO to the store. (subjunctive)
WRONG:	*He ASKED THAT she SHOULD GO to the store.*

ATTRIBUTE

RIGHT:	We ATTRIBUTE the uprising TO popular discontent.
WRONG:	*We ATTRIBUTE the uprising AS popular discontent.*

AVERAGE

RIGHT:	Tech COMPANIES are as likely as the AVERAGE COMPANY to fail.
WRONG:	*Tech COMPANIES are as likely as the INDUSTRY AVERAGE to fail.* (Compare apples to apples.)

AWARE

RIGHT:	AWARE OF the danger, he fled.
	AWARE THAT danger was near, he fled.
WRONG:	*WITH AN AWARENESS THAT danger was near, he fled.*
	WITH AN AWARENESS OF the danger, he fled.

BAN

RIGHT:	They passed a BAN PROHIBITING us FROM CARRYING bottles.
WRONG:	*They passed a BAN that we CANNOT CARRY bottles.*

BASED ON

RIGHT: The verdict was BASED ON the evidence.

                 The jury reached a verdict BASED ON the evidence.

WRONG: *BASED ON the evidence, the jury reached a verdict.* (The jury was not itself BASED ON the evidence.)

BEGIN

RIGHT: The movement BEGAN AS a protest. (= was born as)

                 The movement BEGAN WITH a protest. (= protest was the first part)

                 The protest BEGAN a movement. (= caused)

WRONG: *The movement WAS BEGUN FROM a protest.*

BETWEEN

RIGHT: A battle ensued BETWEEN the reactionaries AND the radicals.

                 A skirmish ensued AMONG the combatants. (Use *among* for more than two parties.)

WRONG: *A battle ensued BETWEEN the reactionaries WITH the radicals.*

                 A battle ensued AMONG the reactionaries AND the radicals.

                 A battle ensued AMONG the reactionaries WITH the radicals.

BORDERS

RIGHT: WITHIN the BORDERS of a country.

WRONG: *IN the BORDERS of a country. INSIDE the BORDERS of a country.*

CHANCE

RIGHT: I have ONE CHANCE IN A THOUSAND OF WINNING tonight.

WRONG: *I have ONE CHANCE IN A THOUSAND FOR WINNING tonight.*

                 I have ONE IN A THOUSAND CHANCES TO WIN tonight.

                 I have ONE CHANCE IN A THOUSAND THAT I WILL WIN tonight.

                 I have ONE CHANCE IN A THOUSAND FOR ME TO WIN tonight.

CLAIM

RIGHT: They CLAIM THAT they CAN read minds.

                 They CLAIM TO BE ABLE to read minds.

WRONG: *They CLAIM BEING ABLE to read minds.*

COMPARABLE

RIGHT: Costs are rising, but incomes have not increased COMPARABLY.

SUSPECT: *Costs are rising, but incomes have not increased TO A COMPARABLE EXTENT.*

COMPARED / COMPARISON

RIGHT: IN COMPARISON WITH (or TO) horses, zebras are vicious.

A zebra can be COMPARED TO a horse in many ways.

COMPARED WITH a horse, however, a zebra is very hard to tame.

Note: The GMAT ignores the traditional distinction between COMPARED TO (emphasizing similarities) and COMPARED WITH (emphasizing differences).

WRONG: *WHEN COMPARED TO horses, zebras are vicious.*

Zebras are MORE vicious COMPARED TO horses.

CONCEIVE

RIGHT: He CONCEIVES OF architecture AS a dialogue.

SUSPECT: *His CONCEPTION OF architecture IS AS a dialogue.*

WRONG: *He CONCEIVES OF architecture TO BE a dialogue.*

CONFIDENCE

RIGHT: We have CONFIDENCE THAT the market WILL RECOVER.

SUSPECT: *We have CONFIDENCE IN the market's ABILITY TO RECOVER.*

WRONG: *We have CONFIDENCE IN the market TO RECOVER.*

CONNECTION

RIGHT: There is a strong CONNECTION BETWEEN his grades AND his effort.

WRONG: *There is a strong CONNECTION OF his grades AND his effort.*

CONTEND

RIGHT: They CONTEND THAT they can decipher the code.

WRONG: *They CONTEND they can decipher the code.*

They CONTEND the code TO BE decipherable.

They CONTEND the ABILITY to decipher the code.

CONTINUE

RIGHT: The danger will CONTINUE TO GROW.

WRONG: *The danger will CONTINUE ITS GROWTH.*

The danger will CONTINUE GROWTH.

The danger will CONTINUE ITS GROWING.

CONTRAST

RIGHT: IN CONTRAST WITH the zoo, the park charges no admission.
              IN CONTRAST TO the zoo, the park charges no admission.
              UNLIKE the zoo, the park charges no admission.

WRONG: *AS CONTRASTED WITH the zoo, the park charges no admission.*
              IN CONTRAST TO the zoo CHARGING admission, the park does not.

CONVINCE

RIGHT: She was CONVINCED THAT she had been robbed.

SUSPECT: *She was OF THE CONVICTION THAT she had been robbed.*

COST

RIGHT: Pollution COSTS us billions IN increased medical bills.

WRONG: *The COST OF pollution TO us is billions IN increased medical bills.*
              Increased medical bills COST us billions BECAUSE OF pollution.

COULD

RIGHT: You COULD DO anything you want.

SUSPECT: *You HAVE (or MAY HAVE) THE POSSIBILITY OF DOING anything you want.*

WRONG: *You COULD POSSIBLY DO anything you want.*

CREATE

RIGHT: We WILL CREATE a team TO LEAD the discussion.

WRONG: *We WILL CREATE a team FOR LEADING the discussion.*

CREDIT

RIGHT: Hugo CREDITS Sally WITH good taste.
              Sally IS CREDITED WITH good taste.

WRONG: *Sally IS CREDITED FOR good taste (or FOR HAVING good taste).*
              Sally IS CREDITED AS a person with good taste (or AS HAVING good taste).
              Sally IS CREDITED TO BE a person with good taste.

DANGER

RIGHT: We ARE IN DANGER OF FORGETTING the past.

SUSPECT: *We ARE ENDANGERED BY FORGETTING the past.*

WRONG: *We ARE IN DANGER TO FORGET the past.*
              We HAVE A DANGER OF FORGETTING (or TO FORGET) the past.

DATE

RIGHT: They DATED the artifact AT three centuries old.

              The artifact WAS DATED AT three centuries old.

....

WRONG: *The artifact WAS DATED TO BE three centuries old.*

              The artifact WAS DATED AS BEING three centuries old.

DECIDE

RIGHT: She DECIDED TO START a company.

....

SUSPECT: *Her DECISION WAS TO START a company.*

DECLARE

RIGHT: I DECLARED the election a fraud. I DECLARED the referendum invalid.

              I DECLARED invalid the referendum that the new regime imposed.

              They DECLARED THAT the election was a fraud.

....

SUSPECT: *They DECLARED the election was a fraud. (DECLARE THAT is preferred.)*

              The judge DECLARED the election TO BE a fraud.

....

WRONG: *The judge DECLARED the election AS a fraud.*

DECLINE   See also NUMBER.

RIGHT: The price of oil DECLINED. Oil DECLINED in price.

              The DECLINE IN the price of oil was unexpected.

              My friend's reputation DECLINED.

....

WRONG: *My friend DECLINED in reputation.*

DEMAND

RIGHT: They DEMANDED THAT the store BE closed.

              Their DEMAND THAT the store BE closed was not met.

....

WRONG: *They DEMANDED the store TO BE closed.*

              They DEMANDED THAT the store SHOULD BE closed.

DESIGN

RIGHT: This window IS DESIGNED TO OPEN.

....

WRONG: *This window IS DESIGNED SO THAT IT OPENS.*

              This window IS DESIGNED SO AS TO OPEN.

DETERMINE

RIGHT: The winner was DETERMINED BY a coin toss.

....

WRONG: *The winner was DETERMINED THROUGH (or BECAUSE OF) a coin toss.*

              The winner was DETERMINED FROM (or AS A RESULT OF) a coin toss.

DEVELOP

RIGHT: The executive DEVELOPED her idea INTO a project.

The idea DEVELOPED INTO a project.

WRONG: *An idea DEVELOPED ITSELF INTO a project.*

DIFFER / DIFFERENT

RIGHT: My opinion DIFFERS FROM yours.

My opinion IS DIFFERENT FROM yours.

WRONG: *My opinion IS DIFFERENT IN COMPARISON TO yours.*

DIFFERENCE

RIGHT: There is a DIFFERENCE IN ability BETWEEN us.

There is a DIFFERENCE BETWEEN what you can do AND what I can do.

There are DIFFERENCES IN what you and I can do.

WRONG: *There are DIFFERENCES BETWEEN what you and I can do.*

DIFFICULT

RIGHT: Quantum mechanics is DIFFICULT TO STUDY.

WRONG: *Quantum mechanics is DIFFICULT FOR STUDY.*

DISCOVERY

RIGHT: I love the DISCOVERY THAT carbon CAN form soccer-ball molecules.

SUSPECT: *I love the DISCOVERY OF carbon's ABILITY TO form soccer-ball molecules.*

WRONG: *I love the DISCOVERY OF carbon BEING ABLE TO form soccer-ball molecules.*

DISINCLINED

RIGHT: She IS DISINCLINED TO WRITE to her parents.

WRONG: *She HAS A DISINCLINATION TO WRITE to her parents.*

There IS A DISINCLINATION ON HER PART TO WRITE to her parents.

Her busy schedule BRINGS OUT A DISINCLINATION IN HER TO WRITE to her parents.

DISTINGUISH / DISTINCTION

RIGHT: The investor DISTINGUISHED BETWEEN trends AND fads.

There is a DISTINCTION BETWEEN trends AND fads.

WRONG: *The investor DISTINGUISHED trends AND fads.*

The investor DISTINGUISHED BETWEEN trends FROM fads.

There is a DISTINCTION BETWEEN trends WITH fads.

There is a DISTINCTION OF trends TO fads.

Trends HAVE a DISTINCTION FROM fads.

DO

RIGHT: I did not eat the cheese, but my mother DID (or DID SO).

WRONG: *I did not eat the cheese, but my mother DID IT (or DID THIS).*

DOUBLE   See TWICE.

DOUBT

RIGHT: We DO NOT DOUBT THAT the apples are ripe.

            We HAVE NO DOUBT THAT the apples are ripe.

            She DOUBTS WHETHER Jan will arrive on time.

SUSPECT: *She DOUBTS THAT Jan will arrive on time.*

            Note: The GMAT claims that DOUBT, used in a positive statement without NOT or
            NO, should be followed by WHETHER or IF, not THAT.

WRONG: *We DO NOT DOUBT WHETHER the apples are ripe.*

            We HAVE NO DOUBT WHETHER the apples are ripe.

DUE TO

RIGHT: The deficit IS DUE TO overspending. (= results from)

            Our policy will not cover damage DUE TO fire. (= resulting from)

            BECAUSE politicians SPEND money, we have a deficit.

WRONG: *DUE TO politicians SPENDING money, we have a deficit.*

            DUE TO THE FACT THAT politicians SPEND money, we have a deficit.

ECONOMIC and ECONOMICAL

RIGHT: The rise in gasoline prices has an ECONOMIC impact on consumers. (= financial)

            Our new car is more ECONOMICAL than our last. (= efficient)

WRONG   *The rise in gasoline prices has an ECONOMICAL impact on consumers.*

EFFECT   See AFFECT.

ELECT

RIGHT: She ELECTED TO WITHDRAW her money early.

SUSPECT: *She ELECTED early WITHDRAWAL OF her money.*

WRONG: *She ELECTED WITHDRAWING her money early.*

ENOUGH   See also SO / THAT
RIGHT: The book was SHORT ENOUGH TO READ in a night.
                              The book was SHORT ENOUGH FOR me TO READ in a night.

SUSPECT: The power plant has found a way to generate energy at an unprecedented scale,
                              ENOUGH FOR powering and entire city.

WRONG: *The book was SHORT ENOUGH THAT I could read it in a night.*
                              The book was SHORT ENOUGH FOR IT TO BE read in a night.
                              The book was SHORT ENOUGH SO THAT I could read it in a night.
                              The book was SHORT ENOUGH AS TO BE read in a night.

ENSURE
RIGHT: He ENSURES THAT deadlines ARE met (or WILL BE met).

WRONG: *He ENSURES THAT deadlines MUST BE met (or SHOULD BE met).*

EQUIPPED
RIGHT: They are EQUIPPED TO FIGHT on any terrain.

WRONG: *They are EQUIPPED FOR FIGHTING on any terrain.*

ESTIMATE
RIGHT: She ESTIMATES the cost TO BE ten dollars.
                              The cost IS ESTIMATED TO BE ten dollars.
                              With a temperature ESTIMATED AT 100 degrees, boiling water can cause severe burns.
                              She ESTIMATES the cost TO BE 10% less than it was last year.

WRONG: *She ESTIMATES the cost AT 10% less than it was last year.*

EVEN
RIGHT: I am EVEN RICHER THAN a prince.
                              I earn AS MUCH money AS EVEN the wealthiest king.

WRONG: *I am RICHER EVEN THAN a prince.*
                              I earn EVEN AS MUCH money AS the wealthiest king.

EVER
RIGHT: The economy is MORE fragile THAN EVER BEFORE.

WRONG: *The economy is MORE fragile THAN NEVER BEFORE.*
                              The economy is MORE fragile AS NEVER BEFORE.
                              The economy is MORE THAN EVER BEFORE fragile.

EVERY
RIGHT: FOR EVERY dollar SAVED, THREE dollars ARE WASTED.

SUSPECT: *FOR EVERY dollar SAVED, you WASTE THREE dollars.*

WRONG: *FOR EVERY dollar SAVED WASTES THREE dollars.*

EXCEPT

RIGHT:	EXCEPT FOR a final skirmish, the war was over.
SUSPECT:	*BESIDES a final skirmish, the war was over.*
	WITH THE EXCEPTION OF a final skirmish, the war was over.
	EXCEPTING a final skirmish, the war was over.

EXPEND

RIGHT:	We EXPEND energy ON neighborhood development.
WRONG:	*We EXPEND energy FOR neighborhood development.*

EXTENT

RIGHT:	We enjoyed the film TO some EXTENT.
	The EXTENT TO WHICH we enjoyed the film was moderate.
WRONG:	*The EXTENT THAT we enjoyed the film was moderate.*

FAULT

RIGHT:	The criminals ARE AT FAULT FOR BREAKING the law.
SUSPECT:	*BREAKING the law IS THE FAULT OF the criminals.*
WRONG:	*THAT the criminals BROKE the law IS AT FAULT.*
	IT IS THE FAULT OF the criminals WHO BROKE the law.

FIND

RIGHT:	The scientist FOUND THAT the reaction WAS unusual.
SUSPECT:	*The scientist FOUND the reaction TO BE unusual.*
WRONG:	*The scientist FOUND the reaction WAS unusual.*

FORBID

RIGHT:	The law FORBIDS any citizen TO VOTE twice.
WRONG:	*The law FORBIDS any citizen FROM VOTING twice.*

GOAL

RIGHT:	The GOAL IS TO EXPAND the company.
SUSPECT:	*The GOAL IS EXPANSION OF the company.*
WRONG:	*The GOAL IS EXPANDING the company.*

HEAR

RIGHT:	She HEARD THAT her investment HAD PAID off.
WRONG:	*She HEARD OF her investment PAYING off.*

HELP

RIGHT: He HELPS RAKE the leaves.
               He HELPS TO RAKE the leaves.
               He HELPS me RAKE the leaves.
               He HELPS me TO RAKE the leaves.
               His HELP IN RAKING the leaves has been welcome.

WRONG: *He HELPS me IN RAKING the leaves.*
               I need him AS HELP TO RAKE the leaves.

HOLD

RIGHT: The law HOLDS THAT jaywalking is illegal.

SUSPECT: *The law HOLDS jaywalking TO BE illegal.*

WRONG: *The law HOLDS jaywalking is illegal.*

INFLUENCE

RIGHT: His example INFLUENCED me.

WRONG: *His example WAS AN INFLUENCE ON me.*
               His example WAS INFLUENTIAL ON me.

INSTANCE

RIGHT: We eat out often; FOR INSTANCE, last week we ate out every night.

WRONG: *We eat out often; AS AN INSTANCE, last week we ate out every night.*

INSTEAD

RIGHT: They avoided the arcade and INSTEAD went to a movie.

WRONG: *They avoided the arcade and RATHER went to a movie.*
               They avoided the arcade, RATHER going to a movie.

INTERACT

RIGHT: These groups often INTERACT WITH ONE ANOTHER (or EACH OTHER).

WRONG: *These groups often INTERACT AMONG ONE ANOTHER.*
               These groups often INTERACT WITH THEMSELVES.

INTERACTION

RIGHT: The INTERACTION OF two nuclei COLLIDING releases energy.

SUSPECT: *The INTERACTION BETWEEN two nuclei COLLIDING releases energy.*

WRONG: *The INTERACTION WHERE two nuclei COLLIDE releases energy.*

INVEST

RIGHT: She INVESTED funds IN research TO STUDY cancer.

WRONG: *She INVESTED funds INTO or FOR research TO STUDY cancer.*
                She INVESTED funds IN research FOR STUDYING cancer.

ISOLATED

RIGHT: The culture was ISOLATED FROM outside CONTACT.

SUSPECT: *The culture was IN ISOLATION.*

WRONG: *The culture was IN ISOLATION FROM outside CONTACT.*

JUST AS … SO   See AS / SO.

KNOW

RIGHT: We KNOW her TO BE brilliant. She is KNOWN TO BE brilliant.
                We KNOW him AS "Reggie." He is KNOWN AS "Reggie."

WRONG: *We KNOW her AS brilliant. (KNOW AS = named)*

LACK

RIGHT: Old gadgets ARE LACKING IN features.
                Old gadgets LACK features.
                The LACK OF features is upsetting.

SUSPECT: *There is A LACK OF engineers TO BUILD new gadgets.*

WRONG: *Old gadgets LACK OF features.*
                It is hard to build bridges LACKING engineers.

LESS   See also THAN.

RIGHT: Our utilities add up to LESS THAN 10% of our income.

WRONG: *Our utilities add up to LOWER THAN 10% of our income.*

LET

RIGHT: My doctor LETS me SWIM in the ocean.

WRONG: *My doctor LEAVES me SWIM in the ocean.*
                The surgery WILL LEAVE me TO SWIM in the ocean.

LIE

RIGHT: Our strength LIES IN numbers. (= resides in)
                Yesterday, our strength LAY IN numbers. (= resided in)
                Tomorrow, our strength WILL LIE IN numbers.
                I lose my books whenever I LAY them down. (present tense of different verb)

WRONG: *Tomorrow, our strength WILL LAY IN numbers.*

LIKELY

RIGHT:　　My friend IS LIKELY TO EAT worms.

IT IS LIKELY THAT my friend WILL EAT worms.

My friend is MORE LIKELY THAN my enemy [is] TO EAT worms.

My friend is TWICE AS LIKELY AS my enemy [is] TO EAT worms.

MORE THAN LIKELY, my friend WILL EAT worms.

WRONG:　　*My friend IS LIKELY THAT he WILL EAT worms.*

RATHER THAN my enemy, my friend is THE MORE LIKELY to EAT worms.

LOSS

RIGHT:　　I have suffered a LOSS OF strength. (= decline of a quality)

They have suffered a LOSS IN the euro. (= decline of an investment)

WRONG:　　*I have suffered a LOSS IN strength.*

MANDATE

RIGHT:　　The general MANDATED THAT a trench BE dug. (subjunctive)

SUSPECT:　　*We HAVE A MANDATE TO CALL an election soon. (= have authority)*

WRONG:　　*The general MANDATED a trench TO BE dug.*

The general MANDATES THAT a trench WILL BE dug.

We HAVE A MANDATE FOR an election in the near future.

MAKE

RIGHT:　　The leader MADE the resistance POSSIBLE.

The leader MADE IT POSSIBLE TO RESIST oppression.

The leader MADE IT POSSIBLE FOR us TO RESIST oppression.

Note: The IT properly refers to the infinitive TO RESIST.

Windshields ARE MADE resistant to impact.

SUSPECT:　　*The leader MADE POSSIBLE the resistance.*

WRONG:　　*The leader MADE POSSIBLE TO RESIST oppression.*

MASS

RIGHT:　　The truck HAS ten TIMES THE MASS of a small car.

WRONG:　　*The truck IS ten TIMES THE MASS of a small car.*

MAYBE

See PROBABLY.

MEANS

RIGHT:　　Music education is A MEANS TO improved cognition.

WRONG:　　*Music education is A MEANS OF improved cognition.*

Music education is A MEANS FOR improved cognition.

MISTAKE

RIGHT: My spouse HAS MISTAKEN me FOR a wealthier person.

WRONG: *My spouse HAS MISTAKEN me AS a wealthier person.*
              My spouse HAS MISTAKEN me TO a wealthier person.

MORE   See THAN.

RIGHT: We observed A 10% INCREASE IN robberies last month.
              MORE AND MORE, we have observed violent robberies on weekends.
              INCREASINGLY, we have observed violent robberies on weekends.

SUSPECT: *We observed 10% MORE robberies last month.*

MOST

RIGHT: OF ALL the Greek gods, Zeus was THE MOST powerful. (superlative)
              He was THE SECOND MOST attractive AND THE MOST powerful.

WRONG: *OF ALL the Greek gods, Zeus was THE MORE powerful.*
              He was THE SECOND MOST attractive AND MOST powerful.

NATIVE

RIGHT: The kangaroo is NATIVE TO Australia. (said of animals, plants)
              My friend is A NATIVE OF Australia. (said of people)

WRONG: *The kangaroo is NATIVE IN Australia.*

NUMBER

RIGHT   A NUMBER OF dogs ARE barking.
              THE NUMBER OF dogs IS large.
              THE NUMBER OF dogs HAS FALLEN, but THE NUMBER OF cats HAS RISEN.
              The grey oyster nearly vanished, but ITS NUMBERS have rebounded.

WRONG: *THE NUMBERS OF dogs HAVE fallen.*
              Dogs HAVE FALLEN IN NUMBER, but cats HAVE RISEN IN NUMBER.

ONCE

RIGHT: We might ONCE have seen that band.

WRONG: *We might AT ONE TIME have seen that band.*

ONLY

RIGHT: Her performance is exceeded ONLY by theirs. (modifies *by theirs*)

WRONG: *Her performance is ONLY exceeded by theirs.* (technically modifies *exceeded*)
              Note: ONLY should be placed just before the words it is meant to modify. In both speech
              and writing, is often placed ONLY before the verb, but this placement is generally wrong,
              according to the GMAT, since we rarely mean that the verb is the only action ever per-
              formed by the subject.

OR

RIGHT: I do NOT want water OR milk.

SUSPECT: *I do NOT want water AND milk. (implies the combination)*

ORDER

RIGHT: The state ORDERS THAT the agency COLLECT taxes. (subjunctive)
            The state ORDERS the agency TO COLLECT taxes.

WRONG: *The state ORDERS THAT the agency SHOULD COLLECT taxes.*
            The state ORDERS the agency SHOULD (or WOULD) COLLECT taxes.
            The state ORDERS the agency COLLECTING taxes.
            The state ORDERS the agency the COLLECTION OF taxes.
            The state ORDERS the COLLECTION OF taxes BY the agency.
            The state ORDERS taxes collected.

OWE

RIGHT: He OWES money TO the government FOR back taxes.

SUSPECT: *He OWES money TO the government BECAUSE OF back taxes.*

PAY

RIGHT: The employer PAYS the same FOR this JOB as for that one.

WRONG: *The employer PAYS the same IN this JOB as in that one.*

PERHAPS

See PROBABLY.

PERSUADE

RIGHT: He PERSUADED her TO GO with him.

WRONG: *He PERSUADED her IN GOING with him.*
            He PERSUADED THAT she GO (or SHOULD GO) with him.

POTENTIALLY

RIGHT: A tornado IS POTENTIALLY overwhelming.

WRONG: *A tornado CAN POTENTIALLY BE overwhelming. (redundant)*

PROBABLY

RIGHT: This situation IS PROBABLY as bad as it can get.
            This situation MAY BE as bad as it can get. (less certain than PROBABLY)
            PERHAPS (or MAYBE) this situation IS as bad as it can get.

SUSPECT: *IT MAY BE THAT this situation IS as bad as it can get.*

WRONG: *This situation IS MAYBE as bad as it can get.*

PROHIBIT

RIGHT: The law PROHIBITS any citizen FROM VOTING twice.

WRONG: *The law PROHIBITS any citizen TO VOTE twice.*
                         The law PROHIBITS THAT any person VOTE (or VOTES) twice.

PRONOUNCE

RIGHT: She PRONOUNCED the book a triumph.

SUSPECT: *She PRONOUNCED the book AS a triumph.*

PROPOSE

RIGHT: The attorneys PROPOSED THAT a settlement BE reached. (subjunctive)
                         The attorneys PROPOSED a new venue.
                         The attorneys PROPOSED TO MEET for lunch.

WRONG: *The attorneys PROPOSED THAT a settlement IS reached.*
                         The attorneys PROPOSED a settlement BE (or TO BE) reached.
                         The attorneys PROPOSED a settlement IS TO BE reached.

PROVIDED THAT   See IF.

RAISE   See RISE.

RANGE FROM/TO

RIGHT: His emotions RANGED FROM anger TO joy.
                         His WIDELY RANGING emotions are hard to deal with. (= changing over time)
                         His WIDE RANGE of accomplishments is impressive. (= a variety)

WRONG: *His emotions RANGED FROM anger AND joy.*
                         FROM anger AND TO joy. FROM anger WITH joy.
                         FROM anger IN ADDITION TO joy.
                         His WIDELY RANGING accomplishments are impressive.

RANK

RIGHT: This problem RANKS AS one of the worst we have seen.

WRONG: *This problem HAS THE RANK OF one of the worst we have seen.*

RATE

RIGHT: The RATES FOR bus tickets are good for commuters. (= prices)
                         The RATE OF theft has fallen. (= frequency or speed)

WRONG: *The RATES OF bus tickets are good for commuters.*
                         The RATE FOR theft has fallen.

REASON

RIGHT: I have A REASON TO DO work today.

She has A REASON FOR the lawsuit.

This observation indicates a REASON THAT he is here.

SUSPECT: *This observation indicates a REASON WHY he is here.*

WRONG: *This observation indicates a REASON he is here.*

The REASON he is here IS BECAUSE he wants to be.

REBEL

RIGHT: The colonists REBELLED AGAINST tyranny.

SUSPECT: *The colonists' REBELLION WAS AGAINST tyranny.*

RECOGNIZE

RIGHT: They RECOGNIZED THAT the entrance fee WAS a bargain.

They RECOGNIZED the entrance fee TO BE a bargain.

They RECOGNIZED the entrance fee AS a bargain.

WRONG: *They RECOGNIZED the entrance fee AS BEING a bargain.*

RECOMMEND

RIGHT: We RECOMMENDED THAT the shelter BE opened.

WRONG: *We RECOMMENDED THAT the shelter SHOULD BE opened.*

REDUCE

RIGHT: The coalition REDUCED prices.

The coalition was considering A REDUCTION IN prices.

SUSPECT: *The coalition MADE (or CAUSED) A REDUCTION IN prices.*

WRONG: *The coalition MADE A REDUCTION OF prices.*

REFER

RIGHT: This term REFERS TO a kind of disease.

REFERRING TO the controversy, the politician asked for calm.

SUSPECT: *This term IS USED TO REFER TO a kind of disease.*

WRONG: *This term IS IN REFERENCE TO a kind of disease.*

IN REFERENCE TO the controversy, the politician asked for calm.

REGARD

RIGHT: He REGARDS the gold ring AS costly.

The gold ring IS REGARDED AS costly.

He IS REGARDED AS HAVING good taste.

WRONG: *The gold ring IS REGARDED THAT IT IS costly.*

RELUCTANT

RIGHT:	They were RELUCTANT TO SAY anything.
WRONG:	*They were RELUCTANT ABOUT SAYING anything.*

REPORT

RIGHT:	A study HAS REPORTED THAT bees ARE DISAPPEARING rapidly.
WRONG:	*A study HAS REPORTED bees AS DISAPPEARING rapidly.*

REQUEST

RIGHT:	I REQUEST THAT he BE removed. (subjunctive)
WRONG:	*I REQUEST him TO BE removed.*

REQUIRE

RIGHT:	She REQUIRES time TO WRITE (*or* IN ORDER TO WRITE). She REQUIRES her friend TO DO work. Her friend IS REQUIRED TO DO work. She REQUIRES THAT her friend DO work. (subjunctive) She REQUIRES OF her friend THAT work BE done. (subjunctive)
SUSPECT:	*In this hostel, there is a REQUIREMENT OF work.* *There is a REQUIREMENT THAT work BE done.*
WRONG:	*She REQUIRES her friend DO work (or MUST DO work).* *She REQUIRES her friend TO HAVE TO DO work.* *She REQUIRES OF her friend TO DO work.* *She REQUIRES THAT her friend DOES work (or SHOULD DO work).* *She REQUIRES THAT her friend IS TO DO work.* *She REQUIRES DOING work (or THE DOING OF work).* *She REQUIRES her friend DOING work.* *In this hostel, there is a REQUIREMENT OF work BY guests.*

RESEMBLE

RIGHT:	A neighbor of mine RESEMBLES my father.
SUSPECT:	*A neighbor of mine HAS A RESEMBLANCE TO my father.*

RESTRICTION

RIGHT:	The government imposed RESTRICTIONS ON the price of gasoline.
WRONG:	The government imposed RESTRICTIONS FOR the price of gasoline.

RESULT

RIGHT: Wealth RESULTS FROM work.

Work RESULTS IN wealth.

Wealth IS A RESULT OF work.

Wealth grows AS A RESULT OF work.

AS A RESULT OF our work, our wealth grew.

The RESULT OF our work WAS THAT our wealth grew.

WRONG: *We worked WITH THE RESULT OF wealth.*

We worked WITH A RESULTING growth of wealth.

RESULTING FROM our work, our wealth grew.

BECAUSE OF THE RESULT OF our work, our wealth grew.

The RESULT OF our work WAS our wealth grew. (THAT is needed.)

The growth of wealth RESULTS.

REVEAL

RIGHT: The analysis REVEALED THAT the comet WAS mostly ice.

SUSPECT: *The analysis REVEALED the comet WAS mostly ice.*

WRONG: *The analysis REVEALED the comet TO HAVE BEEN mostly ice.*

RISE

RIGHT: Oil prices ROSE sharply last year.

A RISE IN oil prices has led to inflation.

RISING prices at the gas pump are hurting consumers.

The RISING OF the SUN always lifts my spirits.

WRONG: *A RAISE IN oil prices has led to inflation. (RAISE = bet or pay increase)*

A RISING OF PRICES at the gas pump is hurting consumers.

RULE

RIGHT: The judge RULED THAT the plaintiff WAS in contempt.

SUSPECT: *The judge RULED the plaintiff WAS in contempt.*

WRONG: *The judge RULED the plaintiff TO BE in contempt.*

The judge RULED ON the plaintiff WHO WAS in contempt.

SAME

RIGHT: The car looks THE SAME TO me AS TO you.

I drove to the store AT THE SAME TIME AS you [did].

WRONG: *The car looks THE SAME TO me AS you. (ambiguous)*

I drove to the store AT THE SAME TIME you did.

SECURE

RIGHT: Our authority IS SECURE.

WRONG: *We ARE SECURE ABOUT our authority.*

SEEM

RIGHT: This result SEEMS TO DEMONSTRATE the new theory.

IT SEEMS THAT this result DEMONSTRATES the new theory.

IT SEEMS AS IF this result DEMONSTRATES the new theory.

SUSPECT: *This result SEEMS TO BE A DEMONSTRATION OF the new theory.*

This result SEEMS DEMONSTRATIVE OF the new theory.

This result SEEMS LIKE A DEMONSTRATION OF the new theory.

WRONG: *This result SEEMS AS IF IT DEMONSTRATES the new theory.*

This result SEEMS LIKE IT DEMONSTRATES the new theory.

SHOULD

RIGHT: A car SHOULD BE TAKEN to the mechanic frequently. (= obligation)

WRONG: *A car SHOULD PASS every two hours. (= probability)*

The owner REQUESTED THAT the car SHOULD BE TAKEN to the mechanic.

(Use the subjunctive BE TAKEN instead.)

SHOW

RIGHT: A discovery SHOWS THAT an object IS strange.

A discovery SHOWS an object TO BE strange.

SUSPECT: *A discovery SHOWS an object IS strange.*

WRONG: *A discovery SHOWS an object AS strange (or AS BEING strange).*

SIGNIFICANT

RIGHT: Your edits HAVE SIGNIFICANTLY IMPROVED the book.

SUSPECT: *Your edits HAVE MADE A SIGNIFICANT IMPROVEMENT IN the book.*

WRONG: *Your edits HAVE BEEN SIGNIFICANT IN IMPROVING the book.*

Your edits HAVE BEEN SIGNIFICANT IN AN IMPROVEMENT OF the book.

SIMILAR

RIGHT: ALL companies HAVE SIMILAR issues. (Comparison requires plural.)

WRONG: *EACH company HAS SIMILAR issues.*

EVERY company HAS SIMILAR issues.

SINCE

RIGHT: Xingo is THE MOST successful new product SINCE 1997. (= up to now)

It is the best new beverage SINCE Prune Cola.

SUSPECT: *Xingo is the best new beverage FOLLOWING Prune Cola.*

WRONG: *Xingo is THE MOST successful new product AFTER 1997.*

SO LONG AS   See AS LONG AS.

SO TOO

RIGHT: Bellbottoms ARE coming back in style, and SO TOO ARE vests.

SUSPECT: *Bellbottoms ARE coming back in style, and ALSO vests.*

WRONG: *Bellbottoms ARE coming back in style, and SO TOO vests.*

SUBSTITUTE

RIGHT: We SUBSTITUTED Parmesan cheese FOR mozzarella.

WRONG: *We SUBSTITUTED Parmesan cheese IN PLACE OF mozzarella.*

SUCCEED

RIGHT: She SUCCEEDED IN REACHING the summit.

WRONG: *She SUCCEEDED TO REACH the summit.*

SUCH

RIGHT: You may enjoy chemistry and physics, but I hate SUCH subjects.

You may enjoy chemistry and physics, but I hate THESE subjects.

Note: THESE means "these specifically." SUCH is more general.

WRONG: *You may enjoy chemistry and physics, but I hate subjects OF THIS KIND.*

You may enjoy chemistry and physics, but I hate subjects LIKE THESE.

SUGGEST

RIGHT: A study SUGGESTS THAT more work IS needed (or WILL BE) needed.

We SUGGEST THAT he BE promoted. (subjunctive)

This artwork SUGGESTS great talent.

SUSPECT: *This artwork IS SUGGESTIVE OF great talent.*

SURFACE

RIGHT: Craters have been seen ON THE SURFACE OF the moon.

SUSPECT: *Craters have been seen AT THE SURFACE OF the moon.*

TARGETED

RIGHT: This intervention is TARGETED AT a specific misbehavior.

WRONG: *This intervention is TARGETED TO a specific misbehavior.*

THINK

RIGHT: She THINKS OF them AS heroes.
          She IS THOUGHT TO BE secretly wealthy.

WRONG: *They ARE THOUGHT OF BY her AS heroes.*
          She THINKS OF them TO BE heroes.
          She THINKS OF them BEING heroes.

TO + verb   See IN ORDER TO.

TRAIN

RIGHT: She WAS TRAINED TO RUN a division.

WRONG: *She WAS TRAINED FOR RUNNING (or IN RUNNING) a division.*

TRY

RIGHT: They WILL TRY TO BUILD a company. (= intent or purpose)

SUSPECT: *We TRIED BREAKING the door down. (= experiment)*

WRONG: *They WILL TRY AND BUILD a company.*
          They WILL TRY THAT THEY BUILD a company.

TWICE

RIGHT: He is TWICE AS tall AS Alex [is].
          Leaves fall TWICE AS quickly AS they grow.
          Naomi wrote TWICE AS MANY letters AS Sara [did].
          Naomi wrote ten letters, DOUBLE THE NUMBER THAT Sara wrote.
          Naomi's income DOUBLED in three years.
          Naomi DOUBLED her income in three years.

WRONG: *He is TWICE AS tall THAN Alex [is].*
          Leaves fall TWICE AS quickly AS their rate of growth.
          Naomi wrote DOUBLE THE LETTERS THAT Sara did.
          Naomi's income INCREASED BY TWICE in three years.

USE

RIGHT: He USES the hammer TO BREAK a board.

He BREAKS a board WITH the hammer.

His hammer BREAKS a board.

He USES the hammer AS a weapon.

....

WRONG: *He USES a hammer FOR BREAKING a board.*

He USES the hammer LIKE a weapon.

He USES the hammer TO BE a weapon.

VARIATION

RIGHT: There are VARIATIONS IN sunspot frequency and strength over time.

....

WRONG: *There are VARIATIONS OF sunspot frequency and strength over time.*

There are VARIATIONS AMONG sunspot frequency and strength over time.

VIEW

RIGHT: I VIEWED this process AS a mistake.

....

WRONG: *I VIEWED this process TO BE a mistake (or LIKE) a mistake.*

WAY

RIGHT: We proposed a WAY OF REACHING the goal.

The WAY IN WHICH we discussed the idea was positive.

The best WAY TO REACH the goal IS TO FOCUS one's energy.

This process was developed TO ACHIEVE the target.

....

SUSPECT: *This process was developed AS A WAY OF ACHIEVING the target.*

....

WRONG: *We proposed a WAY FOR REACHING the goal.*

The best WAY TO REACH the goal IS FOCUSING one's energy.

WEIGH

RIGHT: My laptop WEIGHS LESS THAN a suitcase.

My laptop IS LIGHTER THAN a suitcase.

....

WRONG: *My laptop WEIGHS LIGHTER THAN a suitcase.*

WHERE

RIGHT: Sussex is the only county WHERE pomegranates grow in this state.

Sussex is the only county IN WHICH pomegranates grow in this state.

This incident represents a case IN WHICH I would call the police.

....

WRONG: *This incident represents a case WHERE I would call the police.*

WHOSE / WHOM

RIGHT: The officer WHOSE task was to be here did not show up.

                The company WHOSE growth leads the industry is XYZ, Inc.

SUSPECT: *The officer, THE task OF WHOM was to be here, did not show up.*

WITH

RIGHT: The lions growled, WITH their fur STANDING on end.

WRONG: *WITH only 25% of the student body, seniors get 50% of the resources.*

WORRY

RIGHT: The committee was WORRIED ABOUT increased prices.

WRONG: *The committee was WORRIED OVER increased prices.*

Appendix B

of

Sentence Correction

Glossary

Appendix B
Glossary

The following is a list of grammatical terms used in this guide.

Absolute Phrase

A phrase that consists of a noun and a noun modifier and that modifies a whole clause or sentence. An absolute phrase cannot stand alone as a sentence, but it often expresses an additional thought. An absolute phrase is separated from the main clause by a comma; it may come before or after that main clause. See Modifier.

> The car fell into the lake, the cold water filling the compartment.
> His arm in pain, Guillermo strode out of the building.

Action Noun

A noun that expresses an action. Action nouns are often derived from verbs. In general, action nouns should be made parallel only to other action nouns or to complex gerunds.

> verb + –TION: construction, pollution, redemption
> verb + –AL: arrival, reversal
> verb + –MENT: development, punishment
> Same as verb: change, rise

Active Voice

The form of a verb in which the subject is doing the action expressed by the verb.

> The driver swerved.
> The tires exploded.
> They broke the lamp.

Additive Phrase

Modifier phrases that add nouns onto another noun. However, additive phrases are not part of the main subject of a sentence.

> along with me; in addition to the memo; as well as a dog; accompanied by her; together with the others; including them

Adjective

A word that modifies a noun.

> wonderful food; green eyes; forest fire; the changing seasons

Adverb

A word that modifies a verb, an adjective, another adverb, or even a whole clause. Most adverbs end in -*ly*, but not all.

> The stone fell slowly.
> A swiftly frozen lake appears cloudy.
> We ran very quickly.

Adverbial Modifier

A word, phrase, or clause that describes a verb.

> Adverb: He walked quickly.
> Prepositional phrase: He walked toward the building.
> Subordinate clause: He walked because he was thirsty.
> Present participle: He walked ahead, swinging his arms.
> Infinitive: He walked to buy a drink.
> Preposition + simple gerund: He walked by putting one foot in front of the other.

Antecedent

The noun that a pronoun refers to.

> The rowers lifted the boat and flipped it over their heads.
> (*Rowers* is the antecedent of *their*. *Boat* is the antecedent of *it*.)

Appositive

A noun or noun phrase that is placed next to another noun to identify it. Often separated from the rest of the sentence by commas.

> The coach, an old classmate of mine, was not pleased.
> (*An old classmate of mine* is an appositive phrase to the noun *coach*.)

Article

The words *a*, *an*, or *the*. An article must be followed by a noun (perhaps with modifiers in between). Articles can be considered special adjectives.

Bare Form

The dictionary form of a verb (what you would look up in a dictionary). A bare form has no endings added on, such as *-s*, *-ed*, or *-ing*. The bare form is the infinitive without the *to* in front.

> assess, bark, command, decide, eavesdrop, furnish, gather

Bossy Verb

A verb that tells someone to do something. Bossy verbs take the command subjunctive or an infinitive (or either construction), depending on the verb.

> I <u>told</u> him to run. He <u>requested</u> that the bus wait another minute.
> (The verb *to tell* [*told*] takes the infinitive. *Request* takes the command subjunctive.)

Case

The grammatical role that a noun or pronoun plays in a sentence.

> Subject case (subject role): I, you, she, he, it, we, they
> Object case (object role): me, you, her, him, it, us, them
> Possessive case (ownership role): my/mine, your(s), her(s), his, its, our(s), their(s)
> Nouns show the possessive case by adding *'s* or *s'*.

Clause

A group of words that contains a subject and a working verb.

> Main or independent:
> > <u>This is nice.</u>
> > <u>Yesterday I ate a pizza in haste.</u>
> Subordinate or dependent:
> > Yesterday I ate a pizza <u>that I did not like.</u>
> > <u>When I think about that pizza</u>, I feel ill.

Collective Noun

A noun that looks singular (it does not end in *-s*) but that refers to a group of people or things. Usually considered singular on the GMAT (but look for clues in the sentence!).

> The <u>army</u> is recruiting again.
> This <u>team</u> was beaten.

Command Subjunctive

Subjunctive form used with certain bossy verbs and similar constructions. Same in form as a direct command. See Subjunctive Mood.

> The draft board required that he register for selective service.

Comparative Form

Form of adjectives and adverbs used to compare two things or people. Regular comparative forms are either the base word plus -er (if the base is short, e.g., greener) or the base word preceded by more (more intelligent). Irregulars are listed below:

Adjective or Adverb	Comparative
good/well	better
bad/badly	worse
much, many	more
little	less
far	farther, further

Comparisons

Structures by which we compare things or people in sentences. Usually marked with signal words such as like, unlike, as, or than. Comparisons can be between two things or people (comparative) or among three or more things or people (superlative).

Complex Gerund

A gerund is an -ing form of a verb that functions as a noun; a complex gerund includes an article or something similar to indicate that the -ing word is definitely functioning as a noun. In general, complex gerunds can be put in parallel with action nouns. Simple gerunds should not be. See Simple Gerund.

> The running of the bulls is a tradition in Spain.
> The volcanic eruption resulted in the melting of the iceberg.

Concrete Noun

A noun that does not represent an action. Concrete nouns refer to things, people, places, and even time periods or certain events. Generally, concrete nouns are not logically parallel to action nouns.

> volcano, hole, proton, senator, area, month, Halloween

Conditional Tense

A verb tense formed by combining the helping verb would with the base form of the verb. See Tense.

> Future as seen from the past:
>   He said that he would write.
> Hypothetical result of unlikely condition:
>   If she liked pizza, she would like this restaurant.

Conjunction

A word that joins two parts of a sentence together. Coordinating and correlative conjunctions give the two parts equal weight. Subordinating conjunctions put one part in a logically junior role, in relation to the other part.

> Coordinating: and, but, or   (less common: for, nor, so, yet)
>
> Correlative: either … or …; neither … nor …; not … but …; not only … but also …
>
> Subordinating: after, although, because, before, if, since, when

Conjunctive Adverb

A transition word or phrase that is used after a semicolon to help connect two main clauses. Conjunctive adverbs are not true conjunctions.

> therefore, thus, consequently, however, nevertheless, furthermore, etc.
>
> The general was stuck in traffic; <u>therefore</u>, the ceremony started late.

Connecting Punctuation

The comma (,), the semicolon (;), the colon (:), and the em dash (—). Used to link parts of the sentence.

Connecting Words

Conjunctions, conjunctive adverbs, and relative pronouns. Used to link parts of a sentence.

Countable Noun

A noun that can be counted in English. For instance, you can say *one hat, two hats, three hats.* Countable nouns can be made singular or plural.

> hat/hats, month/months, thought/thoughts, person/people

Dangling Modifier

A noun modifier that does not properly modify or describe any noun in the sentence. In fact, the noun that should be modified has been omitted from the sentence. Likewise, a verb modifier that requires a subject but lacks one in the sentence is considered dangling. Dangling modifiers are always incorrect. See <u>Modifier</u>.

> <u>Walking along the river bank</u>, the new tower can be seen.
>
> (The modifier *walking along the river bank* has no subject. The sentence could be rewritten thus: *Walking along the river bank, one can see the new tower.*)

Demonstrative Pronoun

The pronouns *this, that, these,* and *those.* Demonstrative pronouns can be used as adjectives *(these plants, that company).* They can also be used in place of nouns, but they must be modified in some way, according to the GMAT. See Pronoun.

> The strategy taken by Livonia is preferable to <u>that</u> taken by Khazaria.
> (The demonstrative pronoun *that* properly stands for the noun *strategy.* The pronoun *that* is modified by the phrase *taken by Khazaria.*)

Dependent Clause

A clause that cannot stand alone without a main or independent clause. A dependent clause is led by a subordinator. Also known as a subordinate clause. See Clause.

Direct Object

The noun that is acted upon by a verb in the active voice. Can be a pronoun, a noun phrase, or a noun clause.

> I broke <u>the lamp</u>.
> Who let <u>the big dogs</u> out?
> I believe <u>that you are right</u>.

Essential Modifier

A modifier that provides necessary information. Use an essential modifier to identify the particular noun out of many possibilities or to create a permanent description of the noun. Do not use commas to separate an essential modifier from the modified noun. See Modifier.

> I want to sell the car <u>that my sister drove to the city</u>.

Fragment

A group of words that does not work as a stand-alone sentence, either because it is begun by a subordinator or because it lacks a subject or a verb.

> Although he bought a pretzel.
> The device developed by scientists.

Future Tense

The form of a verb that expresses action in the future. Also known as simple future. See Tense.

> The driver <u>will swerve</u>.
> The tires <u>will be punctured</u>.
> They <u>will break</u> the lamp.

Gerund

An *-ing* form of a verb used as a noun.

> <u>Skiing</u> is fun.
> She enjoys <u>snowboarding</u>.
> She often thinks about <u>sledding</u>.

Gerund Phrase

A phrase centered on an *-ing* form of a verb used as a noun.

> Simple: <u>Skiing difficult trails</u> is fun.
> Complex: We discussed <u>the grooming of the horses</u>.

Helping Verb

A verb used with another verb. Helping verbs create various grammatical structures or provide additional shades of meaning.

Primary:	be, do, have
	I <u>am</u> running. He <u>did</u> not run. She <u>has</u> run.
Modal:	can, could, may, might, must, shall, should, will, would
	We <u>must</u> go to the bank. He <u>should</u> take his medicine.

Hypothetical Subjunctive

Subjunctive form that indicates unlikely or unreal conditions. This form is used in some cases after the words *if*, *as if*, or *as though*, or with the verb *to wish*. The hypothetical subjunctive is equivalent to the simple past tense of every verb, except the verb *to be*: the hypothetical subjunctive of *be* is *were* for every subject. See <u>Subjunctive Mood</u>.

> If he <u>were</u> in better shape, he would win the race.

Idiom

An expression that has a unique form. Idioms do not follow general rules; rather, they must simply be memorized.

If … Then Statement

A sentence that contains both a condition (marked by an *if*) and a result (possibly marked by a *then*). Either the condition or the result may be written first in the sentence. The verbs in *if … then* statements follow particular patterns of tense and mood.

> If he were in better shape, he would win the race.
> They get sick if they eat dairy products.
> If she swims, then she will win.

Imperative Mood

The form of a verb that expresses direct commands. Identical to the bare form of the verb as well as to the command subjunctive. See <u>Mood</u>.

<u>Go</u> to the store and <u>buy</u> me an ice cream cone.

Indefinite Pronoun

A pronoun that does not refer to a specific noun. Most indefinite pronouns are singular.

anyone, anybody, anything	no one, nobody, nothing
each, every (as pronouns)	someone, somebody, something
everyone, everybody, everything	whatever, whoever
either, neither *(may require a plural verb if paired with or/nor)*	

A few indefinite pronouns are always plural.

both, few, many, several

The SANAM pronouns can be either singular or plural, depending on the noun in the *of*-phrase that follows the pronoun.

some, any, none, all, more/most

Independent Clause

A clause that can stand alone as a grammatical sentence. Contains its own subject and verb. Also known as a <u>Main Clause</u>.

Indicative Mood

The form of a verb that expresses facts or beliefs. Most verbs in most English sentences are in the indicative mood. See <u>Mood</u>.

I <u>went</u> to the store and <u>bought</u> an ice cream cone.
I <u>will do</u> so again.

Indirect Object

The noun that expresses the recipient or the beneficiary of some action. Can be a pronoun, a noun phrase, or a noun clause.

I gave <u>him</u> the lamp.
She found <u>the man</u> a good book.

Infinitive

The bare form of the verb plus the marker *to*. Used as a noun or as a modifier within a sentence.

I prefer <u>to read</u> novels.
She drove many miles <u>to see</u> her uncle.

-ing Form

The bare form of the verb plus the ending *-ing*. When used as a noun, the *-ing* form is called a gerund. When used as a modifier or as part of the progressive tense, the *-ing* form is called a present participle.

> Present participle (part of verb): I am <u>eating</u> an apple.
> Gerund (noun): <u>Eating</u> an apple is good for you.
> Present participle (noun modifier): The man <u>eating</u> an apple is my friend.
> Present participle (verb modifier): I sat on the porch, <u>eating</u> an apple.

Intransitive Verb

A verb that does not take a direct object. Intransitive verbs cannot be put in the passive voice.

> I <u>went</u> to the library.
> The driver <u>swerved</u>.
> (Intransitive verb *-ing* forms followed by nouns are usually adjectives: *The <u>swerving</u> driver wound up on the sidewalk.*)

Linking Verb

A verb that expresses what a subject is, rather than what it does. The most important linking verb is *to be.*

Main Clause

A clause that can stand alone as a grammatical sentence. A main clause contains its own subject and verb, and is not introduced by a subordinator. Also known as an <u>Independent Clause</u>.

> <u>I prefer to read novels.</u>
> While eating lunch, <u>she finished reading the report.</u>

Marker

Words that serve as clues that the GMAT is testing a particular issue. For example, *and* is a parallelism marker and *which* is a modifier marker.

Middleman

Words that the GMAT inserts between the subject and the verb to hide the subject. Middlemen are usually modifiers of various types.

Misplaced Modifier

A noun modifier that is not positioned next to the noun it needs to describe in the sentence. Misplaced modifiers are incorrect. See <u>Modifier</u>.

> I collapsed onto the sofa <u>exhausted by a long day of work</u>.
> (The modifier *exhausted by a long day of work* refers to *sofa*, but a sofa can't be exhausted. The modifier needs to be placed as close as possible to the noun it modifies: *Exhausted by a long day of work, I collapsed on the sofa.*)

Modal Helping Verb

See Helping Verb.

Modifier

Words, phrases or clauses that describe other parts of the sentence. Noun modifiers modify nouns. Adverbial modifiers modify anything other than nouns (verbs, clauses, adjectives, etc.).

Mood

The form of the verb that indicates the attitude of the speaker toward the action.

> Indicative: I drive fast cars. We drove to Las Vegas.
> Imperative: Drive three blocks and turn left.
> Command Subjunctive: I suggested that he drive three blocks.
> Hypothetical Subjunctive: If he drove three blocks, he would see us.

Nonessential Modifier

A modifier that provides extra information. If this modifier were removed from the sentence, the core meaning of the sentence would still make sense. Use commas to separate a nonessential modifier from the modified noun. See Modifier.

> I want to sell this beat-up old car, which my sister drove to the city.

Noun

A word that means a thing or a person. Nouns can be the subject of a verb, the direct or indirect object of a verb, or the object of a preposition. Nouns can be modified by an adjective or another noun modifier.

Noun-Adjective

A noun that is placed in front of another noun and that functions as an adjective.

> A government survey; the stone wall
> (A government survey is a type of survey; a stone wall is a type of wall.)

Noun Clause

A subordinate clause (with its own subject and verb) that acts as a noun in the sentence. That is, it is the subject of a verb, the object of a verb, or the object of a preposition. Led by relative pronouns *which, what, when, why, whether,* or *that.*

> I care about what he thinks.
> Whether I stay or go is unimportant.
> I believe that you are right.

Noun Modifier

A word, phrase, or clause that describes a noun.

> Adjective: <u>This big</u> window needs to be replaced.
> Past participle: <u>Broken in the storm</u>, this window needs to be replaced.
> Present participle: The window <u>rattling against the sill</u> needs to be replaced.
> Prepositional phrase: The window <u>on the right</u> needs to be replaced.
> Appositive: This window, <u>an original installation</u>, needs to be replaced.
> Infinitive: The window <u>to replace</u> is on the second floor.
> Relative clause: The window <u>that needs to be replaced</u> has a missing pane.

Noun Phrase

A phrase that acts as a noun in the sentence. A noun phrase typically consists of a noun and its modifiers.

> <u>A new government survey of taxpayers</u> is planned.
> (The subject of the sentence is the noun phrase consisting of the noun *survey* and its modifiers: *a, new, government, of taxpayers*.)

Object Case

The form of a pronoun used as the object of a verb or of a preposition. Nouns do not change form in the object case. See <u>Case</u>.

Parallel Element

A part of a sentence made parallel to another part or parts of the sentence through the use of parallel markers.

> We will invite both <u>his friends</u> and <u>her family</u>.

Parallel Marker

The words that link or contrast parts of a sentence, forcing them to be parallel.

> We will invite both his friends <u>and</u> her family.

Parallelism Category

A type of word, phrase, or clause. Something in one parallelism category can be made parallel to something else of the same type, but it should not be made parallel to anything in another category.

> Concrete nouns: I like to eat <u>peanut butter</u> and <u>ice cream</u>.
> Action nouns and complex gerunds: I like to watch <u>the release of the doves</u> and <u>the changing of the guard</u>.
> Simple gerunds: I like <u>eating ice cream</u> and <u>watching birds</u>.
> Working verbs: I <u>like</u> ice cream but <u>hate</u> sorbet.

Infinitives: I like <u>to eat</u> ice cream and <u>to watch</u> birds.

Adjectives and participles: I like ice cream, either <u>frozen</u> or <u>warm</u>.

Clauses: She knows <u>that I like ice cream</u> and <u>that I hate sorbet</u>.

Participle

One of two kinds of words derived from verbs. Present participles typically end in *-ing* and can be used as a verb, a noun, a noun modifier, or a verb modifier. Present participles typically indicate ongoing action (though not necessarily in the present). Past participles typically end in *-ed* and can be used as a verb or a modifier. Past participles tend to indicate a completed action relative to the given time frame in the sentence.

Present Participle: hiking, growing, doing

She will be <u>hiking</u> next week. <u>Studying</u> for the GMAT is fun. He slipped on the ice, <u>injuring</u> his ankle.

Past Participle: hiked, grown, done

The tires will be <u>punctured</u>. The tires were <u>punctured</u>. <u>Punctured</u> by a nail, the tire slowly deflated.

Parts of Speech

The basic kinds of words. A word's part of speech is determined both by what the word means and by what role or roles the word can play in a sentence.

Noun: peanut, lake, vacuum, considerations, opportunity

Verb: swim, proceed, execute, went, should

Adjective: wonderful, blue, the, helpful

Adverb: slowly, very, graciously

Preposition: of, for, by, with, through, during, in, on

Conjunction: and, but, or, although because

Passive Voice

The form of a verb in which the subject is receiving the action expressed by the verb.

The driver <u>was thrown</u> from the car.

The crystal vases <u>have been broken</u> by the thieves.

Past Participle

The participle used in perfect tenses and passive voice. A past participle may also be used as an adjective. Past participles tend to indicate completed action, although not necessarily in the past (relative to now).

The tires will be <u>punctured</u>. They have <u>broken</u> the lamp. A <u>frozen</u> lake.

Regular past participles are formed by adding -d or -ed to the base form of the verb. Many irregular past participles are listed below, together with irregular past tense forms. Sometimes the past tense form and the past participle are identical. Non-native English speakers should study this list. Native English speakers likely already know most or all of these forms.

Base Form	Past Tense	Past Participle	Base Form	Past Tense	Past Participle
be	was, were	been	lose	lost	lost
become	became	become	make	made	made
begin	began	begun	pay	paid	paid
break	broke	broken	put	put	put
bring	brought	brought	rise	rose	risen
build	built	built	say	said	said
buy	bought	bought	see	saw	seen
catch	caught	caught	seek	sought	sought
choose	chose	chosen	sell	sold	sold
come	came	come	send	sent	sent
cost	cost	cost	set	set	set
cut	cut	cut	show	showed	shown
do	did	done	shrink	shrank	shrunk
draw	drew	drawn	speak	spoke	spoken
drive	drove	driven	spend	spent	spent
eat	ate	eaten	spread	spread	spread
fall	fell	fallen	stand	stood	stood
fight	fought	fought	steal	stole	stolen
find	found	found	strike	struck	struck
forget	forgot	forgotten	sweep	swept	swept
freeze	froze	frozen	take	took	taken
give	gave	given	teach	taught	taught
go	went	gone	tell	told	told
grow	grew	grown	think	thought	thought
hold	held	held	throw	threw	thrown
keep	kept	kept	understand	understood	understood
know	knew	known	win	won	won
lead	led	led	write	wrote	written

Past Perfect Tense

The form of a verb that expresses action that takes place before another past action or time. The past perfect tense is formed with the verb *had* and the past participle.

The officer said that the driver <u>had swerved</u>.
By 2005, she <u>had visited</u> India three times.

Past Tense

The form of a verb that expresses action in the past. See Tense.

> The driver <u>swerved</u>.
> The tires <u>were punctured</u>.
> They <u>broke</u> the lamp.
> (Common irregular past tense forms are listed under the entry for <u>Past Participles</u>.)

Person

Indicates whether the word refers to the speaker or writer (first person), the listener or reader (second person), or someone/something else (third person). Personal pronouns are marked for person. Present tense verbs in the third person singular add an -s: *the doctor writes*.

> First person: I, me, my, we, us, our
> Second person: you, your
> Third person: she, he, it, its, they, them, their

Phrase

A group of words that has a particular grammatical role in the sentence. The type of phrase is often determined by one main word within the phrase. A phrase can contain other phrases. For instance, a noun phrase can contain a prepositional phrase.

> Noun phrase: <u>The short **chapter** at the end of the book</u> is important.
> Verb phrase: The computer <u>must have been **broken**</u> in the move.
> Adjective phrase: The employee <u>most **reluctant** to volunteer</u> was chosen.
> Prepositional phrase: The wolf <u>**in** the cage</u> has woken up.

Plural

A category of number that indicates more than one. Nouns, pronouns, and verbs can be made plural. See Singular.

> <u>Many dogs are</u> barking; <u>they are</u> keeping me awake.

Possessive Case

The form of a pronoun or a noun that owns another noun. In possessive case, nouns add -'s or -s'. See Case.

Preposition

A word that indicates a relationship between the object (usually a noun) and something else in the sentence. In some cases, prepositions can consist of more than one word.

> of, in, to, for, with, on, by, at, from, as, into, about, like, after,
> between, through, over, against, under, out of, next to, upon

Prepositional Phrase

A prepositional phrase consists of a preposition and an object (a noun). The preposition indicates a relationship between that object and something else in the sentence.

> I would like a drink <u>of water</u>. (*Of* is the preposition; *of water* modifies *drink*.)
> The man <u>in the gray suit</u> is the CEO. (*In* is the preposition; *in the gray suit* modifies *man*)

Present Participle

The participle used in progressive tenses. A present participle may also be used as a noun, a noun modifier, or a verb modifier. Present participles tend to indicate ongoing action, although not necessarily at the present moment. To form a present participle, add *-ing* to the base form of the verb, possibly doubling the last consonant.

> The tires were <u>rolling</u>.
> She jumped into the <u>swimming</u> pool.
> <u>Hiking</u> is great.

Present Perfect Tense

The form of a verb that expresses action that began in the past and continues to the present or whose effect continues to the present. The present perfect tense is formed with the verb *has* or *have* and the past participle.

> The tires <u>have been punctured</u>. (The tires were punctured in the past, and it is still true in the present that they were punctured.)
> You <u>have broken</u> my lamp! (The lamp was broken in the past, and it is still broken now.)

Present Tense

The form of a verb that expresses action in the present. The simple present (nonprogressive) often indicates general truths. See <u>Tense</u>.

> The driver <u>swerves</u>.
> The tires <u>are</u> on the car.
> They <u>speak</u> English.

Primary Helping Verb

See <u>Helping Verb</u>.

Progressive Tense

The form of a verb that expresses ongoing action in the past, present, or future. See <u>Tense</u>.

> The driver <u>is swerving</u>.
> The tires <u>were rolling</u>.
> They <u>will be running</u>.

Pronoun

A pronoun stands in for another noun elsewhere in the sentence or for an implied noun. The noun is called the antecedent. For example, in the sentence, "When Amy fell, she hurt her knee," the pronouns *she* and *her* refer to the antecedent *Amy*.

> When it started to rain, the tourists pulled out their umbrellas. (*Their* refers to *tourists*.)
> The term bibliophile refers to someone who loves books. (*Someone* is a pronoun but does not need to have a specific antecedent; *who* refers to *someone*.)

Relative Clause

A subordinate clause headed by a relative pronoun. Relative clauses may act as noun modifiers or, more infrequently, as nouns.

> The professor who spoke is my mother.
> What you see is what you get.

Relative Pronoun

A pronoun that connects a subordinate clause to a sentence. The relative pronoun plays a grammatical role in the subordinate clause (e.g., subject, verb object, or prepositional object). If the relative clause is a noun modifier, the relative pronoun also refers to the modified noun. If the relative clause is a noun clause, then the relative pronoun does not refer to a noun outside the relative clause.

> The professor who spoke is my mother.
> (The relative pronoun *who* is the subject of the clause *who spoke*. *Who* also refers to *professor*, the noun modified by the clause *who spoke*.)
> What you see is a disaster waiting to happen.
> (The relative pronoun *what* is the object of the clause *what you see*. *What* does not refer to a noun outside the clause; rather, the clause *what you see* is the subject of the sentence.)

Reporting Verb

A verb, such as *indicate, claim, announce*, or *report*, that in fact reports or otherwise includes a thought or belief. A reporting verb should be followed by *that* on the GMAT.

> The survey indicates that CFOs are feeling pessimistic.

Run-on Sentence

A sentence incorrectly formed out of two main clauses joined without proper punctuation or a proper connecting word, such as a coordinator or subordinator. Also called a comma-splice.

> The film was great, I want to see it again.
> (This sentence could be fixed with a semicolon as follows: *The film was great; I want to see it again*. Alternatively, the two clauses could be joined by a coordinating conjunction: *The film was great and I want to see it again*. Finally, one of the clauses could be made into a subordinate clause: *Because the film was great, I want to see it again*.)

SANAM Pronouns

An indefinite pronoun that can be either singular or plural, depending on the object of the *of*-phrase that follows. The SANAM pronouns are *some, any, none, all, more/most*.

> <u>Some</u> of the milk <u>has</u> gone bad.
> <u>Some</u> of the children <u>are</u> angry.

Sentence

A complete grammatical utterance. Sentences contain a subject and a verb in a main clause. Some sentences contain two main clauses linked by a coordinating conjunction, such as *and*. Other sentences contain subordinate clauses tied to the main clause in some way.

> My boss is angry. (This sentence contains one main clause. The subject is *boss*; the verb is *is*.)
> He read my blog, and he saw the photos that I posted. (This sentence contains two main clauses linked by *and*. In the first main clause, the subject is *he*, the verb is *read*. In the second main clause, the subject is *he*, the verb is *saw*. There is also a subordinate clause, *that I posted*, led by the relative pronoun *that*.)

Simple Gerund

A gerund is an *-ing* form of a verb that functions as a noun. A simple gerund typically does not include an article or something similar (as a complex gerund does).

> <u>Swimming</u> is fun.
> She likes <u>running</u> and <u>hiking</u>.
> (In general, simple gerunds should not be put in parallel with action nouns. Complex gerunds can be put in parallel with action nouns. See <u>Complex Gerund</u>.)

Singular

A category of number that indicates one. Nouns, pronouns, and verbs can be made singular. See <u>Plural</u>.

> <u>A</u> <u>dog</u> <u>is</u> barking; <u>it</u> <u>is</u> keeping <u>me</u> awake.

Split

Differences in the answer choices. When working on a Sentence Completion problem, compare the answers to find splits; these differences will help you to determine what the problem is testing.

State Verb

A verb that expresses a condition of the subject, rather than an action that the subject performs. State verbs are rarely used in progressive tenses.

> Her assistant <u>knows</u> Russian.
> I <u>love</u> chocolate.
> This word <u>means</u> "hello."

Subgroup Modifier

A type of modifier that describes a smaller subset within the group expressed by the modified noun.

French wines, <u>many of which I have tasted</u>, are superb.

Subject

The noun or pronoun that goes with the verb and that is required in every sentence. The subject performs the action expressed by an active-voice verb; in contrast, the subject receives the action expressed by a passive-voice verb. The subject and the verb must agree in number and in person.

The <u>market</u> closed.
<u>She</u> is considering a new job.
<u>They</u> have been seen.

Subjunctive Mood

One of two verb forms indicating desires, suggestions, or unreal or unlikely conditions.

Command subjunctive: She requested that he <u>stop</u> the car.
Hypothetical subjunctive: If he <u>were</u> in charge, he would help us.

Subordinate Clause

A clause that cannot stand alone without a main or independent clause. A subordinate clause is led by a subordinator. Also known as a dependent clause. See <u>Clause</u>.

Her dog, <u>which is brown</u>, is friendly.
<u>Although he barely studied</u>, he scored well on the test.

Subordinator

A word that creates a subordinate clause.

Relative pronoun: which, that, who, whose, whom, what
Subordinating conjunction: although, because, while, whereas

Superlative Form

Form of adjectives and adverbs used to compare three or more things or people. The reference group may be implied. Regular superlative forms are either the base word plus -*est* (if the base is short, e.g., *greenest*) or the base word preceded by *most* (*most intelligent*). Irregulars are listed below:

Adjective or Adverb	Superlative
good/well	best
bad/badly	worst
much, many	most
little	least
far	farthest, furthest

Tense

The form of the verb that indicates the time of the action (relative to the present time). The completed or ongoing nature of the action may also be indicated.

> *Examples:*
> Present: She <u>speaks</u> French.
> Past: She <u>spoke</u> French.
> Future: She <u>will speak</u> French.
> Present progressive: She <u>is speaking</u> French.
> Past progressive: She <u>was speaking</u> French.
> Future progressive: She <u>will be speaking</u> French.
> Present perfect: She <u>has spoken</u> French.
> Past perfect: She <u>had spoken</u> French.

That Clause

A clause that begins with the word *that*.

> Relative clause: The suggestion <u>that he made</u> is bad. (The clause *that he made* modifies *suggestion. That* is the object of the clause. In other words, *he made that = the suggestion.*)
> Subordinate clause: He suggested <u>that the world is flat</u>. (The clause *that the world is flat* is the object of the verb *suggested*.)
> Subordinate clause: The suggestion <u>that the world is flat</u> is bad. (The clause *that the world is flat* modifies *suggestion*. However, *that* is not the object of the clause, nor is it the subject. Rather, *that* provides a way for the idea in the sentence *the world is flat* to be linked to *the suggestion*.)

Transitive Verb

A verb that takes a direct object. Transitive verbs can usually be put in the passive voice, which turns the object into the subject.

> The agent <u>observed</u> the driver. The driver <u>was observed</u> by the agent. (Transitive verb *-ing* forms followed by nouns are usually simple gerund phrases: *The agent was paid for <u>observing the driver</u>.* Some verbs can be either transitive or intransitive. In particular, verbs that indicate changes of state can be either: *The lamp <u>broke</u>. I <u>broke</u> the lamp.* This duality means that some *-ing* forms in isolation can be ambiguous. The phrase *melting snow* could mean "the act of causing snow to melt" or "snow that is melting." Use context to resolve the ambiguity.)

Uncountable Noun

A noun that cannot be counted in English. For instance, you cannot say *one patience, two patiences, three patiences*. Most uncountable nouns exist only in the singular form and cannot be made plural.

> patience, furniture, milk, information, rice, chemistry

Verb

The word or words that express the action of the sentence. The verb indicates the time of the action (tense), the attitude of the speaker (mood), and the role of the subject (voice). The verb may also reflect the number and person of the subject. Every sentence must have a verb.

Verbal

A word or phrase that is derived from a verb and that functions as a different part of speech in the sentence: as a noun, as an adjective (noun modifier), or as an adverb (verb modifier).

> Infinitive: He likes to walk to the store.
> Gerund: I enjoy walking.
> Present participle: The man walking toward us is my father.
> Past participle: The facts given in the case are clear.

Voice

The form of the verb that indicates the role of the subject as performer of the action (active voice) or recipient of the action (passive voice).

> Active voice: She threw the ball.
> Passive voice: The ball was thrown by her.

Warmup

Words that the GMAT inserts at the beginning of the sentence to hide the subject in question. Warmups are either modifiers of various types or "frame sentences" (that is, you really care about the subject of a subordinate clause, not the subject of the main clause).

Working Verb

A verb that could be the main verb of a grammatical sentence. A working verb shows tense, mood, and voice, as well as number and person in some circumstances. The use of this term helps to distinguish working verbs from verbals, which cannot by themselves be the main verb of a sentence.

GO BEYOND BOOKS.
TRY A FREE CLASS NOW.

IN-PERSON COURSE

Find a GMAT course near you and attend the first session free, no strings attached. You'll meet your instructor, learn how the GMAT is scored, review strategies for Data Sufficiency, dive into Sentence Correction, and gain insights into a wide array of GMAT principles and strategies.

Find your city at manhattanprep.com/gmat/classes

ONLINE COURSE

Enjoy the flexibility of prepping from home or the office with our online course. Your instructor will cover all the same content and strategies as an in-person course, while giving you the freedom to prep where you want. Attend the first session free to check out our cutting-edge online classroom.

See the full schedule at manhattanprep.com/gmat/classes

GMAT® INTERACT™

GMAT Interact is a comprehensive self-study program that is fun, intuitive, and driven by you. Each interactive video lesson is taught by an expert instructor and can be accessed on your computer or mobile device. Lessons are personalized for you based on the choices you make.

Try 5 full lessons for free at manhattanprep.com/gmat/interact

Not sure which is right for you? Try all three!
Or give us a call and we'll help you figure out
which program fits you best.

Toll-Free U.S. Number (800) 576-4628 | International 001 (212) 721-7400 | Email gmat@manhattanprep.com

PREP MADE PERSONAL

Whether you want quick coaching
in a particular GMAT subject area
or a comprehensive study plan developed
around your goals, we've got you covered.
Our expert, 99th percentile GMAT tutors
can help you hit your top score.

CHECK OUT THESE REVIEWS FROM MANHATTAN PREP TUTORING STUDENTS.

CALL OR EMAIL US AT **800-576-4628** OR **GMAT@MANHATTANPREP.COM**
FOR INFORMATION ON RATES AND TO GET PAIRED WITH YOUR GMAT TUTOR.